SLIPWARE AND ST IVES

THE LEACH POTTERY 1920-1937

SLIPWARE AND ST IVES

THE LEACH POTTERY 1920-1937

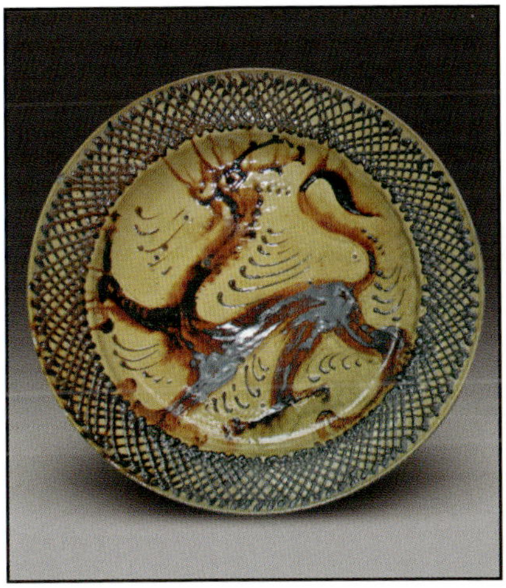

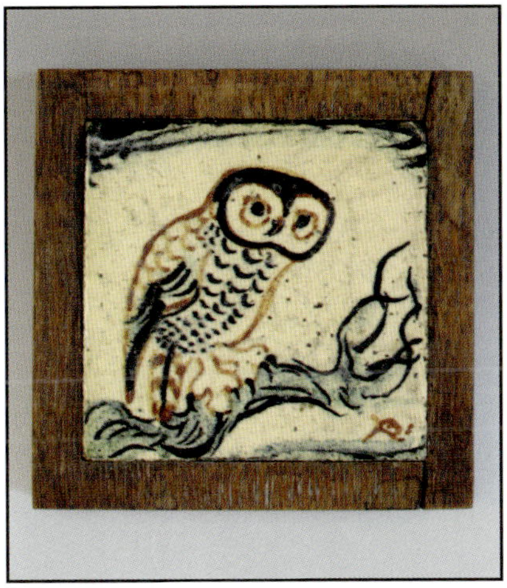

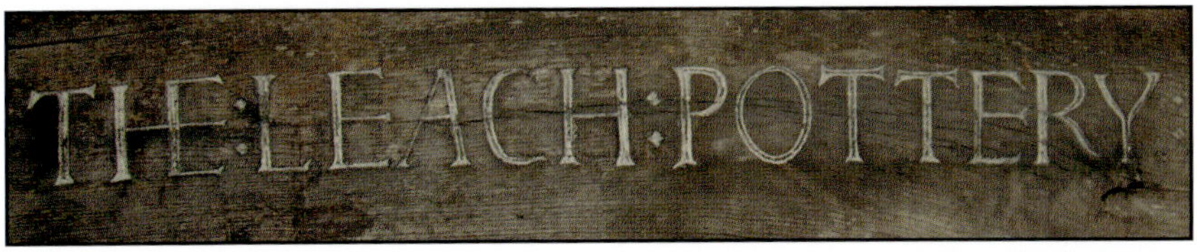

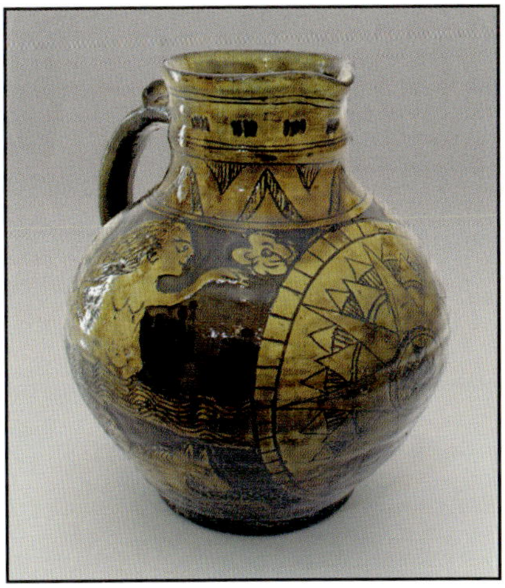

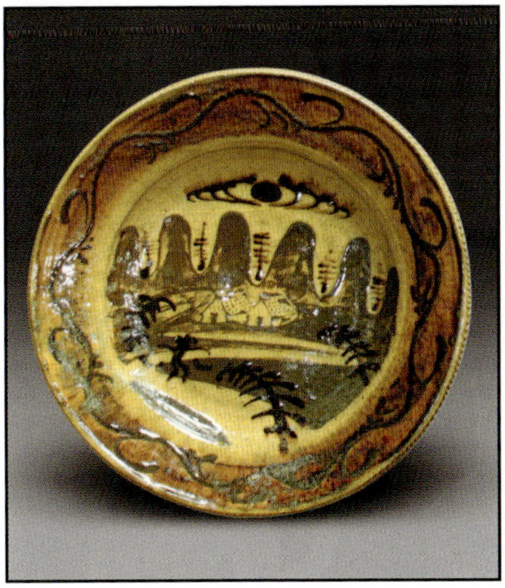

JOHN EDGELER

First published in 2010 by Cotswolds Living Publications,
Queen Anne House, High Street, Winchcombe GL54 5LJ (Tel 01242 602319)

ISBN 0-9550315-5-9 (soft cover) 0-9550315-6-7 (hardback).

Main text set in Gill Sans and Trajan

Printed in Wales by Cambrian Printers

Collections and archive photograph copyright
York Art Gallery and Museum: pages 87, 90, 113, 114, 137
UW Aberystwyth: pages 7, 34, 63, 76, 88, 90
Victoria & Albert Museum: pages 47, 58, 59, 60, 61, 69
Stoke-on-Trent Museums Service: pages 9, 13, 16, 18, 22, 43, 49, 51, 54, 62
Southampton City Art Gallery: pages 44, 52, 87, 89
High Cross House, Dartington: pages 95, 103
Royal Cornwall Museum, Truro: pages 23, 25, 26, 50, 77-80, 94
Craft Study Centre, Farnham: pages 9, 12, 14, 27, 37-39, 43, 55, 57, 85, 100, 102, 104, 111, 112, 126, 131, 157
Walker Art Gallery, Liverpool: page 72

Bernard Leach line drawings from *A potter's book* are used with the kind permission of the Leach family and Messrs Faber & Faber, London

Photography credit
John Edgeler

Previous titles
Sid Tustin, Winchcombe Potter: a celebration (ISBN 0-9550315-0-8)
Ray Finch, Craftsman Potter of the modern age (ISBN 0-9550315-1-6)
Michael Cardew and the West Country slipware tradition (ISBN 0-9550315-2-4)
Michael Cardew and stoneware: continuity and change (ISBN 0-9550315-3-2)
The Fishleys of Fremington: a Devon Slipware Tradition (ISBN 0-9550315-4-0)

Graphic Design
Petersen Creative, www.petersencreative.com

Measurements
Where Imperial measurements are shown, 1 inch = 2.54cm, 1 foot = 30.5cm

SLIPWARE AND ST IVES

THE LEACH POTTERY 1920-1937

CONTENTS

INTRODUCTION AND ACKNOWLEDGEMENTS

My last few years of research, writing and publishing have concentrated on areas close to home, focussing initially on those leading figures of 20th century Studio ceramics associated with our Greet Pottery on the outskirts of Winchcombe, a place of making of practical pots for over 200 years. So the team and tradition that Michael Cardew (1901-1983) established during his 13 years here were the initial focus, with titles on Sid Tustin (2005) and subsequently Ray Finch and his own team (2006) the starting point. Subsequent books on Cardew's output in Slipware (2007) and Stoneware (2008) only served to emphasise the core role of traditional pots and potters in the foundation of the Studio Pottery movement of the 20th century, inspiring a prequel on the dynasty of Devon potters that were Cardew's wellspring, the Fishleys of Fremington (2008).

The influence of the central father figures of Studio Pottery in this country, Bernard Leach (1887-1979) and Shoji Hamada (1889-1978), proved to be recurring themes throughout these titles, as were those other, primarily Midlands and Northern, traditional ceramics of the British Isles that were in turn a significant early and in the case of Hamada a continuing influence in their potting careers. Yet despite the undoubted standing and importance of Leach and Hamada, the output of the Leach Pottery in its early years has received relatively little attention in publications, with much biographical detail printed by and about Leach but little by way of coherent analysis of the product.

Indeed, we have inevitably encountered much legend and lore about those early days at St Ives, with written recollections where they exist brought together some 50 years and more after the event. However, by and large, pots bear the evidence of the inspiration and perspiration that went behind their making, so this primarily visual history of the slipware period of the Leach Pottery, St Ives focuses on those examples available in primarily national but also some private collections. The pots have wherever possible been examined by hand and a photographic record established for research and analysis after the event. Lastly, I have taken the opportunity to say something of the dissemination from those early days, with some analysis of pots subsequently produced in both the East and West, and showing an influence of those western traditions that were core to the foundation of the Leach Pottery in the 1920s.

It is the manifest kindness, generosity and help of those individuals with responsibility for the care of these wonderful pots that has been pivotal in making this book happen. My thanks go to Helen Walsh of the York

Art Gallery and Museum, Tim Craven of Southampton City Art Gallery, Moira Vincentelli of UW Aberystwyth, Alun Graves of the Victoria and Albert Museum, Miranda Goodby of the Potteries Museum, Stoke, Sarah Lloyd-Durrant of the Royal Cornwall Museum, Truro, Heather and Yvonne at High Cross House, Dartington and Jean Vacher of the Crafts Study Centre, Farnham. The 'Brotherhood of the pot' of private collectors and enthusiasts has again been immensely supportive, and particular thanks are due to David and Susan Attenborough, and also to Martin Harrison, Robert Buscombe, Jacqui Hopwood and Margaret Williams. Lastly I am very appreciative of the support received from Julia Twomlow and her team at the Leach Pottery Studio and Museum, St Ives and Philip Leach of Springfield Pottery, Hartland.

A special mention is owed to Dr Oliver Kent for his paper *Firing Technology and the search for the 'English Tradition'*, to the potter, Peter Smith for his insight into kilns, materials and making and the ceramics of both East and West, to Lawrence Osborne for his thoughts on the origin of the St Ives workshop seal, and to Eileen Hampson for her help on Henry Bergen. Thanks are again due to Steve Tustin for his sensitive and complimentary graphic design and to John Shakeshaft for his patient proof reading and ceramic expertise.

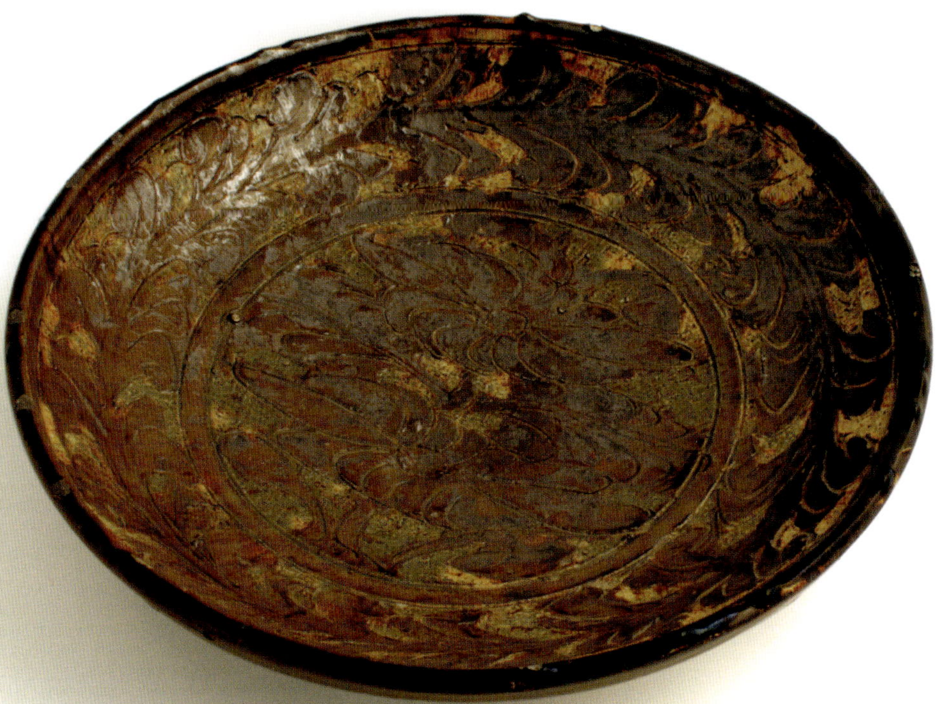

Shoji Hamada sgraffito bowl
(c. 1923). 39cm x 13cm.

PREAMBLE

In the pre-industrial world of localised markets and relatively closed communities, slipware potters established workshops close to the raw materials of their trades – clay to throw, iron ore to glaze and wood or coal to fire. Good forms were handed down from generation to generation, later changing their practical usage over time as the early stages of industrialisation made new materials available to rural communities. A staple form such as a handled cup or bowl might later be found a new role as a paint container for scene painters or coach builders.

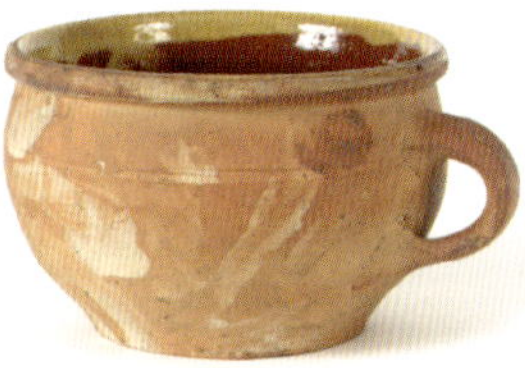

Gallipot (c. 1900). Height 9cm.

Similarly, styles of decoration, whether using the sgraffito (scratching) tradition of the West Country or the slip trailing of the Midlands and Northern England and Wales, persisted, even on coarse earthenwares, to gladden the heart of the user and encourage a sale. In its more illustrious rural expression, this embellishment might be on celebratory jugs, or large chargers primarily for decoration and very occasional use. In the West Country, traditional potteries persisted in the Bideford area of North Devon and in Dorset and Somerset as well as Cornwall into the 20th century, with Lakes of Truro finally closing its doors in 1980 and C H Brannam Ltd of Barnstaple, North Devon, in the early years of the new Millennium.

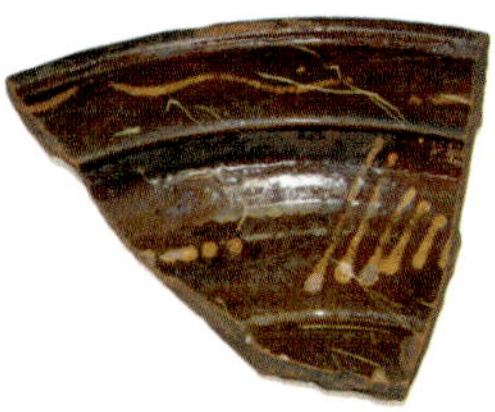

Plate shards (c. 1700).

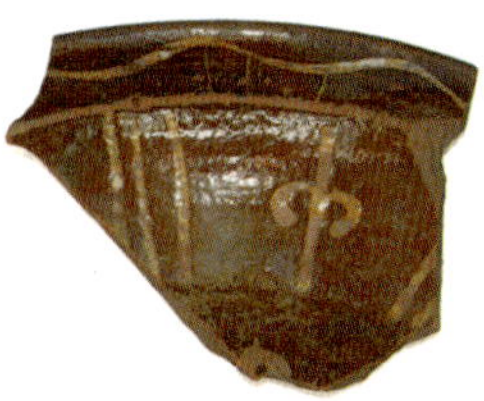

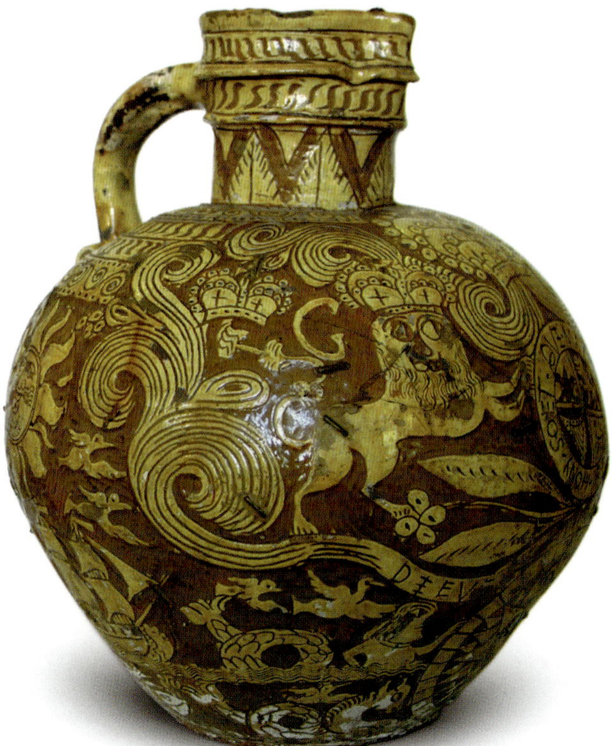

Thomas Fields of Bideford (c. 1750). Height 37.5cm.

Similarly in the Midlands and the North, whilst the country potteries of Staffordshire were swamped or succeeded by the industrial manufacturers of Stoke and the Six Towns by the end of the 18th century, traditional potteries of the Buckley area of North Wales continued in production until the Second World War. Amongst remaining rural workshops, even if the market for more elaborately finished wares declined, easier production methods using moulds and casting were developed to compete, and the urge to decorate never quite disappeared.

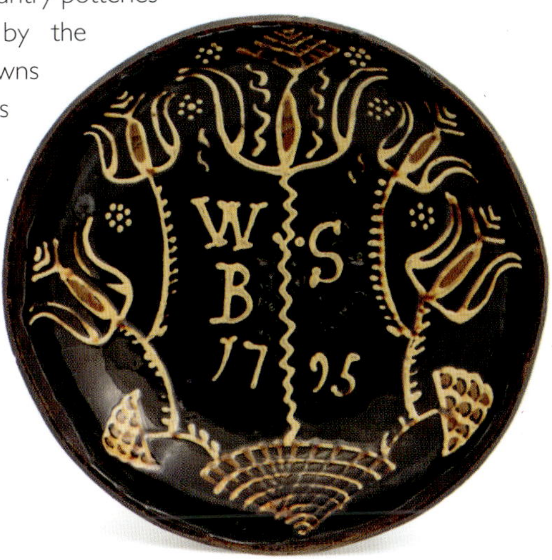

Bristol or Midlands (dated 1795). Diameter 40cm.

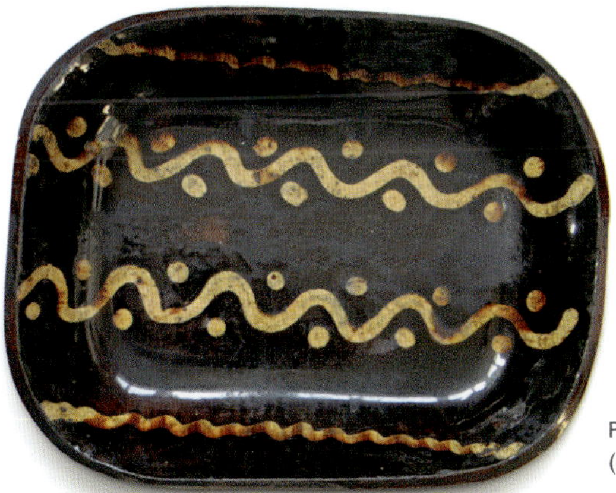

Powell pottery, Buckley (c. 1900-1920). Length 31cm.

Over time international trade grew, bringing exotic porcelains from China and Asia, and a taste for such ceramic products of the East was established in the homes of the aspirational middle classes in the 18th century. Home manufacturers in Liverpool, Bristol, Worcester and elsewhere in the Midlands responded by discovering, through trial and error, the secrets of porcelain, and by imitating the look by the use of surface slip and glaze to disguise the red fabric of local pottery.

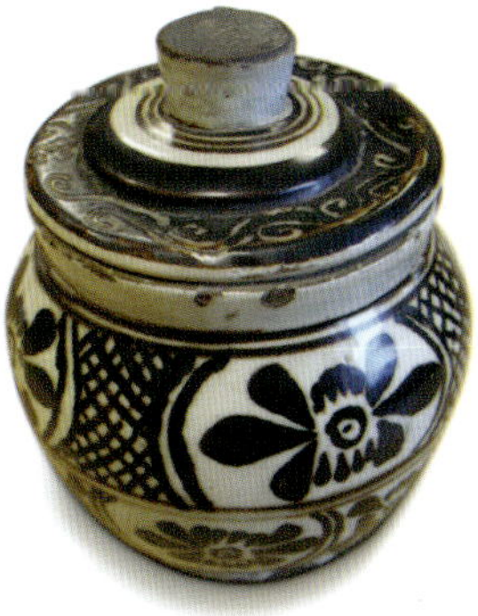

Chinese stoneware (possibly 12th century). Height 13cm.

As a nation whose wealth was built on international commerce, a taste for the exotic and for novelty became entrenched, and in the early years of the 20th century, a strong vogue developed for older, newly excavated Chinese ceramics of the Sung period. Middle-class artist potters, such as Howson Taylor of Ruskin Pottery in 1900-1910 and, in the very early 1920s, Reginald Wells with his 'Soon' wares, responded to this taste by developing their own wares inspired by China and 'the East'. The establishment in St Ives by Bernard Leach and Hamada Shoji of the first oriental climbing kiln to be built in the West should be viewed in this wider context, representing as it did a transplanting of an exotic approach to making and firing ceramics.

1 BEGINNINGS

Our study of the slipwares and raku wares from the Leach Pottery starts with an overview of the early influences on its leading figures. In the case of Leach and Hamada, it was primarily the traditions of Korea, China and Japan, and a broadly Eastern philosophy and aesthetic, whilst for Michael Cardew, Leach's first apprentice and lead thrower from 1923 to 1926, it was very much the English tradition in general and the slipwares of the West Country in particular that were pivotal. Additionally, the indirect stylistic influences of the slipwares of the Midlands (Thomas Toft and followers) and the North (the moulded wares of Buckley and Shropshire) must be taken into account, as well as the artistic community encountered and established in and around St Ives in the 1920s and elsewhere.

EAST

Bernard Leach and Shoji Hamada

There are strong parallels between the early interests and aspirations of the Asian born Leach and Hamada. Both hoped to make careers as artists, but were to choose ceramics as their eventual vocation. Whilst they had been aware of each other indirectly for some time and Hamada first saw pots by Leach at an exhibition in 1914, they did not meet until 1919.

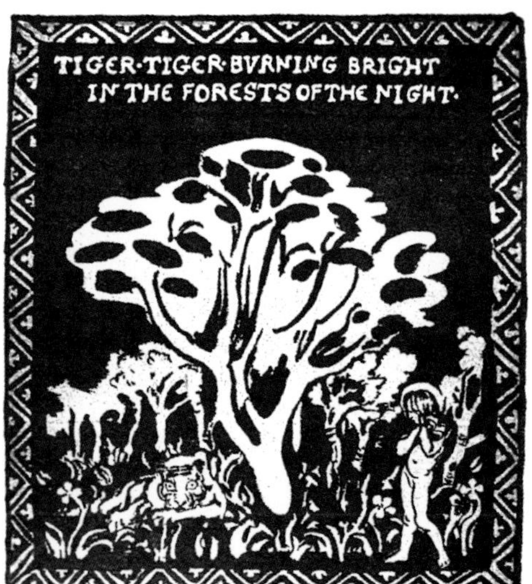

Leach woodcut (c. 1913).

Bernard Howell Leach was born in Hong Kong in 1887, and after the early death of his mother spent many of his most formative years with his grandparents in Japan, and later in Singapore, only living in England from 1897 where he attended Public School. He then trained initially at the Slade School of Art from 1903, later attending the London School of Art in 1908 where he learnt etching under Frank Brangwyn (1867-1956), before moving to Tokyo in the spring of 1909 with the intention of making a living there using his print-making skills. His advertising of lessons in etchings brought him into contact with leading members of the Shirakaba (Silver Birch) artists and writers group, who had a fascination with Western art and aesthetics. With Leach's background and training he was a natural collaborator, and contributed articles to the Shirakaba magazine from as early as 1911, notably providing a woodcut illustration on the theme of the artist and visionary poet William Blake (1757-1827) in 1913.

Artist or Craftsman

Hamada Shoji, born in 1894 at Mizonokuchi in Kawasaki City, had similarly intended in his youth to be an artist, and won prizes for his woodcuts both at school and college. Kozo Yoshida's article *The ceramic art of Shoji Hamada*, written for the retrospective exhibition of Hamada at the National Museum of Modern Art, Tokyo in 1977 recounts something of the latter's early influences and decisions:

'He accidentally came across the following statement by Renoir at the house of his friend, Shohachi Kimura; "There certainly is an extremely large number of prospective artists in France. But I wonder why almost all of them want to paint? If half, or even one-third of them entered the crafts, there would be a great improvement in the quality of the crafts, and this would probably relieve the excessive competition among painters as well." These were just like the voice of heaven to Mr. Hamada, and he decided to strike off on the potter's way.'

'Hamada felt that he could not be a first-class painter and would be fated to work only by compromise: conversely he felt that even if one makes an error in producing craft, some value might come of it so long as the product is usable.'

Early experiences of making

The widely recounted story of Leach's introduction to pottery is of his attendance at a raku party in the outskirts of Tokyo in February 1911 where he was invited to decorate pots made and biscuit-fired in advance, which were then glaze-fired at a relatively low temperature during the gathering. However, this was not the only early pottery influence, as in Tokyo in the years preceding WW1, a middle class vogue for making and decorating ceramics as a hobby was comparatively widespread. The researches of Brian Moeran, published in the Journal of Design History Vol. 2 Nos. 2 & 3 (1989) in the article *Bernard Leach and the Japanese Folk Craft Movement; the Formative Years*, provide further insight on the involvement of Hamada and two other eminent potters Tomimoto Kenkichi (1886-1963) and Kawai Kanjiro (1890-1966) in such sociable gatherings.

Tomimoto had been introduced to ceramics whilst studying at the Central School of Arts in London in 1908-1909, and became a close friend of Leach by 1910 who nicknamed him 'Tomi', later together 'discovering' Oriental crafts – in particular Korean ceramics. By the spring of 1911, Leach and Tomimoto were spending time decorating pots in a small shop near the Colonial Exposition (Takushoku Hakurankai) in Ueno Park, Tokyo, close to where they first saw an exhibition of Korean wares. At around the same time, both Hamada and Kanjiro separately used to visit the same ceramic workshop on the other side of the capital to make and decorate pots, which lead to their later meeting. These three Japanese potters along with the philosopher and critic Yanagi Soetsu (1889-1961) were to be the co-founders of highly influential Japanese Mingei folk craft movement in the 1920s.

Ceramic training and development

Hamada's early professional training was strongly technical, giving him wide experience of both glazes and kilns. After graduating from school in 1913, he enrolled in the Ceramics department of Tokyo Advanced Technical College. In 1916 he entered the Kyoto Municipal Institute of Ceramics and rejoined his friend Kawai Kanjiro who was working there, and Hamada undertook over one hundred experimental glaze firings in just a year covering a range of the main traditional stoneware finishes. In his later years before departing to England with Leach, he also took lessons in throwing at weekends and this in conjunction with the knowledge of kiln materials and construction gained from his college training and his visits to Seto and other pottery centres would have proved vital in the early days at St Ives.

Raku ware cake dish by Kenzan.

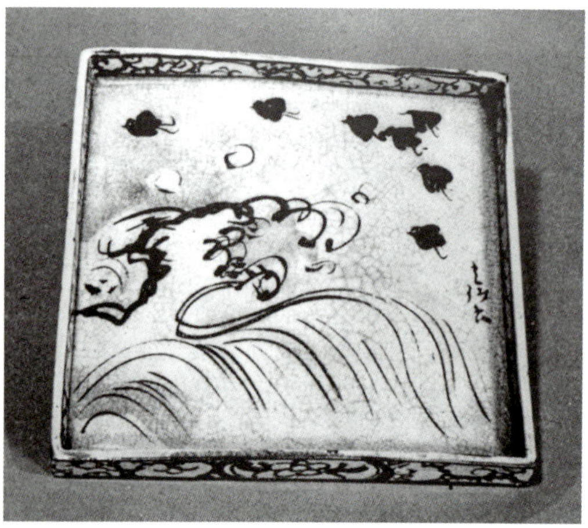

Leach's development was in contrast more informal and artistically based. Influenced by his experience of decorating raku in 1911, later that year he took lessons with Ogata Kenzan 6th (1853-1923) a master potter of a dynasty of potters and a specialist in raku. Notably, Leach was taught to throw on a Japanese wheel, which relies on the use of a stick to provide momentum and is best suited to the making of relatively small objects. Kenzan built a kiln for Leach at the latter's workshop in 1913, and this same kiln was later rebuilt on Yanagi's land at Abiko in 1916, where Leach is known to have used a Japanese wheel to throw pottery. The model kiln illustrated was made by him at Abiko in 1917; it has a dense greyish-white raku body with brush-painted oxide and sgraffito decoration direct on the fabric under a clear (probably lead) glaze. This is a stylised version of reality, and from a contemporary photo we know that the kiln was protected by an extension of the roof of his workshop. Unfortunately, the kiln was built too close to the roof. This led to a disastrous fire in

Abiko (1917).
Length 17.5cm.

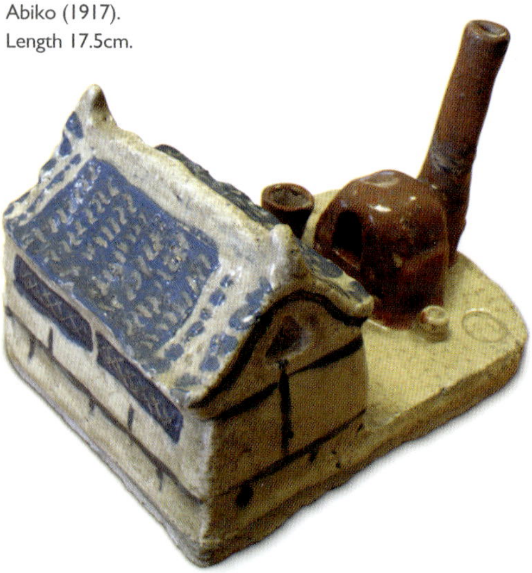

1919 which destroyed his workshop as well as technical notes and records that Leach had accumulated during his time in Japan.

Oliver Watson, writing in *Bernard Leach, Potter and Artist* in 1997, says of his collaboration with Kenzan 6th:

'Leach found a teacher in Ogata Kenzan 6th. Kenzan came from a line of sophisticated, urban, fine-art, gentleman-ceramicists. He was not a country potter, and was far from being an "anonymous craftsman"; and Leach similarly had no desire to follow the ways of either.'

Leach seems to have developed an early preference for the separation of the physical and technical acts of making and firing from the higher art disciplines of design and decoration, a philosophy and approach which he retained throughout his life. He consequently valued in particular the contrasting and complementary skills of a series of collaborators over the years, and was generously appreciative of their contribution to the output of the St Ives workshop bearing his name, the traditional division of labour in the studio of a master artist between teacher and acolytes.

From surviving examples of Leach ceramics of the two periods of making, 1913-1914 and 1916-1920, it is raku that dominates, with some stoneware and belatedly porcelain produced in his last years in Tokyo. It is now the increasing view of commentators that the higher-fired wares were produced with the help of professional throwers working to his designs, for him subsequently to decorate, primarily with the brush. Useful wares feature strongly, showing the influence of both continental European Delft and stoneware as well as oriental examples.

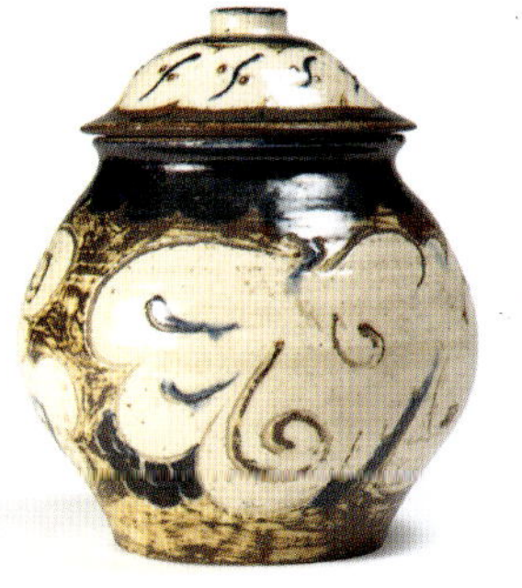

Raku style jar (St Ives c. 1922).

In the area of particular interest for this book; low-temperature raku, continental Delft and English earthenware were clear influences. The method for raku production, with making in advance and later decoration of biscuit-fired pots probably suited Leach's approach, skills and priorities well, and implies at the very least an initial collaboration with his friend Tomimoto who took raku lessons alongside Leach with Kenzan 6th, and showed an immediate flare as a thrower. Tomimoto committed himself to the life of a potter in advance of Leach, and set up a raku kiln and workshop from 1913 on family land at Ando, Nara Prefecture. There are examples of Tomi's decorated raku in Japanese museums.

Quaint Old English Pottery by Charles J Lomax

This title was probably owned by Leach by 1913, and features the work of the Midlands potter, Thomas Toft and other English slipwares: it was to influence Leach's work in both raku and slipware for the following 15 years. For further information, please refer to page 17.

China: An aesthetic and philosophical pilgrimage

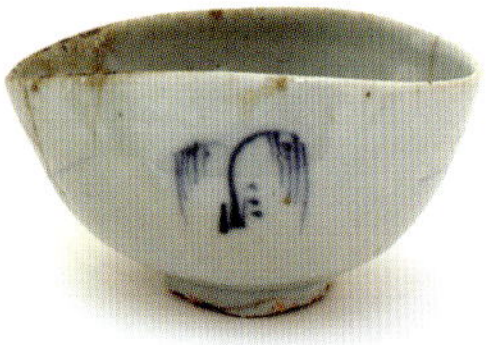

Arita (Japan) porcelain bowl given to Leach by Hamada (c.1610).

Leach had been aware of Korean ceramics since his 1911 visit to the Korean Hall in the Colonial Exposition at Ueno Park, accompanied by Tomimoto. Brian Moeran (op cit) believes that he was he was disappointed with what he found in Japan, and with the way in which (quoting Leach) 'the art of old Japan has passed away with the old life and that which lingered on not only lacked all vitality, but was a hindrance to progress on new lines' . In turn, a material part of Japanese ceramic traditions owed a legacy to a group of Korean potters, so a ceramic pilgrimage searching out the historic roots elsewhere in Asia may have been a factor. Leach also developed an interest in Chinese art, and this was probably a motivation for his trip to China in 1914, his continuing commitment to fine rather than applied art made clear by his inclusion of drawing and etching equipment in his luggage.

His trip was additionally a spiritual and philosophical journey, as he had been in correspondence with Dr Alfred Westharp, a doctor of philosophy and music, a resident of Peking and some five years his senior. Emmanuel Cooper, in Bernard Leach, Life and Work writes; "It seemed to Leach that Westharp offered 'a deep and wide perception in art, education and philosophy to focus my own groping thoughts between the Occident and the Orient"'. Westharp's influence on Leach led to some friction with his family when they joined Leach in Peking in 1915.

It was, however, the two-week visit of Yanagi to Peking in 1916 following the latter's one-month trip to Korea looking at pots, historical and archaeological sights that, in the view of Cooper, 'rekindled Leach's appreciation and enjoyment of pots' , and Yanagi and Leach were later to visit Korea together in 1918. During Yanagi's visit, he and Leach toured China by train and donkey, seeing the sights and subsequently searching antique shops for Sung pottery among other objects. Whilst Leach's stay in China did not result in great artistic production, some of his drawings and etchings inspired by Chinese art and scenery were included in an exhibition organised by Yanagi after their return to Japan together, later that year.

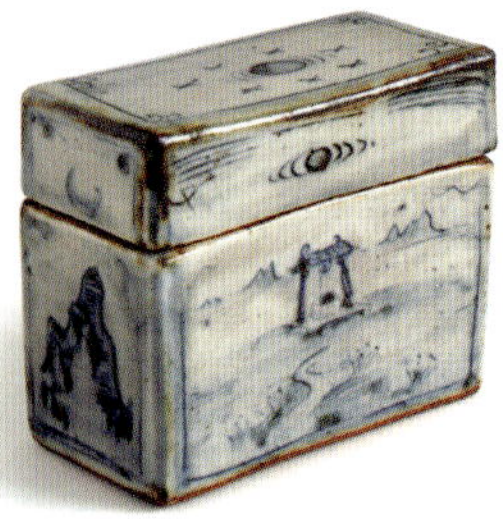

Lidded box in porcelain by Leach (c.1931).

It is difficult to discern any aesthetic impact of his two years in China on his ceramic output once he was back in Japan. Some of his earliest ceramics of 1912-1913 involving cobalt blue brushwork on porcelain blanks were strongly influenced by the Ming porcelains produced at centres such as Jingdezhen, and stylised Chinese landscapes dominate. But the similar white-bodied wares in porcelain and white stoneware decorated by him in 1919-1920 feature stylised brushwork motifs, with a bird design particularly favoured. A similar motif was used by him in raku work from around 1917 featuring the verse of William Blake (see page 57), and this may have been in his mind.

The landscape around Jingdezhen is very distinctive, and while it is not known whether Leach and Yanagi visited there in 1916, a range of hump-backed mountains resembling the Guilin hills near

Jingdezhen feature prominently on a woodcut produced by Leach for the Shirakaba magazine in 1918. Similar motifs – the winding road, the high village, a distant mountain range – appear on his St Ives output in both slipware and stoneware. An image similar to the Shirakaba woodcut is also found on large Toft-style chargers decorated by him in 1929, one of which is listed as 'Hills in China' in the records of the owners, High Cross House, Dartington (see page 95).

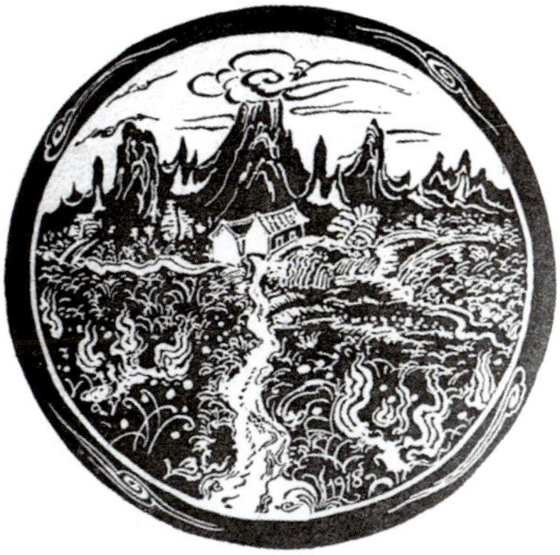

Leach woodcut (c. 1918).

The Japanese peasant tradition

Simple designs also feature on peasant stonewares produced in the Seto region of Japan. Motifs in brushwork on these wares, which were normally painted by children, range from abstract designs such as Una-No-me or 'horse eye' to motifs from nature including weeping willow trees. Seto peasant dishes were purchased and valued by both Leach and Hamada; examples remain in their respective reference collections, and Seto-type motifs were used on ceramics by Leach and Cardew throughout their careers.

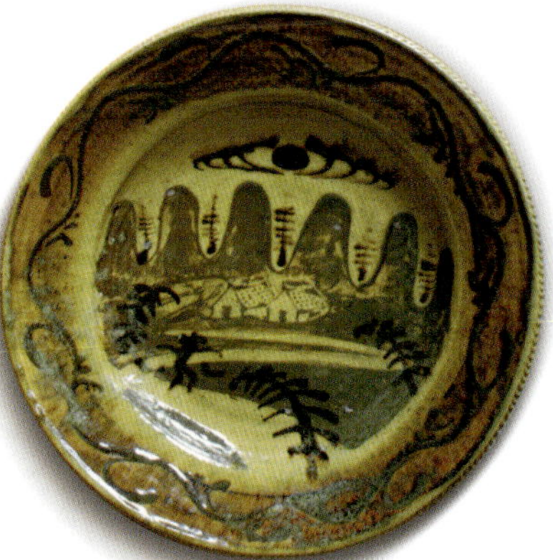

Slipware charger
(St Ives 1929).

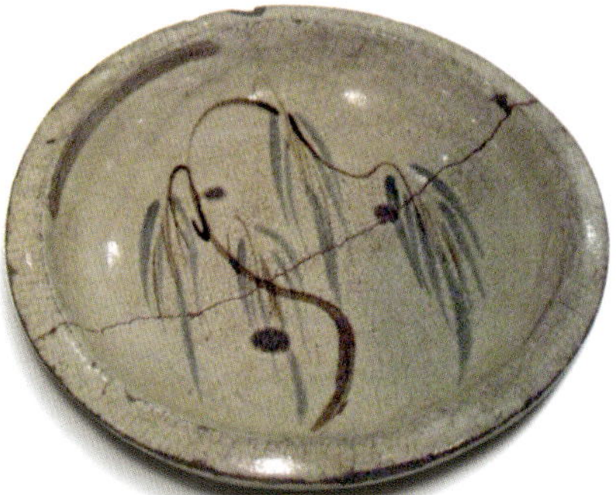

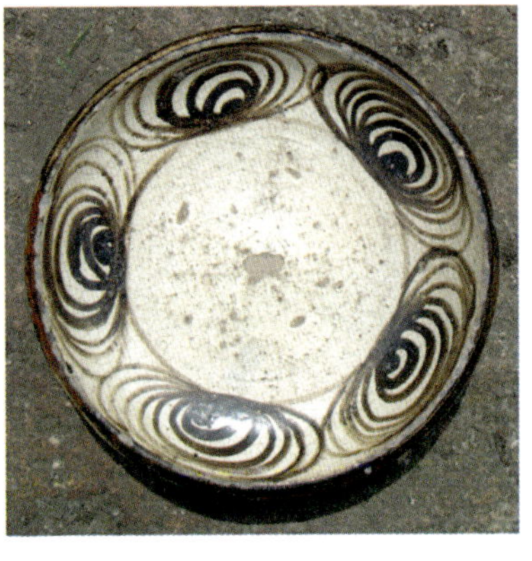

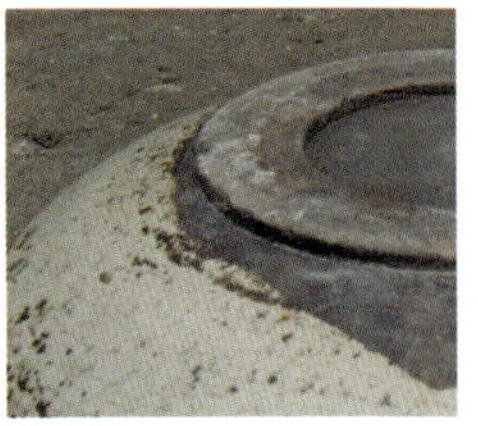

Seto stoneware dishes
(19th century).
Both diameter 31cm.

The anonymous craftsman

The leading members of the Japanese Mingei folk craft movement valued highly such unthinking and untutored everyday ceramics. There developed as a result a cult of 'the anonymous craftsman' and examples of rural craftwork from around Japan and elsewhere were collected by Yanagi and his circle of friends and a museum was built to house them, the Mingeikan in the outskirts of Tokyo.

The nature of creation

After his return to Japan from St Ives in 1924, Hamada sought to rethink his approach to ceramics, and Kozo Yoshida provides an eloquent summary in his 1977 article (op cit):

'He has come to believe that all the charm of pottery comes from its material, clay, and the flame at the time of firing ... He feels that he himself does not produce it, but that it is something which is born out of nature ... After Mr. Hamada took up residence at Mashiko he referred to himself as a craftsman. This was because he did not want to appear to be an artist who likes to create through conscious intent and intelligence.'

The Mingei movement aspiration to honour as far as possible the practice, procedures and time-served skills of the anonymous rural craftsman was reflected in the ethos of Hamada's establishment of a workshop at Mashiko from 1924, a true revivalist approach which may in turn have influenced Cardew in his recreation of a rural earthenware workshop in Winchcombe from 1926.

The status of the craftsman

This is a difficult subject for discussion but needs to be raised here, underpinning as it does the impact of the oriental ceramic culture brought to England by Leach and Hamada in the 1920s. Even now, some Japanese craftsmen still venerate their forbears by acknowledging their dynastic heritage, and 20th or 30th generation potters are not uncommon. There is additionally almost a 'nobility of craft' element to this practice, which has survived decades of heavy industrialisation in Japan in the 20th century, a reflection of the impact on educated Japanese society of the Mingei ethos of Yanagi and his followers.

In the western context to which we now turn, the role of craftsman whilst valued in the pre-industrial economy, had became a role of common toil (as was the case for the rural potteries of 19th century Japan), and it was Leach who above all made it acceptable and fashionable for well-to-do British people of a good background to take on the role of craftsman. It was however the central influence of Hamada, Yanagi and the Mingei movement in creating a fashion for peasant craftsmanship that underpinned this ethos, subsequently propagated in St Ives and in the subsequent Studio Pottery movement of the 20th century.

WEST

In Japan, in part a reflection of the fashionable interest in western art and aesthetics in Japan (see page 10), Leach had been shown respect up to the time of his departure and had a developed a circle of practical and personal supporters; the West was however to prove a comparative 'baptism of fire'. Turning now to western ceramic influences on the early Leach Pottery, probably the most significant in terms of the output of the Leach Pottery in the period to 1926 predated Leach's arrival in England:

Quaint Old English Pottery by Charles J Lomax

This title published privately in 1909 was the catalogue of an important private collection of English earthenwares, since dispersed to public and private collections both in the USA and Britain. It was purchased for Leach by Tomimoto in Maruzen bookstore in Tokyo, probably in 1913, and features the Midlands potter, Thomas Toft, and his family and fellow potters with full page photographic illustrations of their work. Toft ware chargers were made on a large scale (up to 50 cm/20 inches in diameter), giving considerable scope for elaborate design and decoration – a ceramic canvas the style of which clearly appealed to Leach. Slip-trailed techniques used by Toft appear on Leach's raku pots from as early as 1916, and Toft designs and the tightly delineated and applied techniques of such wares were later to dominate the finer slipware output of Leach, Hamada and Cardew at the St Ives workshop from 1923.

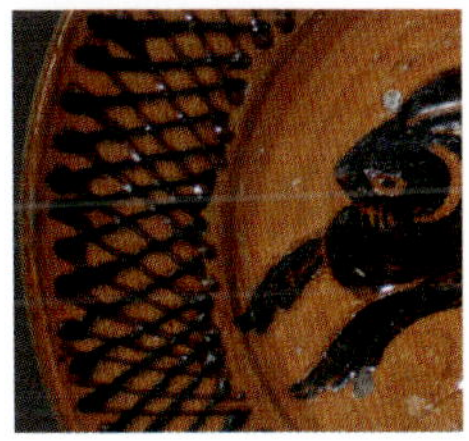

St Ives charger detail (c. 1923-1925).

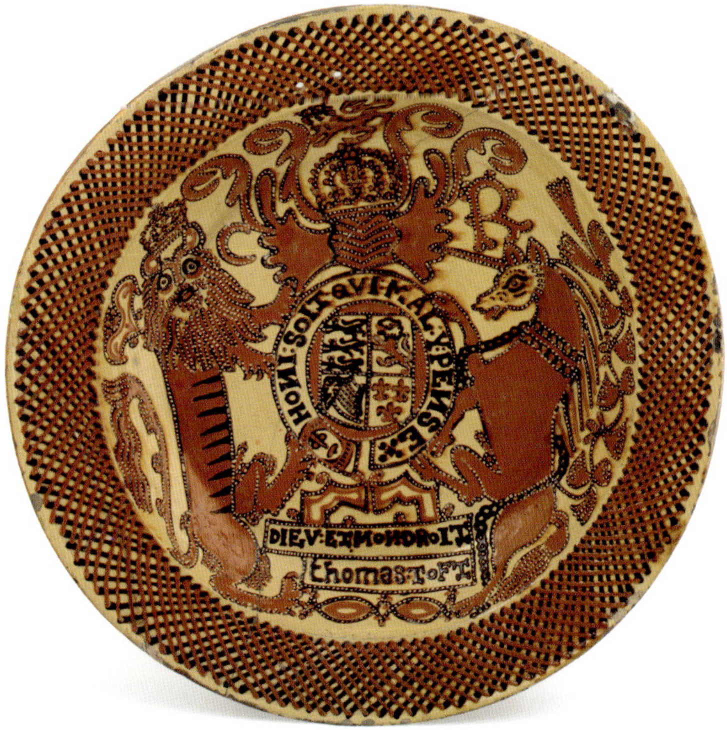

Toft slipware charger (c. 1670). Diameter 56cm.

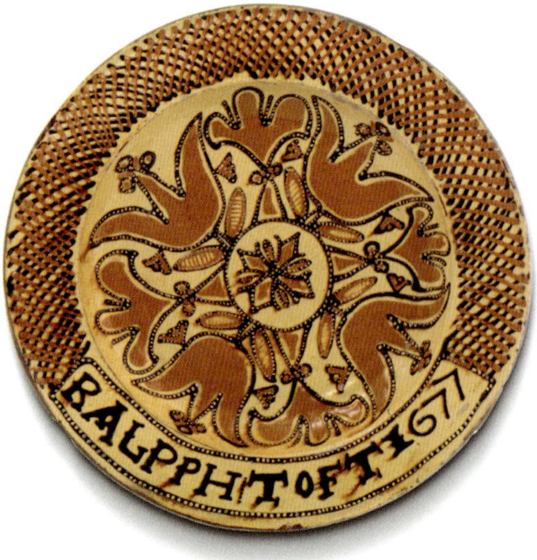

Toft slipware charger (dated 1677). Diameter 45cm.

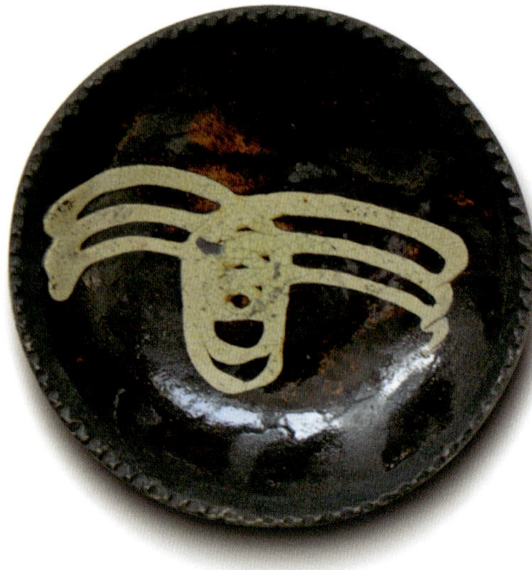

Staffordshire moulded dish (c. 1700). Diameter 35cm.

Notably, however, examples of the hump-moulded and freely slip-trailed dishes produced by rural English and Welsh workshops in the Midlands and Buckley in North Wales are not represented at all as Lomax did not own any. Soon after his arrival in England in 1920, Hamada sought out London public collections of English and other slipwares at the Guildhall Museum and the Victoria & Albert Museum, in his search for the roots of the rural tradition of British ceramics. These studies paralleled the interest of the Mingei group of Yanagi and others in Japanese country craftsmanship. Such wares were avidly collected by Hamada during his time in England, and some 30 are on display at the Mashiko Reference Collection Museum.

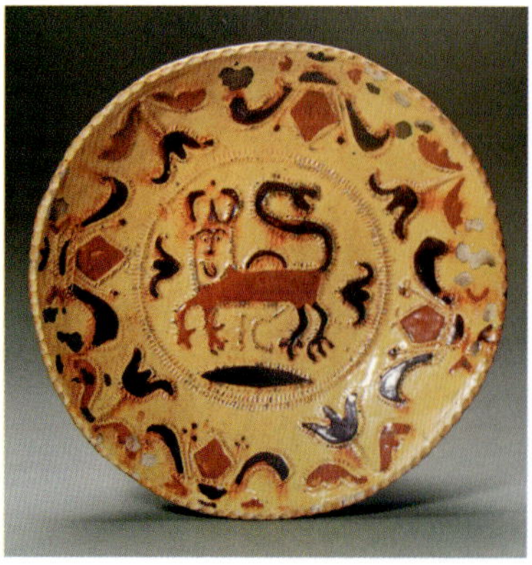

Midlands moulded dish (18th century). Diameter 20cm.

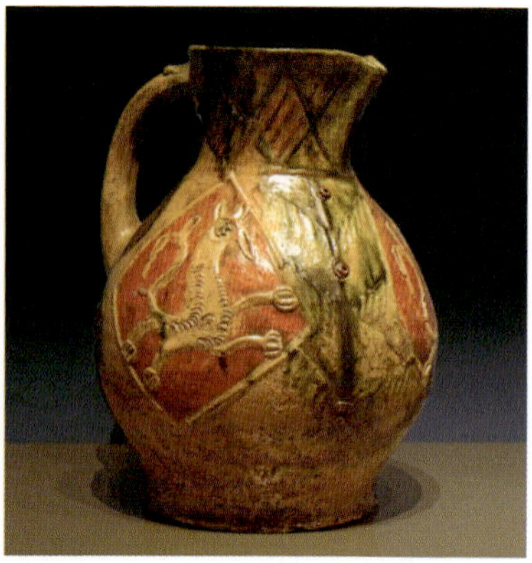

English medieval slipware jug.

Although the cultured circle of friends and followers surrounding Leach and Hamada from 1921, lacked the cosmopolitan quality of the circle of Yanagi, it had a clear regional flavour. Additionally, contacts were readily established with craft colonies such as the Ditchling Guild in Sussex headed by the calligrapher Edward Johnston (1872-1944) and the sculptor and letter-cutter Eric Gill (1882-1940), and London whilst not close at hand was visited regularly with contributions made to exhibitions in the West End from autumn 1921.

The following provides background information on some of the leading primarily local and regional figures and influences which are mentioned elsewhere in the book, here arranged in broad chronological order:

Frances Horne and the St Ives Handicraft Guild

The wife of a rice merchant and a lady of considerable financial resources, Frances Horne established a craft guild in St Ives in 1919, primarily as a personal diversion reflecting the frequent absences of her husband on business. A wide range of handcrafts were encompassed, including basket-making, weaving and embroidery, with an emphasis on craft skills suitable primarily for women. Her offer of help to Bernard Leach to establish a pottery was seen as an extension of the Guild, and she provided him with a loan of £2,500 of capital for the necessary land and building together with a payment of £250 per annum for the first three years towards running costs. In establishing the Guild, Mrs Horne had hoped to foster the active involvement of local women and provide employment in the light of the continuing decline of the traditional fishing industry of the area. Sadly, the sudden and early death of her husband in 1923 left Leach's first sponsor impoverished and obliged to sell the family home at Carbis Bay and move away. The Handicraft Guild did, however, have the effect of broadening the cultural environment of St Ives, previously dominated by the fine arts, and Frances Horne was pivotal in the establishment of what was to become a Pottery workshop of international renown.

The Art Colony of St Ives

The town's art colony had its roots in the building of a railway line linking the area to London in 1877, which facilitated the visits of artists attracted by the unspoilt beauty of the local countryside and the quality of light offered by its maritime situation. The colony did not achieve full prominence until the period around WW2 and the arrival of Barbara Hepworth, Ben Nicholson and others, but it established travelling exhibitions to the South West and Midlands. One in 1925 was unique in that the ceramics of Leach were included alongside wall-hung art, but in general the geographic separation of the Pottery on the outskirts of the town was mirrored by a practical separation, although Leach provided lectures to local St Ives societies on subjects close to his heart – notably William Blake – on several occasions in the 1920s.

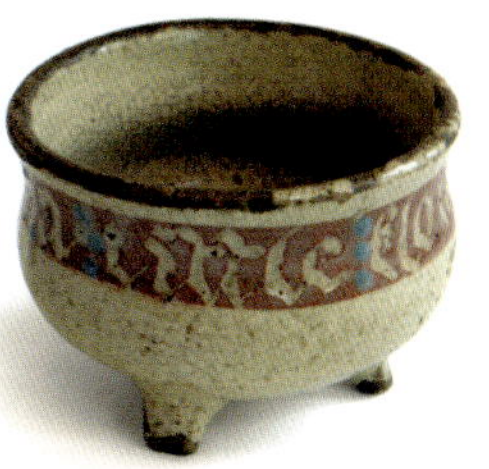

St Ives incense burner (c. 1922).

Lakes of Truro

First established as a business in 1872 and as the leading surviving traditional slipware pottery in Cornwall, Lakes were a natural point of reference for Leach and Hamada in their researches into English and regional ceramic traditions that in the early days were necessarily foreign to them. The everyday products of Lakes such as water jugs of varying sizes and other wares were in general use in St Ives, and Hamada investigated this pottery by visits in 1921 and 1923. The effect of such visits was evident in technical areas such as glazes as described later, but not in the forms of pottery, aside from the detailing on some handles of stoneware jugs made by Hamada whilst at St Ives (see page 44).

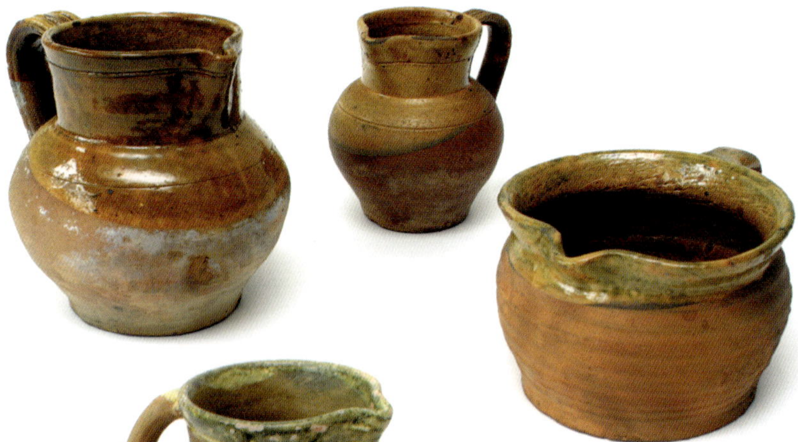

Group of Lakes jugs (1920s).
Heights 9 – 15cm.

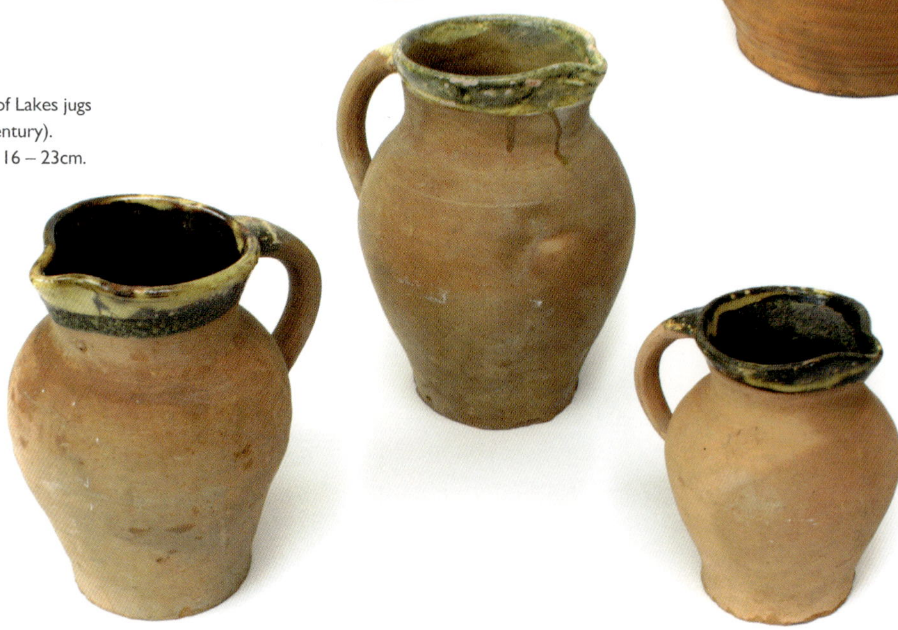

Group of Lakes jugs
(20th century).
Heights 16 – 23cm.

Robert Morton Nance

R M Nance (1873-1959) was born in Cardiff of Cornish parents. After school and college, and an early career as an artist primarily of marine subjects, some exhibited at the Royal Academy, he moved to Cornwall in 1906, subsequently buying a property at Carbis Bay, close to St Ives, in 1914. He was the leading revivalist of the Cornish language in the period after WW1, was co-founder of the Old Cornwall Society, and became an antiquarian and marine archaeologist probably best known for his researches into and publication of *Sailing ship models* (1924).

Robert was the brother of the ceramic historian Ernest Morton Nance (cf. Henry Bergen), so had an interest in ceramics and was one of Leach's earliest friends in St Ives. His direct involvement in the Leach pottery dated from the autumn of 1922 when he collaborated with Hamada in decorating a number of raku style pots thrown by the latter (see pages 55-56). His son Robin ('Dicon') was subsequently apprenticed to Leach, and made a significant practical contribution to the Pottery through his woodworking, design and engineering skills as we will later learn.

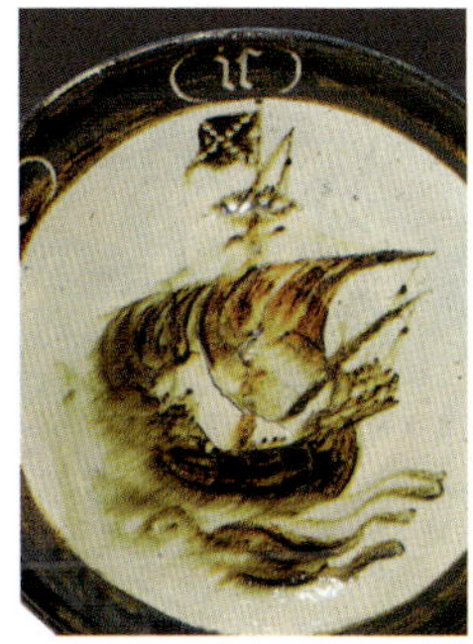

Detail of Nance decorated St Ives charger (1922).

Henry Bergen

Henry Vanderveer Bergen (1873-1950) was born in Bay Ridge, New York, in 1873 to parents of Dutch extraction, and read History at Yale University before studying in Heidelberg and then Munich, where he took a degree of Doctor of Philosophy in 1906. He subsequently followed a literary career, writing, translating and editing, which brought him to London and the British Museum. He came on to the St Ives scene through meeting Leach at an Artificers Guild exhibition in Conduit Street, London, probably in autumn 1921, in which Leach was an exhibitor. This area has been under-researched, but correspondence from 1924 preserved in the Leach archive indicates that Bergen spent some weeks in St Ives in the summer of 1922 taking pottery lessons and also decorating raku pots thrown for him by Hamada, and a date of 1922 date is assigned to a photo of him at the wheel reproduced in the album section of *Hamada Potter*.

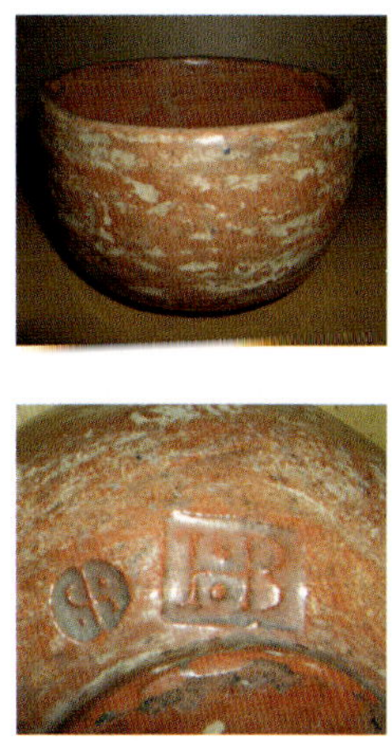

Bergen mixed clay tea bowl (1922). Height 10 cm.

Bergen's friendship with Leach was to prove an enduring one, and later in the 1920s he used contacts to promote Leach on the London scene. Bergen is probably best known for the encouragement he provided to Leach to set down his theories and approach to ceramics in writings that coalesced into A potter's book which was extensively proof read and refined by Bergen prior to its publication in 1940.

Bergen was politically to the left, and is regarded as having provided a social conscience to Leach and later Cardew in promoting the idea of making well-designed everyday ceramics available to the common man. His influence may

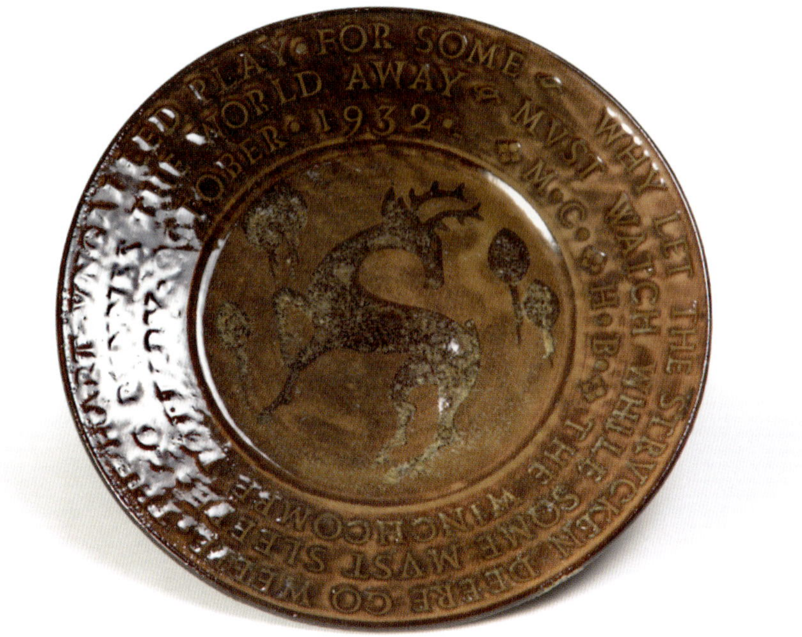

Bergen decorated platter (dated 1932).
Diameter 35cm.

perhaps be seen in the development of standardised forms both at St Ives and at Winchcombe Pottery, and David Leach was later to develop a range of Standard Wares to designs originated by his father in the late 1930s.

Bergen was an occasional visitor over the years to St Ives, but worked particularly closely with Cardew in his Winchcombe days, providing designs based around slip-resist techniques and impressed lettering for forms thrown by Cardew or, on occasions, Sidney Tustin (1913-2005). Bergen's extensive collection of early wares from St Ives in the 1920s and slipwares from 1930s Winchcombe was donated by him to The Potteries Museum, Stoke in 1948. He was also a friend of Ernest Nance, Robert's brother, and proof read Ernest's book *The Pottery & Porcelain of Swansea & Nantgarw* (1942).

Those wanting to learn more of Bergen are recommended to read Eileen Hampson's essay *Henry Bergen: Friend of Studio Potters*, Journal of the Northern Ceramics Society, Volume 8 (1991).

Johnston, Gill and Ditchling

Perhaps reflecting the interest of Francis Horne in craft communities, Leach, Hamada, Cardew and Matsubayashi visited Ditchling on several occasions in the early to mid-1920s, and Leach later spent some weeks there in 1936, visiting friends and walking and sketching on the nearby South Downs.

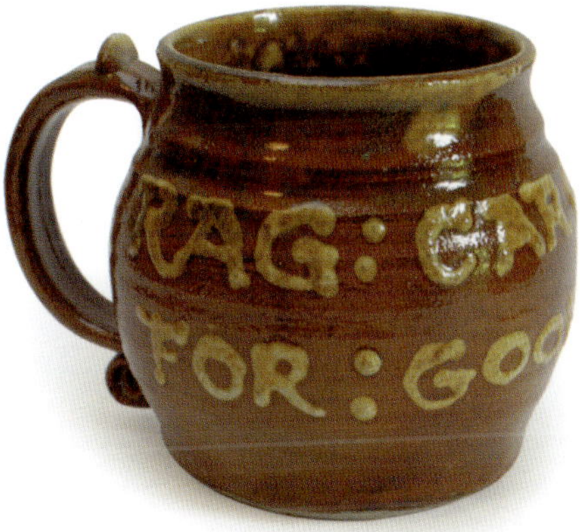

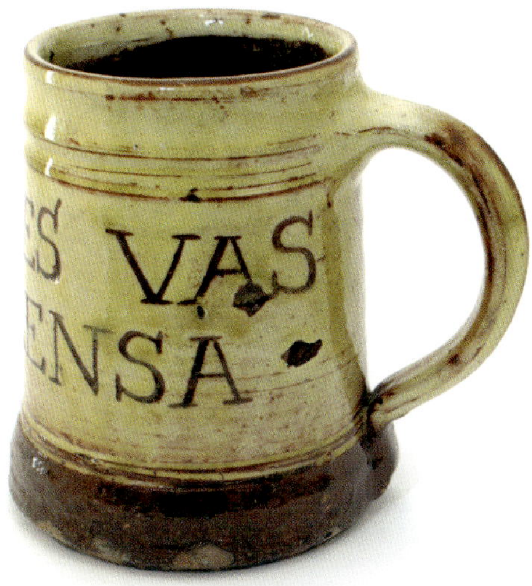

Winchcombe slipware (c. 1926). Height 11cm.

St Ives slipware tankard (1923-1924). Height 10cm.

Gill alphabet for St Dominic's Press (c. 1918).

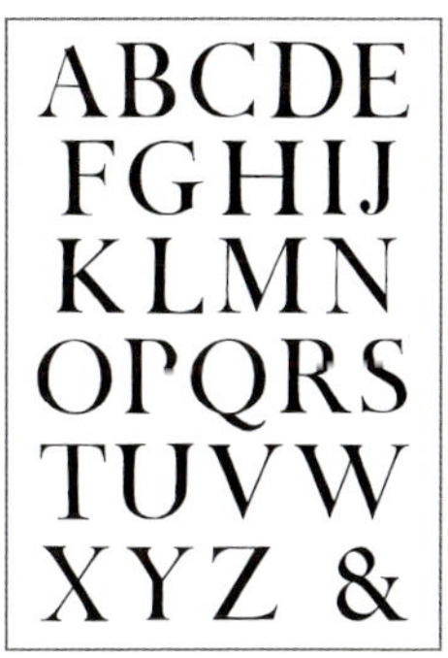

Aside from the philosophical and organisational aspects of the Gill craft guild, probably the most obvious influence on ceramic output at the Leach Pottery was the use of incised lettering on jugs and tankards produced in the period 1923-1926. Prior to this, any lettering was usually slip trailed. Edward Johnston, a calligrapher famed for his alphabets (Johnston Sans being the typeface of the London Underground to this day), was one of the founders at Ditchling, and his pupil Eric Gill developed a series of now widely used Alphabets including Perpetua and Gill Sans, which in turn influenced the incised lettering used by Cardew on his slipwares at St Ives and subsequently at Winchcombe during 1926-1939. A fuller account of the visits of Leach, Hamada, Cardew (and later Yanagi) to Ditchling, and its consequent influence on the Japanese Mingei movement, is given in our publication *Michael Cardew and the West Country Slipware Tradition* (2008).

Edwin Beer Fishley (c. 1890).

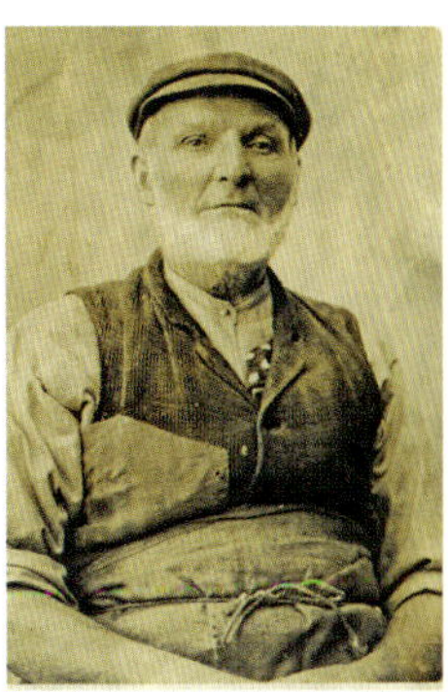

Michael Cardew and North Devon

Michael Ambrose Cardew was born in Wimbledon in 1901 and brought up in London, but the family owned a holiday home at Saunton near Barnstaple, North Devon, which Cardew visited regularly in his youth. His father Arthur was a collector of slipware and an occasional writer on English ceramics and was a friend of Edwin Beer Fishley (1832-1912) of Fremington, perhaps the best known of the Fishley dynasty of potters. Their Saunton house was full

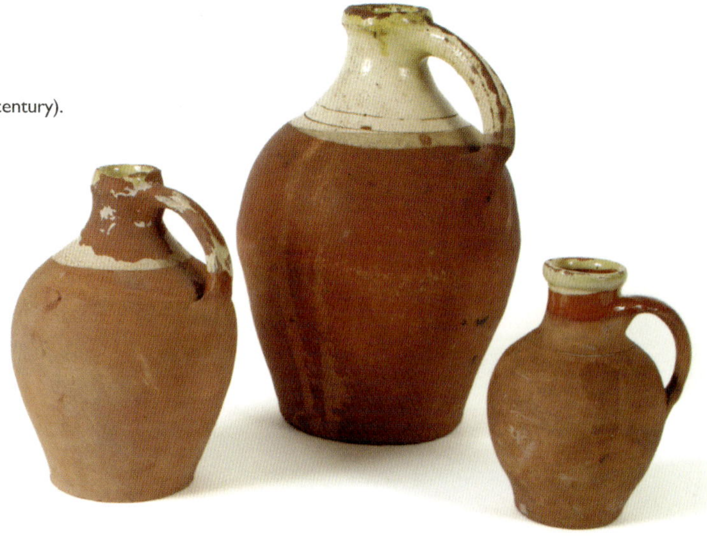

Fremington bottles (late 19th century). Height of largest 25cm.

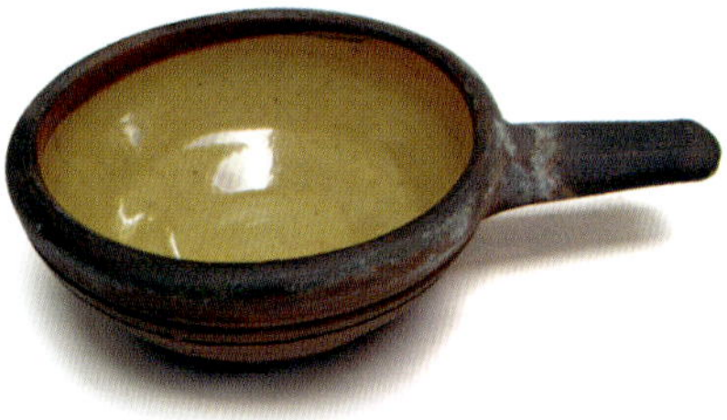

St Ives egg coddler with BL seal (c. 1930). Diameter 8cm.

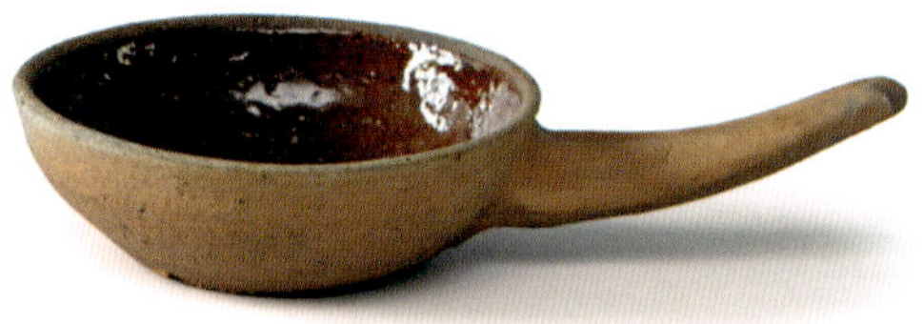

Fremington scoop or egg coddler (c. 1900). Diameter 11cm.

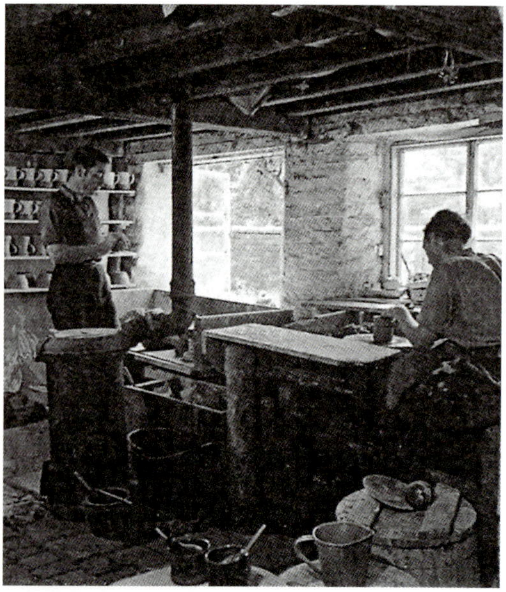

Ray Finch at Cardew's kick wheel (c. 1938).

of Fremington slipware, and Cardew subsequently took Leach on a visit there in 1924, where Leach particularly admired the utilitarian Fishley pots in the family kitchen. Cardew first learnt to pot in the summer of 1921 at the Braunton Pottery of Willie Holland (1889-1969), Edwin Beer's grandson, and was taught the Devon method of 'bowing' a handle onto pots – a skill he later shared with Leach at St Ives. A further account of Devon slipware traditions is given in our publication '*The Fishleys of Fremington*' (2008). With his father's help, Cardew also commissioned a Braunton-based blacksmith and carpenter to build him a kick wheel at a total cost of £7, and later used this at the Leach Pottery after he joined in the autumn of 1923. The kick wheel remained at St Ives until 1929, and may have influenced the potter's wheel designed by Dicon Nance in conjunction with David Leach, whose name it bears.

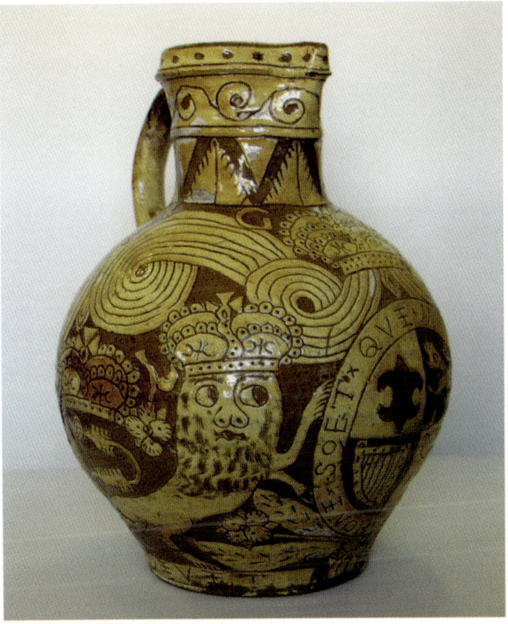

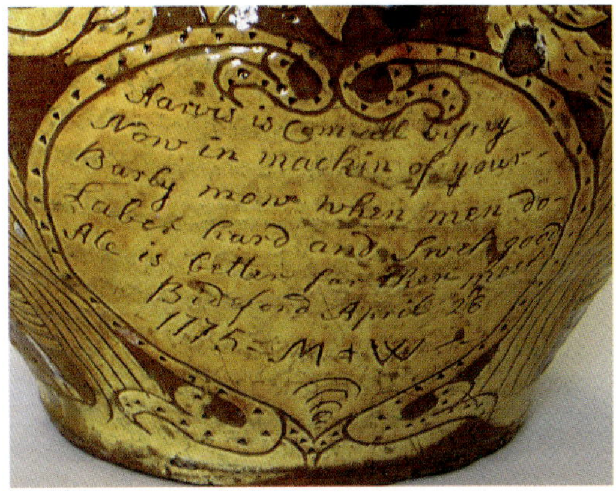

Bideford sgraffito Harvest Jug (late 18th century).

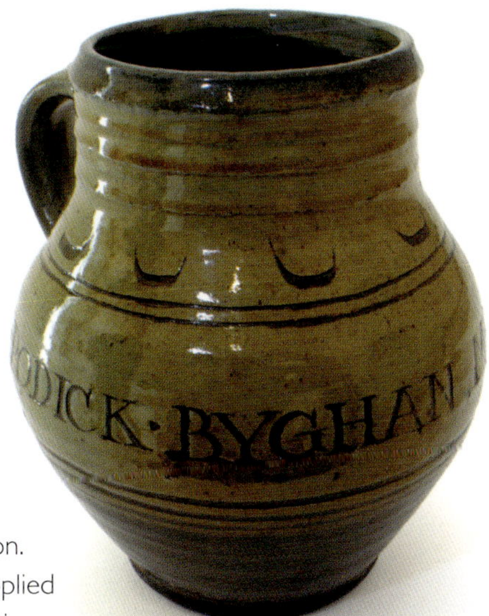

St Ives (c. 1925).
Height 16cm.

Cardew was imbued by a deep love of North Devon pottery, a tradition typified by jugs of full-bellied form for celebration and the home. Aside from galena glazes coloured various shades of yellow by the iron in local clays, the Devon tradition relied almost exclusively on sgraffito techniques for decoration. A thin layer of white slip made from ball clay was applied to the red wheel-thrown body, and then the decoration was scratched through to reveal the contrasting body-colour. Lettering was a feature of Devon slipware from the earliest days of volume production in the 18th century, applied both cursively and using a more formal seriffed lettering and capitals. Cardew subsequently recreated pots in this full-blooded tradition at St Ives, occasionally copying individual jugs as we will later see.

The Cardew family were of Cornish origin, and the call of his roots increasingly came to bear on Michael, leading him to establish a stoneware pottery at Wenford Bridge on Bodmin Moor in 1939. Probably one of the founding factors in this rediscovery was his early and close friendship with R M Nance (see above), for whom he made several jugs and tankards with inscribed verse in Cornish whilst at the Leach Pottery and subsequently at Winchcombe (see pages 79 and 23).

R J Noall

Virtually no mention is made of Richard John Noall (1871-1944) in publications on and by Bernard Leach. I am indebted to the researches of the potter Peter Smith, for shedding light on this interesting yet overlooked character. Noall was a well-known St Ives antiquarian and amateur archaeologist, and contributed articles for the Old Cornwall Society where he met Cardew at a Cornish language class in 1924 (as was recalled by the latter in his autobiography). A self-educated man of local upbringing, Noall saw active service in WWI and was injured in action causing him to be invalided out in 1916.

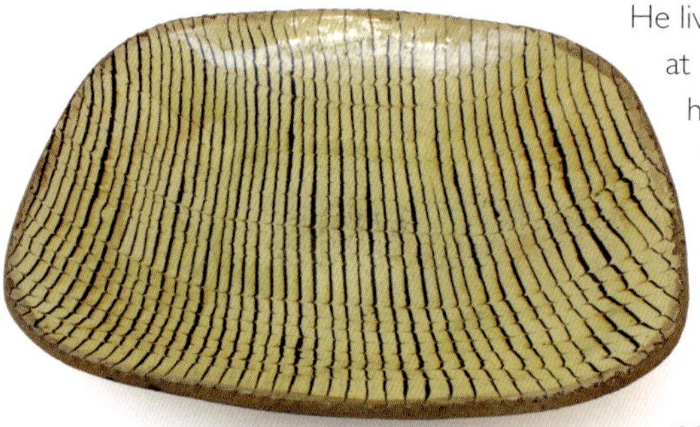

Hump moulded feather-decorated dish (c. 1800). Length 50cm.

He lived in a period house just 300 yards from the Pottery at Hellesvean, on the edge of open countryside, and had constructed a 'Dark Age' house in his garden with a museum including Mesolithic pieces gathered from field-walking and archaeological digs around St Ives. Judging by pieces in the collection of the Royal Cornwall Museum, Truro, donated by Noall, he was a collector of early English pottery and traditional slipwares. He was also an important early patron of the Leach Pottery, purchasing pottery made by both Hamada and Cardew, who may well have made as a presentation piece for Noall, the three handled tyg in over-fired slipware illustrated here.

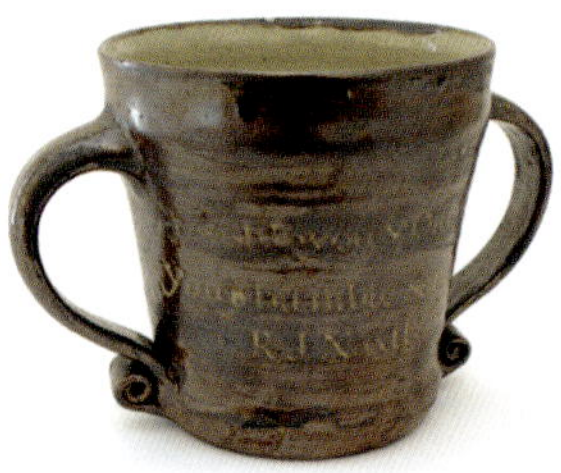

St Ives slipware tyg (c. 1924). Height 15cm.

In *Hamada Potter* (pages 53 and 54), it is related that Hamada recalled visiting a neighbour for tea during the building of the first kiln in 1920-1921, and seeing '...large dishes one and a half feet across, with black backgrounds and simple white stripe designs. I was simply amazed by them.' He subsequently acquired one from an antique shop in Plymouth, it was 'Yellow with black lines – very quiet, almost Sung in feeling.' Although unnamed, this neighbour was almost certainly Richard Noall, whose strong interest in hump-moulded and slip-trailed wares was clearly an important early influence on Hamada.

Leonard and Dorothy Elmhirst and the Dartington Estate and Pottery

Leonard Elmhirst was the son of a Yorkshire clergyman, and Dorothy Straight a wealthy American widow, who in the mid-1920s set up a broadly based craft and educational community at Dartington in South Devon. Leach had lost his first sponsor, Frances Horne, in 1923, and the first decade of operations in St Ives saw continuing operating losses, culminating in a record deficit of £901 in 1931. The Elmhirsts were keen to establish a working pottery on their estate, and approached first Leach and later Cardew in the 1920s before finally getting Bernard's agreement in 1932. The set up and output of this workshop is covered in the main illustrated section of this book.

Leach's involvement at Dartington was to prove short-lived although some slipware was produced there both in 1932-1934 and around 1936. In addition to supporting pottery operations in St Ives financially when necessary through the early to mid-1930s, the Elmhirsts sponsored Bernard's son David to follow a three-year course in pottery management at North Staffordshire Polytechnic, Stoke-on-Trent (1934-1937). This gave David the thorough technical grounding that he recognised would not be available from his father, and the intervention was critically important for the professionalization and survival of the Leach Pottery in the late 1930s and its growing commercial success after WW2.

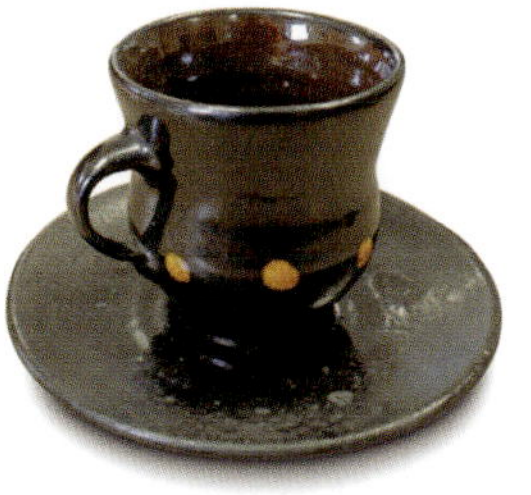

Dartington cup and saucer (c. 1932).

Under the tutelage of Leach, Dorothy and Leonard Elmhirst built up a substantial collection of art and ceramics, including studio pottery by Leach, Hamada and Cardew as well as English slipware and Oriental stonewares.

George Fishley Fremington jug (c. 1830). Height 37cm.

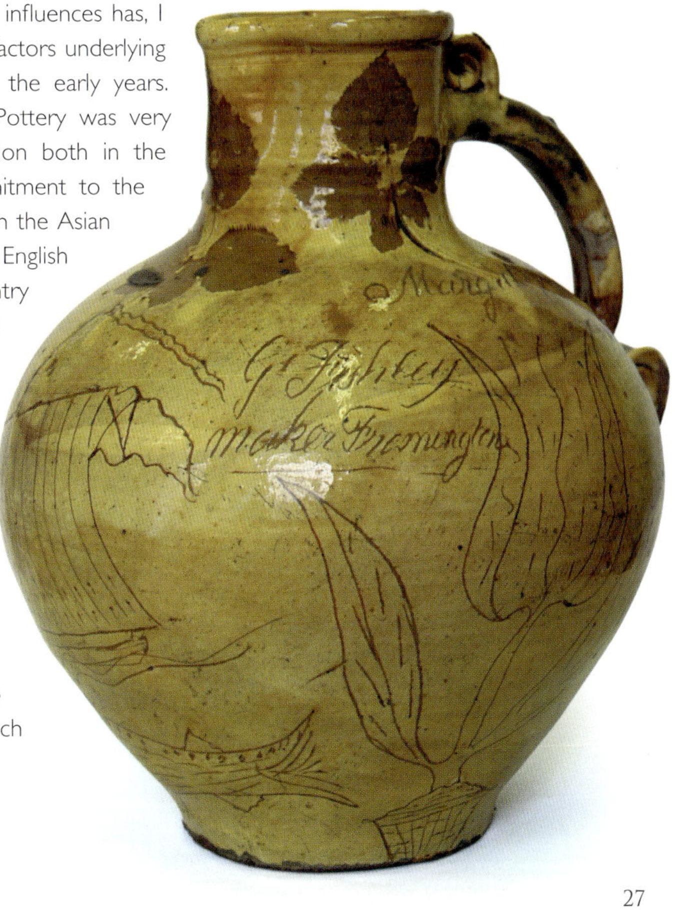

In summary

This overview of the key figures and influences has, I hope, provided some insight on the factors underlying production at the Leach Pottery in the early years. While the original concept of the Pottery was very much oriental in ethos and operation both in the choice of kiln and long term commitment to the production of high-fired stonewares in the Asian tradition, it was Western culture and English and more specifically West Country tradition that held equal sway in the formative years, as will be seen in our illustrated overview of pottery output (page 48 onwards).

It must not be forgotten that Leach and Hamada had the loyal support of a number of local people in addressing the physical and practical problems of the building and running of the new workshop. Let us turn now to the day-to-day operations at the Leach Pottery from its inception in 1920:

2 THE FOUNDATION OF THE LEACH POTTERY AND ITS SITE

INTRODUCTION

As readers have learnt, it was the generous funding provided by Frances Horne that was pivotal to the establishment of the workshop, using a hundred-yard long strip of land on the outskirts of the town. Leach had required rising ground to facilitate the construction of a climbing kiln and, with water being a being a necessity in clay preparation, proximity to the Stennack stream was an obvious consideration. However, from a commercial viewpoint, its position on the outskirts and at the top of a steep hill was perhaps ill-considered in the likelihood of attracting visitors.

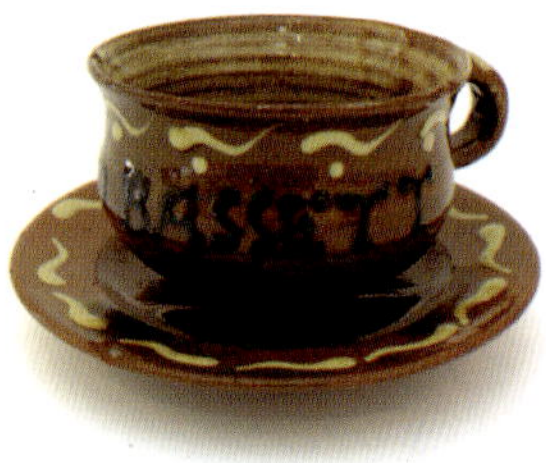

St Ives cup and saucer by Leach (c. 1922-1923). 13 x 6cm.

The kiln was built personally by Hamada with the assistance of Leach using second-hand bricks from the local gasworks together with blocks made primarily from raw china clay fired on site in a temporary kiln. Extensions and improvements to make a workshop from an existing granite building were achieved with the help of a former miner and fisherman, George Dunn, who stayed on to act as general handyman, clay worker and wood cutter. Financial and secretarial matters were initially looked after by Edgar Skinner, a friend of the family of Leach's first wife, Muriel, and he was also the original informant of Francis Horne's plans for a Handicraft Guild in the town. Great kindness was also shown by a number of locals, notably Edward Basset ('Old Bassett'), a retired fisherman who befriended Hamada, taking him on a fishing trip on one occasion and providing the Pottery with a generous supply of seafood and fish. Memoirs of these individuals may be found in the reminiscences of the two founders recounted in *Hamada Potter* (op cit).

The St Ives seal

The classic SI seal appears to have been inspired consciously or unconsciously by the Yang and Yin characters from Chinese tradition, and Leach reproduces these symbols on pages 105-106 of *A potter's book* (see illustration). The active and passive principles represented by this symbol chimes well with Leach's interpretations of the differing qualities of 'East and West' underlying the foundation of the Leach Pottery (see Oliver Watson's title *Bernard Leach potter and artist*, page 12, op cit), and indeed, from the first use as an impressed seal in circular form, (see illustration of seal on 1922 Leach jug), dots are retained alongside the SI lettering, a residual feature of its likely original inspiration. As

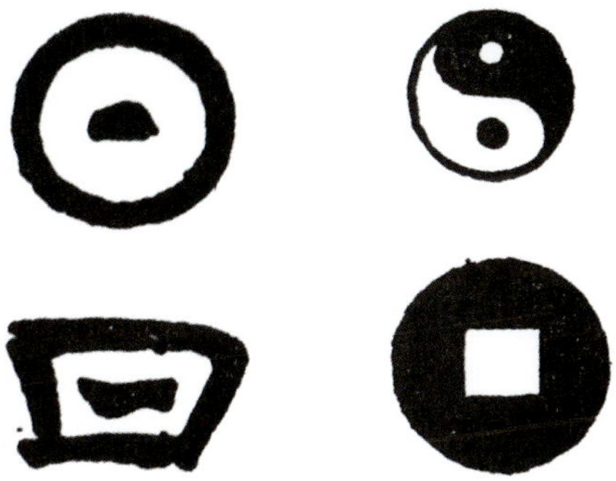

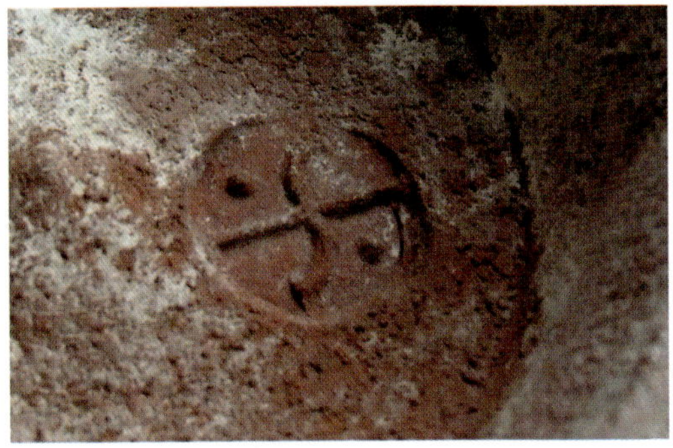

to the transition of this brushwork motif into a calligraphic form, an educated guess suggests the indirect influence of the letterist Edward Johnston at Ditchling, and the interval in between the visit of Leach and Hamada to the Guild headed by Eric Gill in 1921 and the first appearance of this distinctive monogram by 1922 and seriffed capital personal seals by 1923-1924 is consistent with such a proposal. The Leach archive at the Craft Study Centre, Farnham contains correspondence between Johnston and Leach, and the former is known to have developed monograms for friends over the years.

Slipware Production and Early Operations

As with my previous studies of the Greet pottery taken on by Michael Cardew in 1926, and the Fishley Pottery at Fremington, I would have hoped to be able to provide readers with details of the early operations of the Leach Pottery. Unfortunately, unlike the kiln and firing records maintained from 1927 by Cardew, and the vivid recollections of William Fishley Holland in his *Fifty years a potter* (Pottery Quarterly 1958), there is an almost total absence of records from the 1920s in the case of the Leach Pottery. This might lead the admirer to assume that this workshop arrived fully formed and perfect in the 1930s through the efforts of Harry Davis and Laurie Cookes (later Leach) and crucially David Leach from 1936-1937, fresh from the experience of his professional training at Stoke-on-Trent.

This silence – partly a reflection of the time that elapsed before there was any conscious effort of recollection in titles such as *Hamada Potter* (Kodansha International, 1975) – veils the inevitable period of trial and error, revealed indirectly by the limited number of wares surviving in Museums and National collections here and in Japan from those early days. We provide here a brief summary to assist the general reader in their understanding of the account of slipware production that follows. Those wishing for a more technical discussion of clays and kilns are directed to the specialised appendices at the end of this title.

Wheels

In the period to 1923, the main wheels were of a small Japanese type (see line engraving) driven clockwise by means of a stick, and a rather inefficient kick wheel. The Japanese wheel was employed primarily by Leach, who had originally been trained on this design by Kenzan in 1911 and used such a wheel for throwing at Abiko from 1916. Its size and method of propulsion limited the scale of pots that could be thrown, and larger material was created on the kick wheel used by Hamada, with Leach possibly helping to drive the wheel on occasions when a more substantial piece was required. To judge from the output of pots in 1924-1926, the wheel that Cardew had made for him at Braunton and delivered for his use at St Ives was relatively efficient (see line engraving and contemporary photograph).

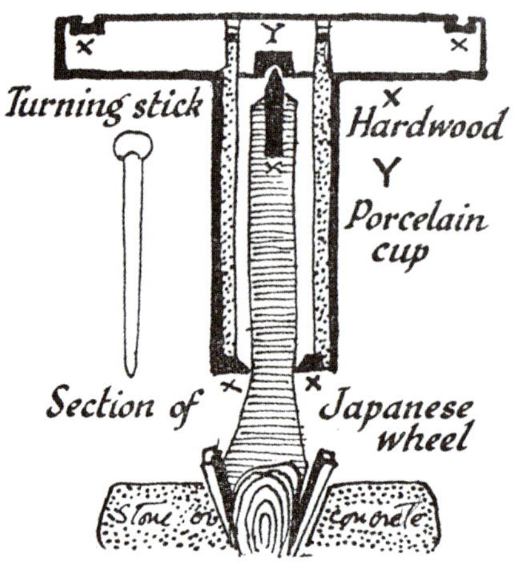

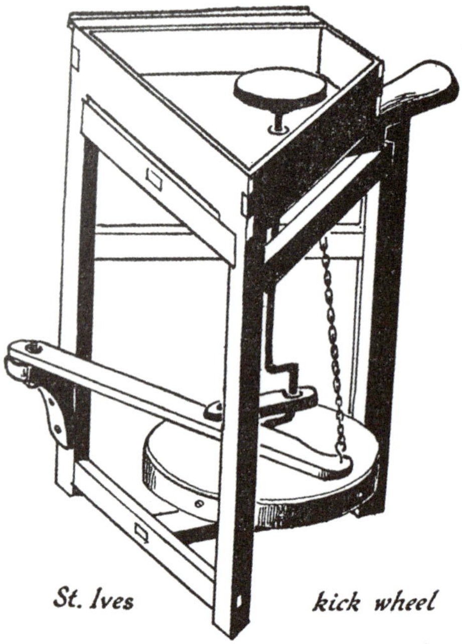

Throwing clays

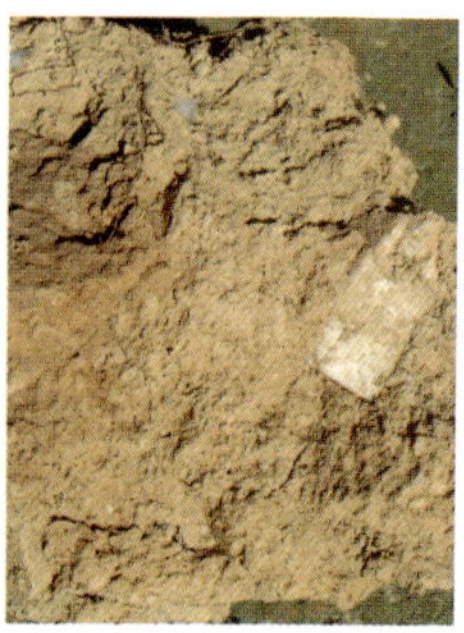
Raw St Erth clay.

The location of the Pottery in St Ives was primarily a consequence of accepting Francis Horne as sponsor, and stands in marked contrast to Mashiko, chosen by Hamada in 1924 as a site rich in the materials needed to make pottery. Cornwall in contrast, whilst a source of kaolin used in the production of porcelains at Worcester and elsewhere from the 18th century, was short of plastic clays suitable for throwing. A letter from Leach to the St Ives Times in August 1923 mentions sourcing china and fire clay materials from Towednack (Porthia China Works on the moors above St Ives), and red and blue plastic clays from St Erth, together with Cornish stone and feldspar from St Austell, and ball clay and white slip clay from Devon.

It now seems likely from an analysis of contemporary correspondence that much of the local prospecting for materials where required was led primarily by Hamada, who from his far superior technical education and grasp of the subject, knew what types of material would work in what was an experimental kiln. The igneous origin of most clays in this granite-dominated region and their coarse nature also had the advantage of offering a wider firing range of 900-1100°C, particularly compared to glaciation clays such as that at Fremington, used widely by North Devon potters over many generations and more locally by Lakes at Truro. Whilst this clay was probably known to Hamada, it matured at the comparatively low temperature of 1000°C, so firing conditions at the Leach Pottery would have made it unsuitable for use in the 1920s.

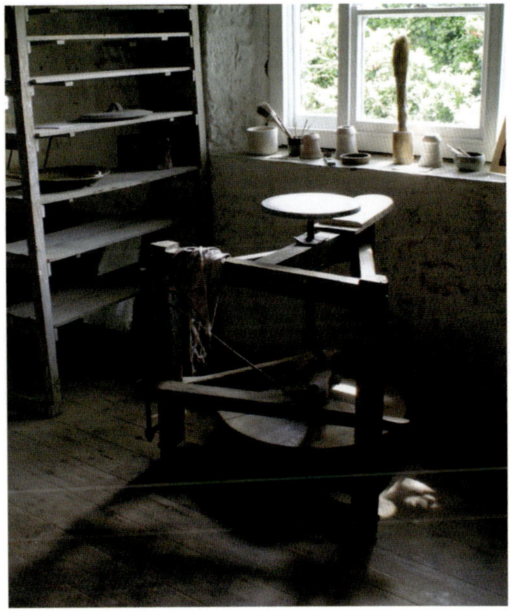

An illustrated description of clay types identified from the examination of slipwares can be found in the appendix to this book, but in summary a number of St Erth based red body mixes were employed in the period 1921-1927, primarily for the throwing of hollow wares and standing forms, including tableware, mugs, tankards and jugs, using varying quantities of coarser material. Low-fired and brush-decorated raku style wares together with higher fired flat wares including plates and large chargers used a cream coloured body based around coarse Porthia china clay. Where a traditional-looking finish was required for cream-bodied forms, notably the largest chargers, iron and sometimes manganese was used to colour otherwise clear lead-based glazes.

Sieved and slaked St Erth clay.

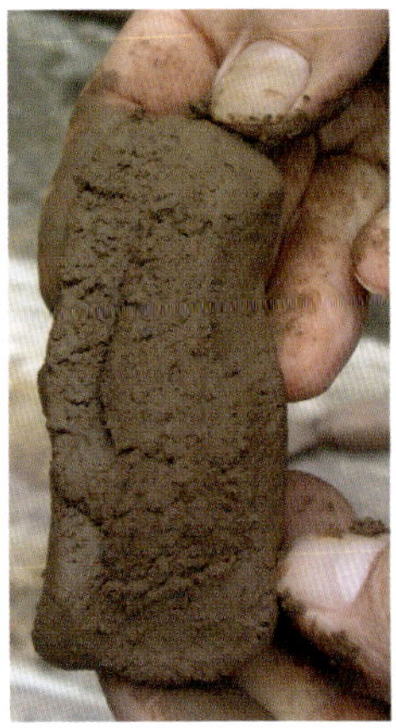

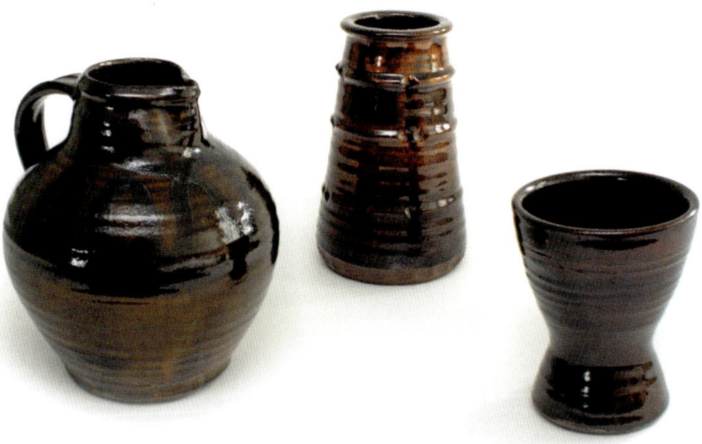

St Ives slipware jug and vase prototypes (c. 1925).

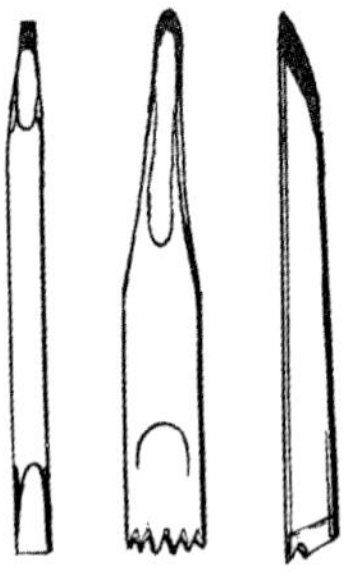

Bamboo graving tools

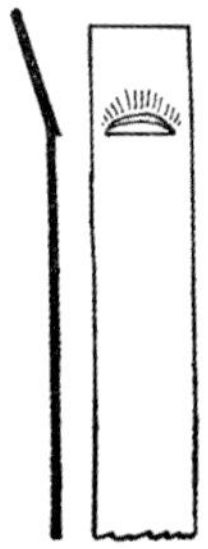

Fluting Tool

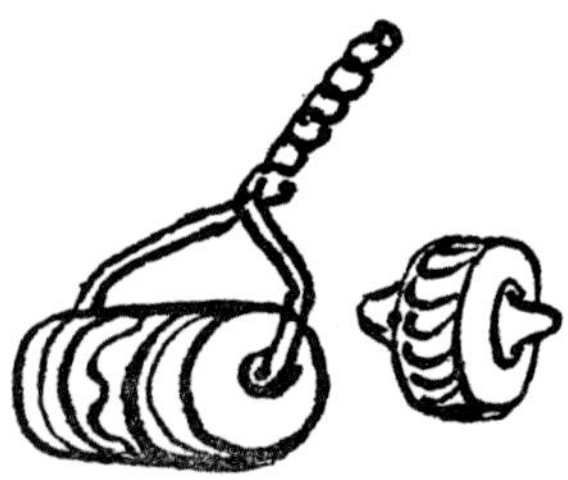

Incised rollers

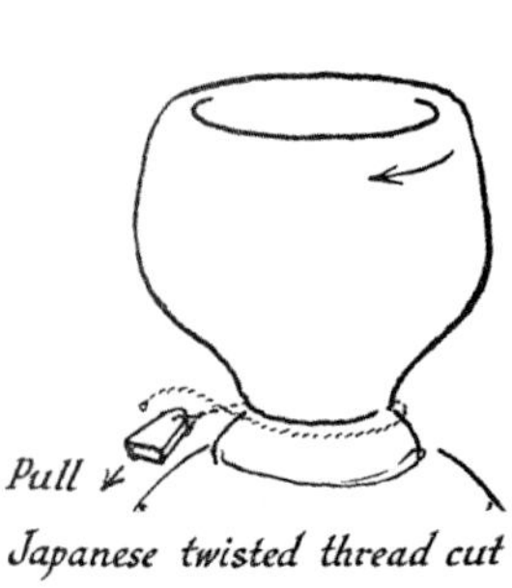

Japanese twisted thread cut

Tools

Prepared and engraved clay moulds were employed to reproduce designs, primarily on the flat but also on some bowls, together with profile moulds for attachment to the top of the wheel head. It is possible that the latter were turned from wood, the method believed to have been used historically to form moulded bowls and dishes. As to the hand tools for fettling and finishing, line engravings by Leach shown in *A potter's book* (see illustrations alongside) imply that a range of metal and wooden tools and blades were employed at the Leach Pottery from the early days. Indeed, in *Hamada Potter*, Hamada recalls their use of curved staves as finishing and trimming tools recycled from barrels originally employed for pickling herrings, rather than the bamboo traditionally used by potters in Japan, which needs to be cut and shaped whilst still green and which was not available in Cornwall.

Using such equipment would also have helped in the forming of foot rims of pots, a particular feature of the slipware output from the Pottery including the first pots exhibited in London at the Artificers Guild in 1921 and 1922. They would have also proved particularly valuable in finishing both the sides and base of wares thrown from coarser clays, and Hamada recalls their necessity in the finishing of saggars "...as the clay that we used was so coarse that, unless we were careful, the skin on our hands was chafed off" (*Hamada Potter*, op cit).

Another hand tool put to good use at the Pottery was a rouletting wheel, notably seen as providing a finishing touch to large chargers in the manner of Thomas Toft. These impressive platters were a major feature of early production, and the employment of this tool possibly made edges less liable to chipping, as well as providing a decorative finish: Leach illustrates such a tool in A Potter's book.

Bases and foot rims

This subject could almost be a study in itself, particularly having in mind the importance of the bottoms of pots in oriental ceramics, the base being frequently the first part examined in detail by the connoisseur. In the St Ives context, in the 1920s many pots were thrown 'off the lump' rather than by using a measured portion of clay (the English tradition), with the required amount of fabric drawn up from the residue centred on the spinning wheel, and the finished form removed using twisted wire (see line engraving). The evidence of this process can be seen on St Ives standing forms, although not all pots bearing a tell-tale wire scar were necessarily thrown in this way, and output under the guidance of Harry Davis in the mid-1930s is unlikely to have employed this technique (see illustration).

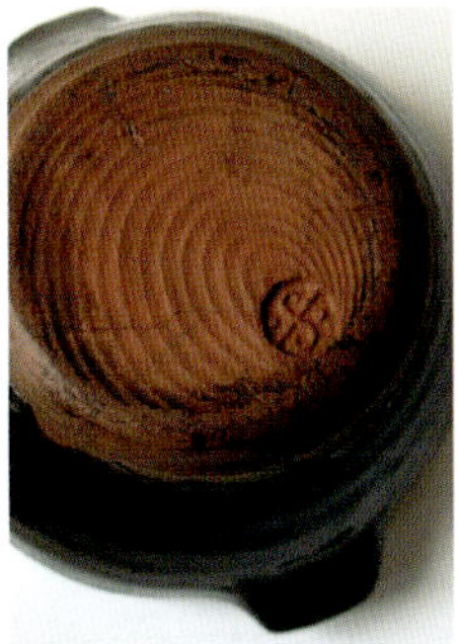

Foot rims, where present, were usually turned from excess clay on the base, but were on occasions made separately and then applied using a Japanese technique. Turned foot rims were sometimes quite shallow, particularly on the very occasional mug or cup finished in this way, whilst on tea- and other bowl forms, this feature was normally deep and pronounced, used perhaps to present the form to the onlooker or user in a more effective way. An elegant spiral finishing was also sometimes used on that part of the base contained by the rim. An illustrated analysis of these topics can be found in the appendix.

Handles

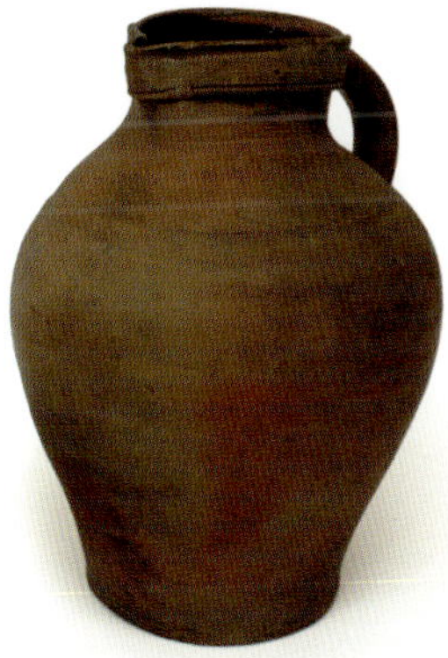

Lakes jug similar to that in handle-pulling photograph of 1923.

Techniques of making and fitting (or 'pulling') handles to jugs, mugs and tankards were important for both Leach and Hamada, perhaps because handles were rarely found in Japanese ceramics. The famous 1923 photo of the founders observing the handling of a pot at Lakes of Truro has become almost a cliché but it emphasises the significance for them of this Western skill. Indeed to this day, a group of specimen handles from early earthenware jugs sits on the mantelpiece of the old Leach Workshop (see illustration) and must have been the subject of more than one fireside lecture. In summary, the fame of the Lakes demonstration notwithstanding, there is no evidence that it altered methods at the Pottery except for a few odd examples – one or two Hamada jugs in stoneware and a few pots by Cardew. On the contrary, jugs and tankards from Cardew's time at St Ives (1923-1926) – the main period of production of handled forms in the 1920s – show a wide variety of styles of handle, presumably made under the direction of Leach, borrowing handle styles from different mediums and sources, including stoneware, which seemed to have formed part of a process of investigation prior to the introduction of an anonymous 'Workshop style'. More information and illustrations may be gleaned from the appendix.

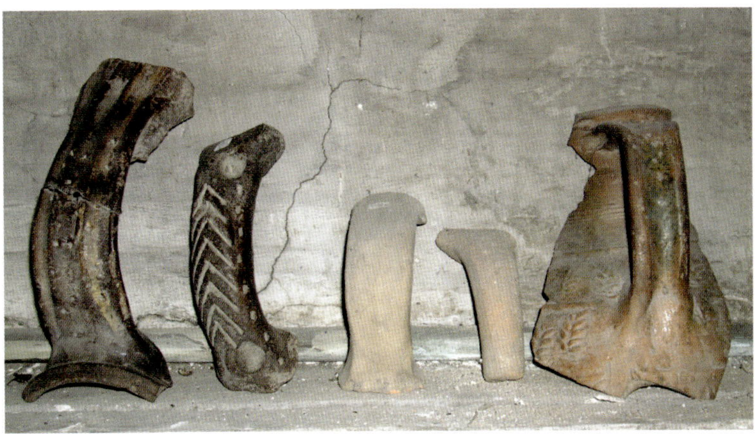

Specimen early earthenware handles with concave and chevron detailing.

Decoration using slips and oxides

As to decoration, in the earlier years the use of plain and coloured slips predominated, applied either with a trailer or a brush, with probably neutral coloured ball clay as the medium which would then have been coloured by the addition of oxide stains as appropriate. On occasions, it seems likely that a throwing clay medium was used for decoration, probably St Erth to give a rich red. Additionally, plain and coloured clay slips were applied to the thrown or moulded pot on the upper or outside surface to provide a background for the decoration then applied, or to disguise the underlying body colour. From as early as 1923, brushwork of diluted iron oxide was also employed under glaze with a proportion of clay sometimes added. While the use of high-lead glazes sometimes led to a dissolving of the iron oxide during firing, the fugitive results were not unpleasing: additionally, decoration 'bled' or was softened by movement under the glaze.

Glazes

Stoneware glazes are outside the scope of this study. A variety of slipware glaze recipes are shown in later material written and published by Leach in both pamphlet and book form. Helpfully, in a contemporary essay, *Memoirs of England: British Slipware* (1933), translated into English and republished in a Mingei magazine article in 2004, Hamada recalls an early visit to Lakes: 'Slipware glaze was made by simply mixing lead ore ground to a powder called galena with an appropriate amount of red clay...Leach and I set on investigating recipes to produce slipware. We started out by acquiring galena and mixing glaze. We took galena powder and added approximately twenty percent clay. The result was surprisingly successful from the beginning.'

A raku glaze is included in *A potter's book* which employs white lead and is probably based on a Japanese formula first developed by Kenzan I and was used in the early days at St Ives: its low melting temperature made it suitable for the raku style wares made principally by Hamada and later by Cardew in the 1920s, for decoration by Leach and others. Further information on slipware and raku kilns, firings and glazes are included in the appendix.

St Ives raku-style wares decorated by Leach (early 1920s).

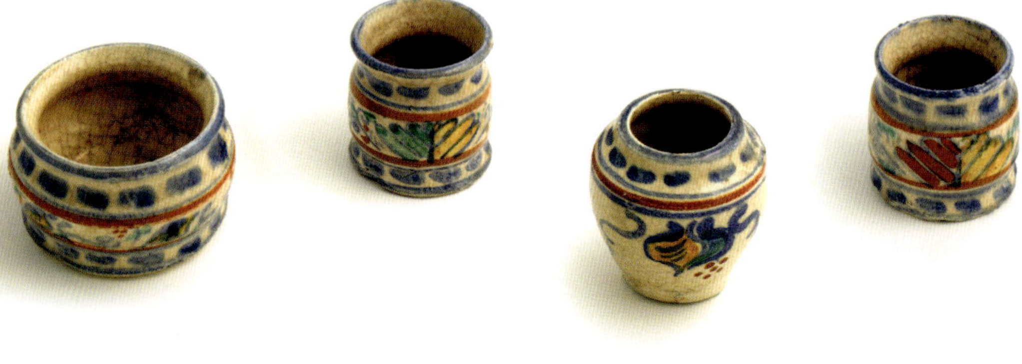

Kilns

Leach had relied on Kenzan to construct his first kiln in 1913, which was later rebuilt for him in 1916 at Abiko, and whilst Hamada conducted many firing tests whilst studying at Kyoto in 1916-1919 and would have studied the principles of kiln construction, this would have been based around Japanese materials. Their aim to build a relatively large kiln at St Ives was therefore a very ambitious one, and it now appears that the first 'noborigama' climbing kiln built in 1920-1921 was a somewhat romantic recreation by Hamada of a rural Japanese design. Something of its construction may be seen in the contemporary photo below, and sections can also be seen in the

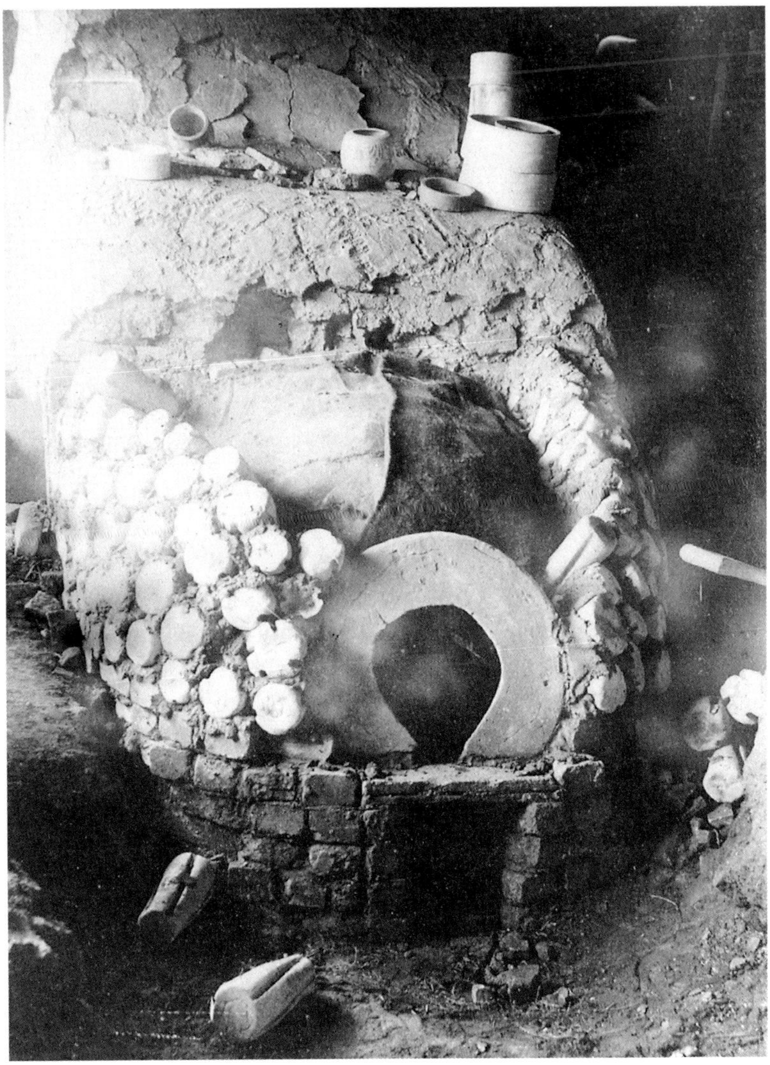

Partially rebuilt firebox of first climbing kiln showing use of cones (c. 1922).

background to photographs of individuals (see *Hamada Potter*, op cit, Album section). The use of local materials by Hamada in its construction followed the traditions of past generations of potters both Japanese and European, although these were clays that were unfamiliar to him. It seems likely that he also consulted those technical books then available on kiln types, brick making and fireclays and their sourcing in England, *A treatise on ceramic industries* (Emile Bourry, 1901) and *Refractory materials, their manufacture and uses* (Alfred B Searle, 1917).

The problems that emerged after firings are now believed to have been caused by the employment of construction blocks made primarily from locally sourced raw china clay (see interview with Peter Smith on pages 125-127). There were additional problems with the firebox, which had not been properly braced, and was rebuilt probably in 1922 using clay cones (see archive photo on page 126), a method of construction common in Japan. When things went wrong, Hamada, who judging by contemporary correspondence reproduced in *Hamada Potter* had tried to prepare well for the kiln-build, called on the help of an old friend from college, Matsubayashi Soetsu (nicknamed Matsu). Matsu was a kiln professional from a family that had been associated over many generations with the Asahi kiln of Uji, near Kyoto. His attendance at St Ives depended on him being able to afford what was then a long and expensive trip, a cost that Leach would not have been able to bear at the time.

The 1924 rebuilding of the climbing kiln

Matsu is known to have visited working kilns shortly after his arrival in England in the summer of 1923, including those of William Staite Murray (1881-1962) at his London workshop and Lakes in Truro, possibly to seek advice as to the renovation of the first St Ives kiln and to gain knowledge of traditional English slipware firing techniques. A contemporary kiln drawing from 1923 bearing Matsu's name (see illustration) has the look of a blueprint and shows a three chambered design with precise details in imperial measurements, including the specified size of saggars, we presume intended to be used in conjunction with the existing chimney. This time around, ready-made fireclay bricks were employed in a substantial kiln which, with a partial rebuild of one chamber, survives to this day.

It is likely that there was a general lack of experience at St Ives of the practicalities of firing a full climbing kiln as opposed to the raku and smaller scale test kilns to which Leach and Hamada had been exposed, although the latter had learned enough to produce two very good final firings in 1923. Similarly, Matsu was not an experienced fire master, and the first firing of the new climbing kiln in May 1924 as recounted by Katharine Pleydell Bouverie

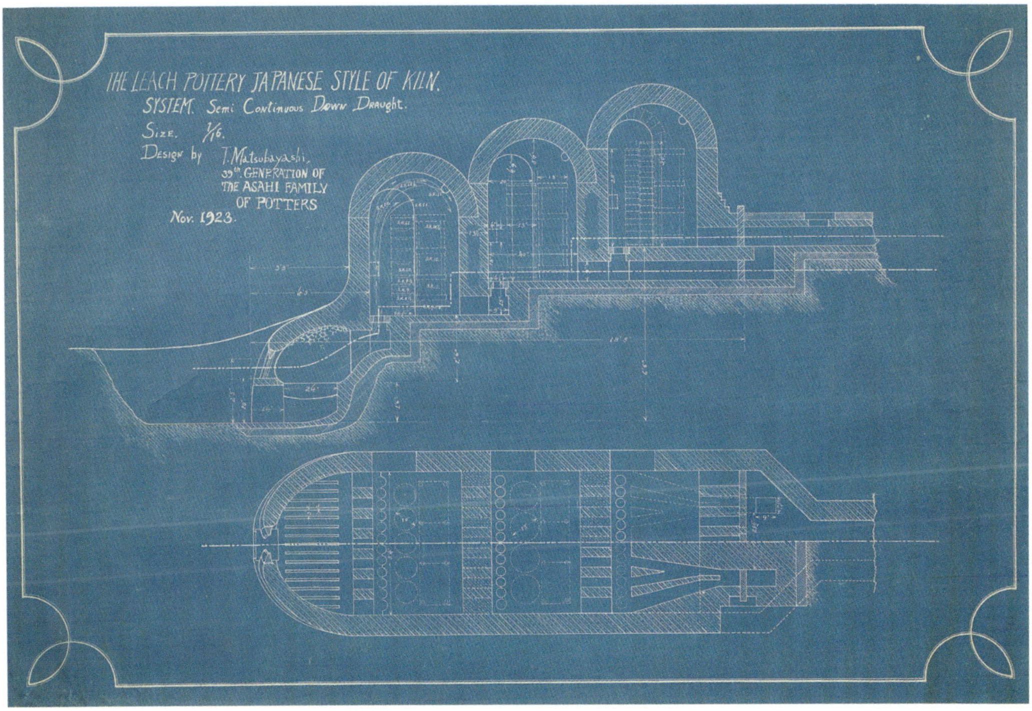

Matsubayashi climbing kiln plan dated November 1923 (for enlargement see page 157).

(1895-1985) resulted in minor disaster as shelving collapsed and wares were spoiled. Temperature control probably relied on a few Seger cones and visual judgement: it would have been difficult to gauge the temperature accurately as firing progressed, so over-firing would have been all too easy to achieve, and the accumulated experience of firings of Hamada was no longer available, having returned to Japan.

Temporary kiln

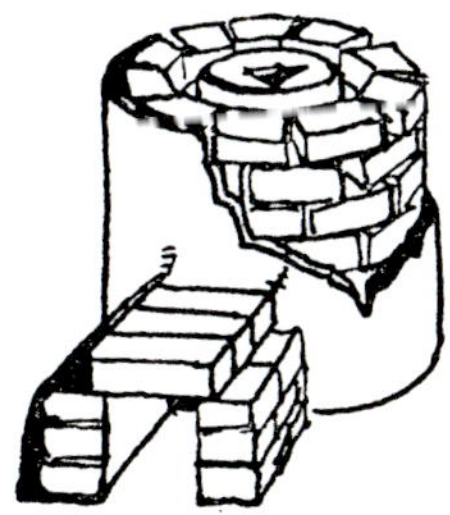

Slipware kilns

Judging from pots researched for this book, the results of using the climbing kiln for slipware proved mixed, a reflection of the narrower temperature tolerances of this medium, and the basic temperature controls available (see above). From the published recollections of Hamada and the pre 1925 slipwares that have survived, it now seems likely that there was at least a small up-draught kiln on site, roughly the shape of an igloo if line drawings in *A potter's book* and a contemporary flier seen are anything to go by, with space provided for firing raku in the top. Hamada refers to the use of a small biscuit kiln for firing large platters thrown by him for decoration by Leach, and Hamada would have been aware of bisque kilns in the Japanese Shigarake tradition of a similar shape (see illustration).

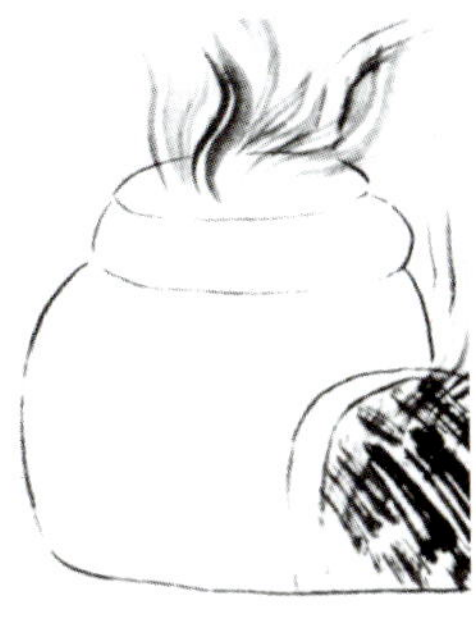

Shigarake kiln.

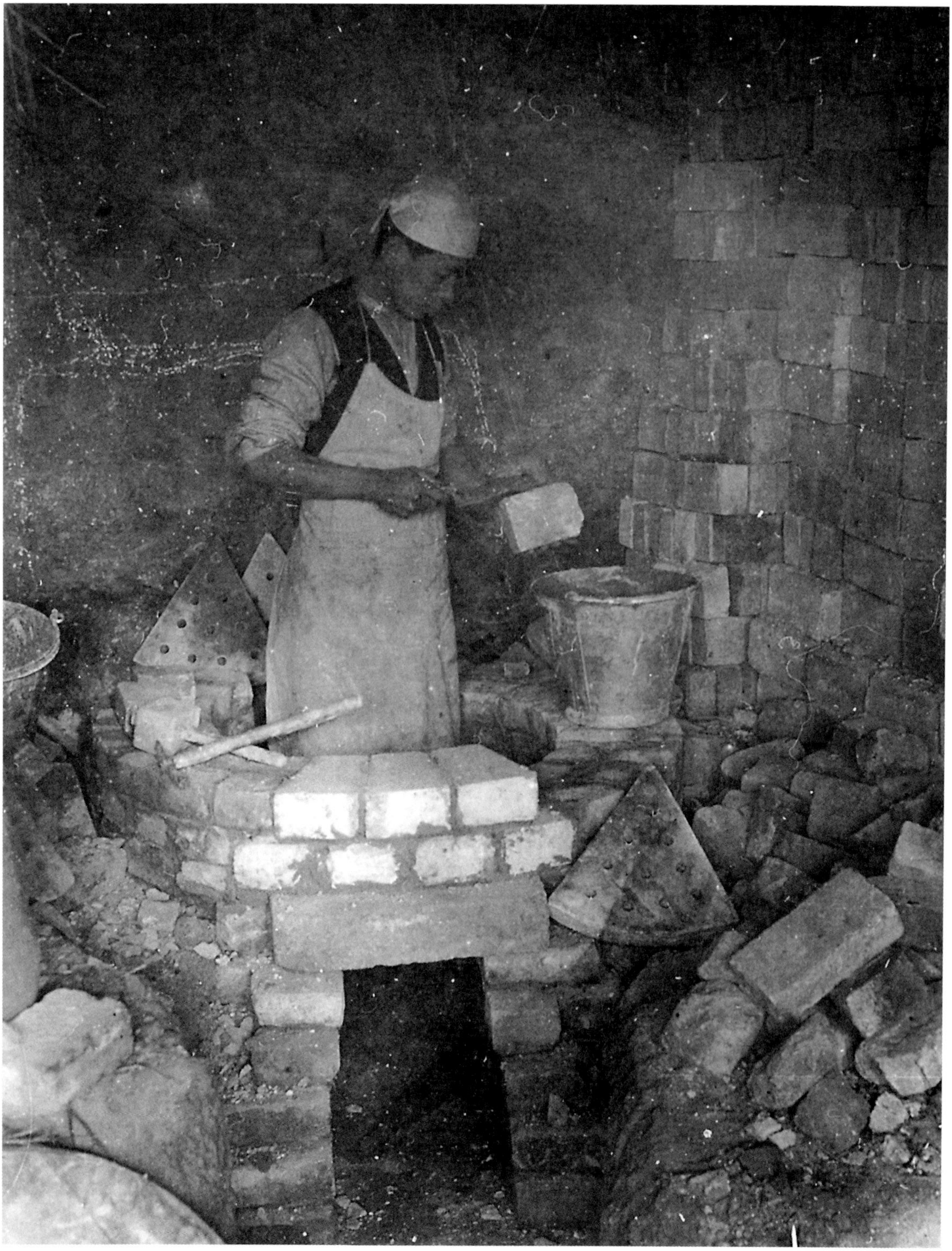

Matsubayashi building the 1925 slipware and raku kiln.

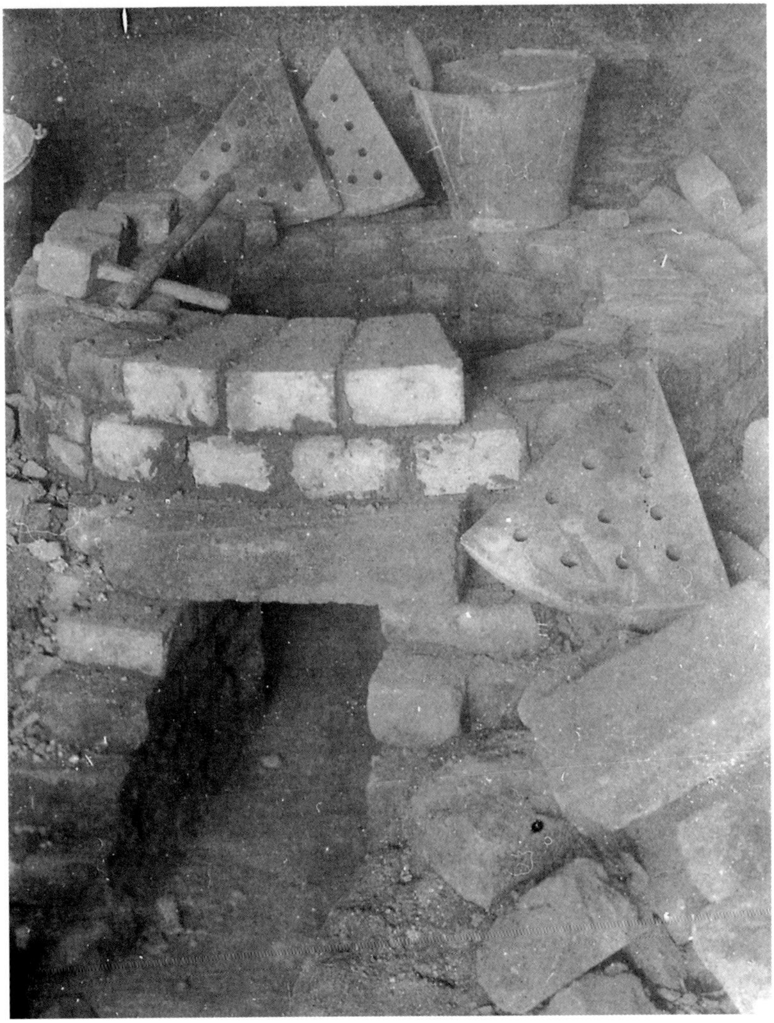

Detail of 1925 round up-draught kiln showing perforated kiln shelves.

A larger round up-draught kiln was then built by Matsu in 1925 (see archive photographs), which employed perforated kiln shelves, and in operation, a 2-inch (5 cm) gap was provided between the kiln shelving and the outside wall, the theory being that this combined with the perforated shelving would allow gases and heat to penetrate to the upper layers. It shows little apparent influence from Matsu's meeting and discussions with the owners of Lakes of Truro in 1923, who had a deep knowledge and experience of firing slipware, albeit using what was by then an old fashioned bottle oven. There is an apparent parallel in the use of a perforated single floor in a round kiln owned by Tomimoto, a line engraving of which appears in *A potter's book*, although the date of construction is unknown. Whether due to its design

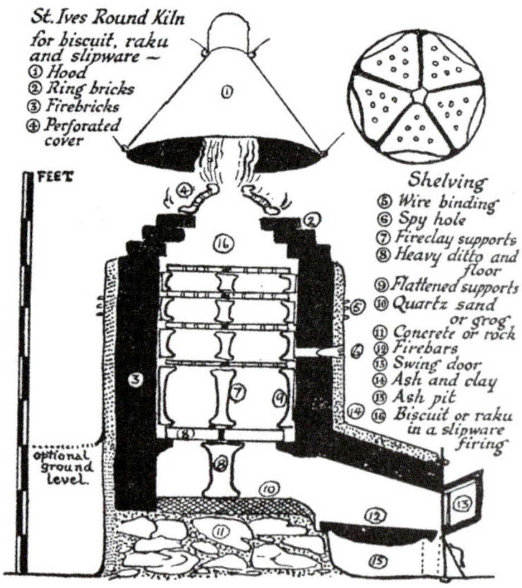

St. Ives round up-draught kiln

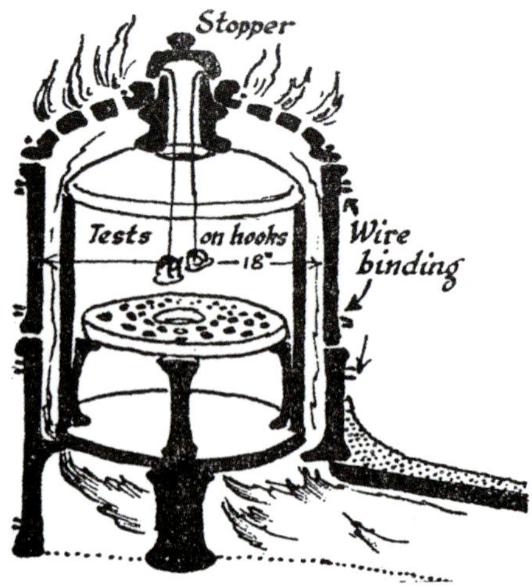

Tomimoto's biscuit, raku or enamel kiln
Three hour firing with thin pine

Leach line engravings from *A potter's book.*

or poor usage, output from the Matsu slipware and raku kiln was of uneven quality, and whilst there were some good results, many pots revealed the effects of uneven heat and gas distribution in the kiln, with under-cooking and poor glaze development seen in some instances and warping of flat forms such as chargers in others.

For a more detailed consideration of related issues, readers should consult Oliver Kent's paper and the interview with Peter Smith in the Technical appendices to this title.

Fuel and kiln firings

Lakes 'bibbed' jug (c. 1930). Height 13cm.

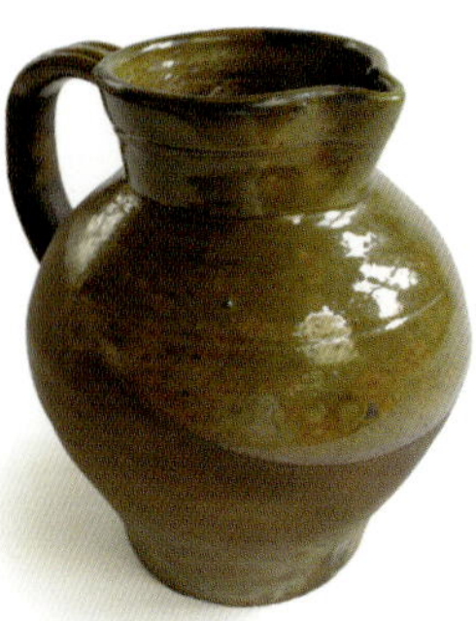

The oriental-style climbing kilns built at the Leach Pottery were of a design predicated on the ready availability of wood (fir or pine being the classic fuel in Japan). The lack of wood in Cornwall necessitated considerable improvisation by Leach and Hamada. In 1920-1921 a large quantity of cut Rhododendron and some pine wood was purchased from the Great Western Railway (GWR), and subsequently Leach acquired disused railway sleepers from the same source, but the problem was not resolved until the conversion of the 1924 Matsu kiln to oil by 1940. The 1925 slipware and raku kiln was fuelled at least initially using sawdust and a paraffin drip, with cut furze (gorse – plentiful throughout Devon and Cornwall) used in the late stage of firings to flash and melt the lead-based glazes. The traditional use of furze for firing slipware was known to Hamada and Leach from their early visit to Lakes, and is recounted in *Memoirs of England: British Slipware* (op cit). Wood is believed to have been used for the main firing later in the 1930s.

Usage of kilns and kiln effects

A potter's book (op cit) makes reference to the use of cooler upper chamber(s) of climbing kilns for lower temperature work, including biscuit firing and raku, a technique long practiced in Japanese noborigama kilns. Cardew also mentions this procedure in his recollections of St Ives in his posthumous autobiography *A Pioneer Potter* (1988), and research of slipwares from 1923 also confirm this possibility, with the variability in firing temperature compensated for by the use of different body clays and glazes in different chambers.

It also seems likely that some large platters were fired in an early up-draught kiln, and a number of early wares show a classic glaze effect from the employment of cut furze, also seen seasonally in glazed wares produced by Lakes – the so-called 'salmons-back' finish. This speckling of lead glazes is caused by the use of furze that is not fully dried to 'flash' (melt) the galena glaze. This causes spots of moisture which boil on the glaze surface and produce consequent colour variations in the finished ware. This tell-tale feature is present on the back of a Hamada sgraffito-decorated wide shallow bowl from 1923 in the UW Aberystwyth collection, which is listed as stoneware but is in fact earthenware (see close-up illustration). It should be born in mind that with the poor control over the firing temperature evident in early firings, pottery intended for slipware and stoneware temperatures may not have been fired as originally intended, albeit that a use of a traditional lead glaze on a pot would imply a low temperature intent in the maker.

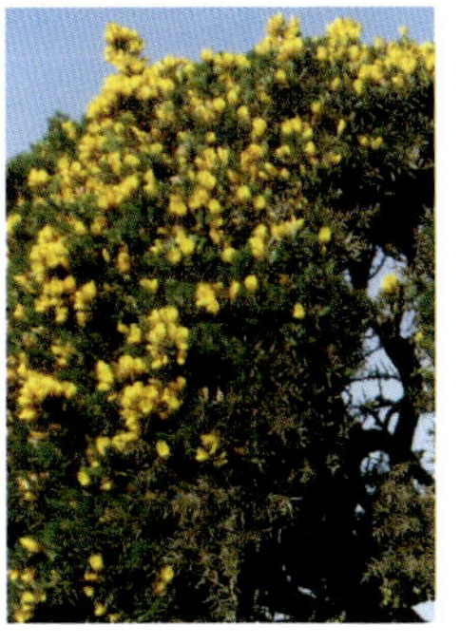

Furze (gorse) bush in flower.

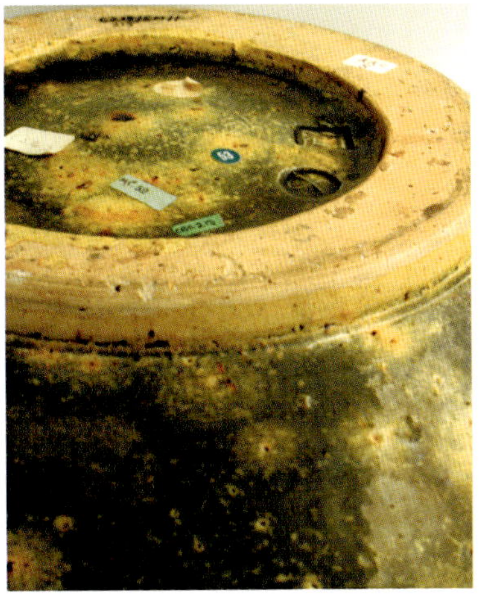

Detail of underside of Hamada sgraffito slipware bowl from 1923.

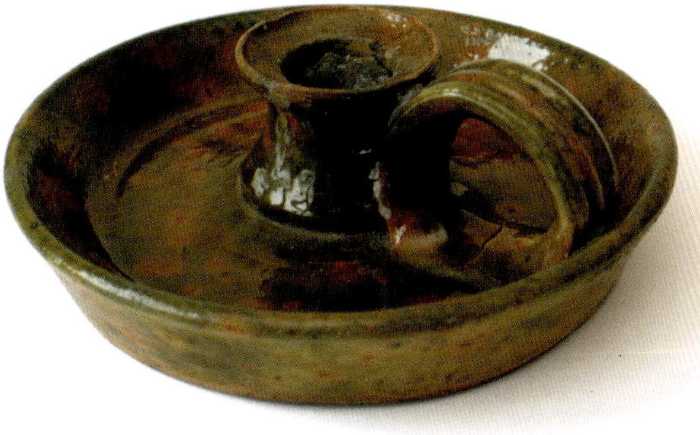

Lakes chamber candlestick (1920-1940). 14.5 x 4.5cm.

Aside from the under- and over-firing and kiln warping already described, the other significant kiln effect seen is on slipwares from 1924 -1925. These are at times very dark in colouration, particularly on those pot faces turned towards the heat source during firing. While the overall colour of such wares is darker than in the traditional slipwares of say North Devon (on account of Leach's preference to add extra iron ore to glazes), pots also exhibit fine pin-pricks not dissimilar from those seen on salt glaze. The explanation appears to be the ill-judged use of railway sleepers as fuel, since these were pickled with preservatives such as saltpetre which volatilised during firing to produce nitric acid. The fumes released during such firings would presumably have drifted downhill to the town, and it is known that there were complaints from their neighbours. Kiln reduction and over-firing may also have had a role in the finish of these and other pots of a darker finish.

A kilns summary

The record of trial and error revealed in our researches is one that any potter will encounter in the building and first firings of a new kiln, magnified in the case of the Leach Pottery by their choice of establishing from scratch a technology of which little was known in the west of England. Any kiln expertise locally would have been primarily in the smelting of tin and other metals, although help may have been available in areas such as Stoke. That Leach and Hamada chose to rely on their own resources is a reflection perhaps of their desire to remain independent and uncontaminated by the industrial processes that they had philosophically rejected, no matter what the cost. Their 1920-1921 recreation of a noborigama kiln of a type in common use in rural Japan reflects this, although the reduction in the number of kiln chambers to two or three as opposed to the multiple chambers in traditional versions would have made it tricky to fire.

Additionally, having sought to establish a name for expertise in an oriental approach, this may have precluded their seeking assistance – hence the recourse to Japan and Matsu in 1923. That they avidly researched but struggled to master traditional methods of making and firing slipware is wholly understandable, since earthenwares were uncommon in Japan and stoneware predominant. It does however remain curious that they failed to capitalise fully on expertise readily available to them at Lakes in Truro.

At a personal level, the picture of Leach that emerges from contemporaries and commentators is of a man at best uncomfortable on kiln issues, with Bernard walking up and down, "mygodding" profusely during firings, with very mixed results. After a period of comparative improvement during Cardew's time, firing and output did not improve more permanently until the 1930s – when the knowledge brought to the Pottery by Harry Davis and later David Leach from their training elsewhere had its effect.

The Wares

For all the manifest technical and practical shortcomings of their decision to set up a pottery at St Ives with relatively little knowledge of kiln building and firing and besides the local shortage of suitable clay and fuel, the wares produced by Leach and Hamada in the early years showed considerable strengths both in their sense of form and synthesis of decorative styles and themes influenced by a wide range of both fine and applied art sources. These core qualities were complemented and broadened particularly in the area of standing forms by the recruitment of Michael Cardew in 1923, as we will subsequently learn.

Hamada bowl with inlaid slip under a celadon glaze (c. 1923).

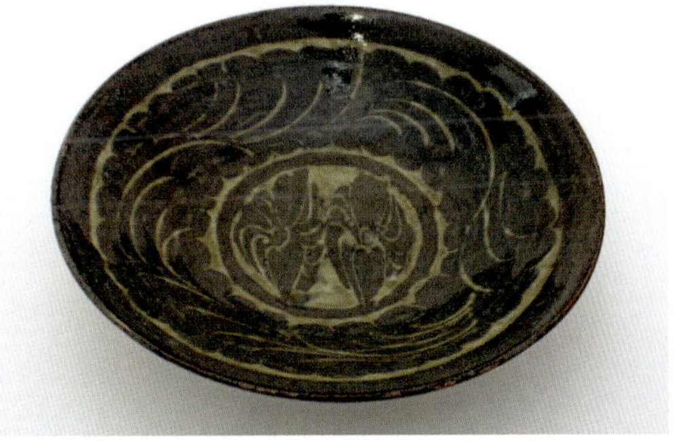

Forms and techniques

Many potters will admit that they start by copying existing forms that they admire, before making these inspirations their own by creating their personal interpretation: the character of the individual cannot help but emerge in this way. In the case of Leach and Hamada in the period 1920-1923, there are significant differences, with Leach emerging as having a strong concept of the forms that he admired and wished to reproduce and Hamada acting as his amanuensis to realise these. As a result, Hamada produced relatively few pieces bearing his mark until his final year in England, when they had two shows at the Paterson Gallery in London, which also marked the early emergence of his individual creative instinct for form that was only to be fully developed when working independently at Mashiko.

Hamada stoneware vase with removed and incised slip in the Cizhou manner. Height 22cm.

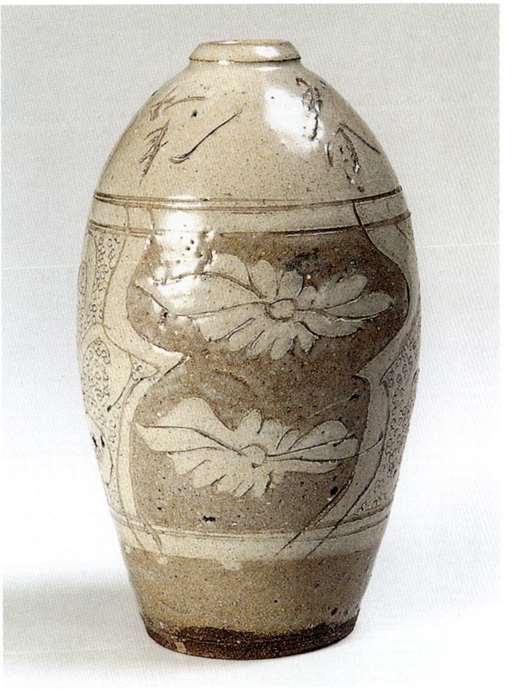

For Hamada, his stay in England and at St Ives served as a technical and cultural apprenticeship complementing his existing strong knowledge of glazes accumulated during his college years in Tokyo and Kyoto with his crucial development of throwing and kiln clays for the new Workshop using primarily local materials. Aside from acting as an early lead thrower for Leach, surviving work shows him trying different techniques of making and decoration, with the use of *Neriage* (similar to the Sussex 'agate ware' thrown with contrasting clays) and the inlaying of clays particularly noteworthy (see illustrations). He probably also had a hand in the making of fired clay moulds, which were incised

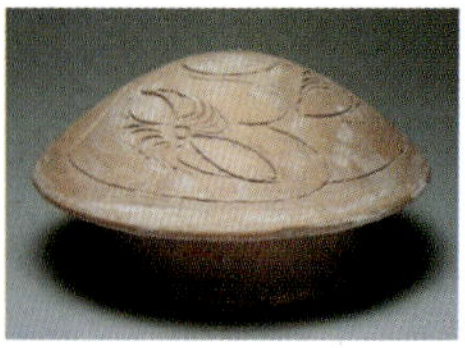

Incised clay hump mould by Hamada (c. 1922-1923).

with a limited number of designs for reproduction by both him and Leach. To judge from marked examples, designs with stylised motifs based on flower heads were by Hamada, and representational forms such as a hare were by Leach. As to applied decoration, Hamada appears to have employed slip trailing rarely, although spectacularly well on two known Bull chargers (see page 62 and 63), and concentrated instead on sgraffito and brushwork. While not relevant to the present study, his knowledge of stoneware glazes was put to good use and this must have been particularly valued by Leach in the light of his underlying desire to introduce and popularise a fundamentally oriental ceramic aesthetic. Notably, Hamada produced a number of jugs and mugs fired to stoneware temperatures but showing a clear inspiration from English and West Country slipwares.

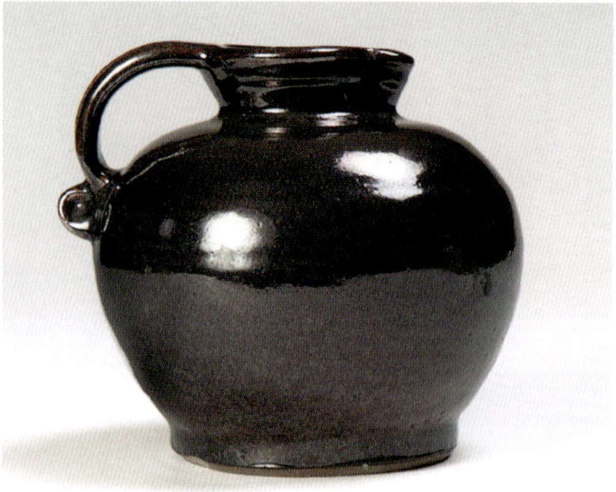

Stoneware scroll-handled jug by Hamada (c. 1922-1923). Height 16.5cm.

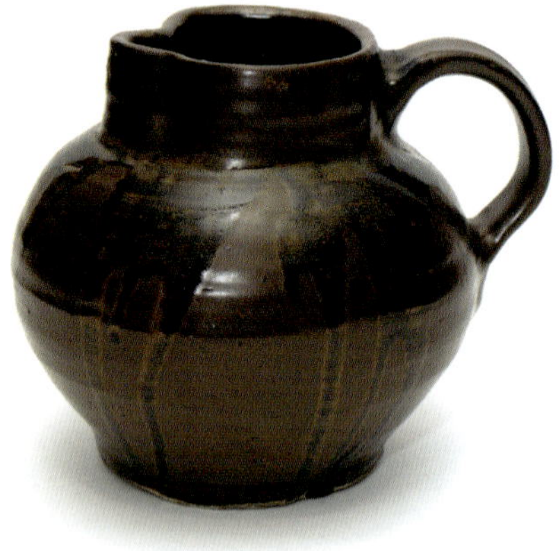

Stoneware jug by Hamada (1928). Height 17cm.

As to Leach's choice of form, it had been Raku wares that dominated his work in Japan, and two forms in particular – platters and lidded jars – and these again make an appearance at St Ives alongside other standing forms, both with and without handles. The graphic artist in Leach responded particularly to flat wares, so it is understandable that large platters dominated early production (see pages 70-76). These were thrown by Hamada over a mould attached to the wheel prior to being turned and refined by Leach to achieve his desired form, with the magnificent chargers of Thomas Toft the clear inspiration. Oriental ceramics were the model for a 'ginger jar' lidded form, and a good example is the illustrated Cizhou brushwork jar in the Sung tradition from the Leach reference collection. Inlaid and other Korean wares of the Koryu dynasty also provided models. Other one-off handled forms were produced – the jugs illustrated on page 57 and the teapot on page 58 being representative– but aside from these, tea bowls and flared open bowls predominate with the occasional vase (page 59).

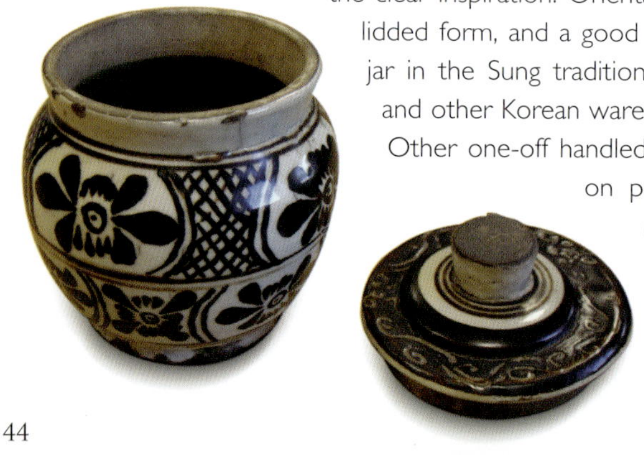

Decorative styles

If the last year of Hamada's stay showed the early emergence of his later mastery of form, it was Leach's decorative instinct that dominated throughout, and in my view led to the production of some of the most interesting ceramics produced at the Leach Pottery before the hushed tones of the Sung Aesthetic emerged there. At this late juncture it is dangerous to be dogmatic about his inspirations, but it is probably safe to draw some overall conclusions about these from our knowledge of his early training and interests. Certainly the art and verse of William Blake, the techniques of etching and engraving from his college days, Chinese and oriental philosophy and aesthetics, a wide range of contemporary art including Vincent Van Gogh (1853-1890) and subsequently earlier artists in the Blake school, notably Samuel Palmer, all emerge as possibilities. Decorative inputs from ceramics include the brushwork designs used on Ming period porcelains, the stylised decoration of Seto peasant wares, and the non-abstract motifs and patterns seen on the English slipwares of the Toft school and other Midlands pottery. Lastly as an inveterate sketcher of the artist manqué, some of his freshest artistic expression is direct from nature and landscape, particularly in his brushwork decoration of stoneware, and the occasional slipware tile.

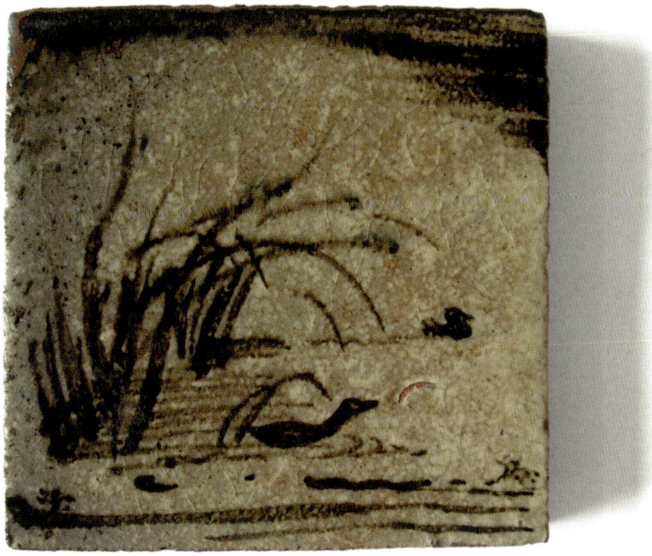

Late 1920's. 10 x 10cm.

This synthetic ability of Leach to absorb and recreate directly and indirectly form and decoration from a wide variety of disparate sources and traditions was his strongest suit, the artist as designer rather than the unconscious craftsman as the creator of truly original form. Following as a central tenet the philosophy of the Artist Craftsman as leader of a group of acolytes, he worked with and actively promoted a succession of individuals with complementary skills. That he was thus able to overcome his own practical shortcomings, producing at a Workshop level ceramics uniting exemplary form and complementary decoration, is to his manifest credit. His technical ability to transpose decoration across different media and techniques, from slip to glaze to sgraffito, was particularly impressive, and whilst there was something of the Edwardian 'gentleman-craftsman' about Leach, ill educated for the role of 'master-potter' – a reflection of his social background and the similar attitudes of some of his pottery peers – it was he above all who put Studio Pottery on the map in England and gave his students ambition and hope.

Themes

Further analysis is included in the appendix to this book but, in short, the main themes were the natural world, heraldry, legend and the Zodiac. Some early Leach slip-trailed designs on wheel head chargers show the direct influence of Toft school and other wares illustrated in *Quaint Old English Pottery* by Lomax, notably a hare (Lomax plate III), mermaid (plate VII), heraldic lion (plate XI) and cockerel (plate XXXV). The hare had been used on a raku plate decorated by Leach in Japan in 1919, and the early slipware emphasis of the Leach Pottery and the pride of its creator are illustrated by Leach's choice of image in the flier for the Pottery illustrated here. A zodiacal influence is also suggested by the choice of Bull (Taurus) and Gemini designs on platters of the period 1923-1927, and the Plough constellation is shown incised and painted on both slipwares and stonewares of the 1920s. Motifs used apparently for (undisclosed, possibly philosophical) symbolic purposes also recur, including mountain ranges, remote habitations, winding roads, pilgrims and well heads, employed initially on slipware but

Detail of 1929 slipware charger.

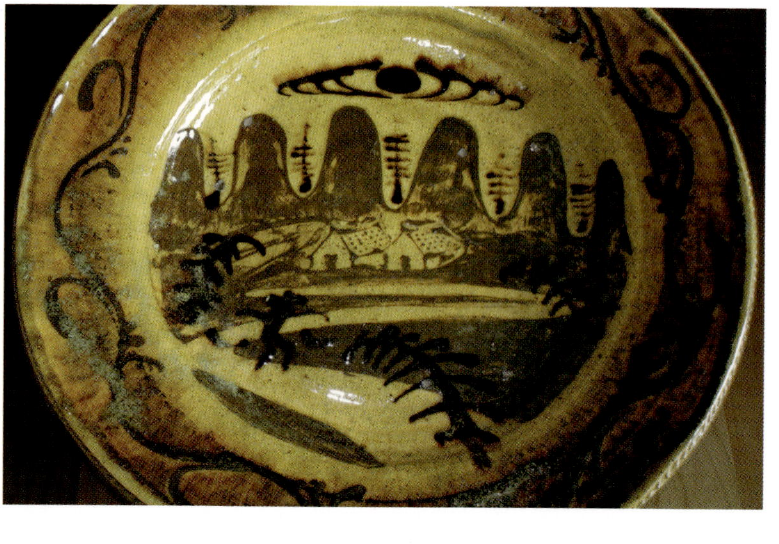

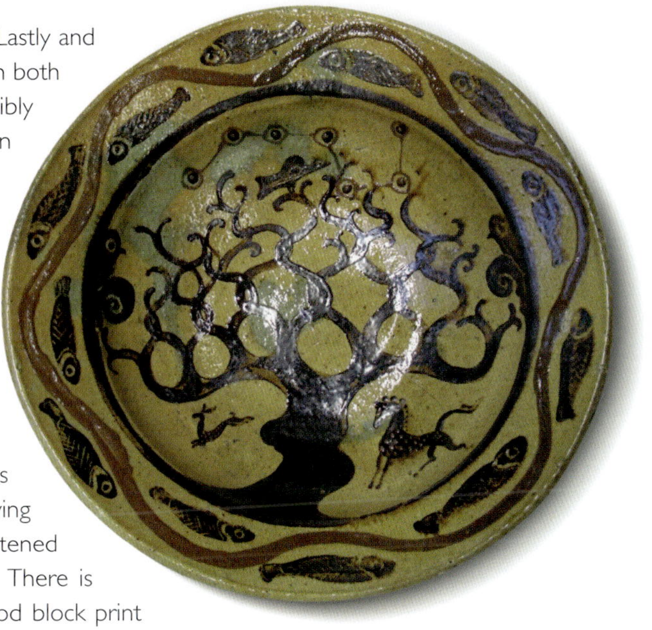

later absorbed into his stoneware idiom. Lastly and famously is the 'Tree of Life' motif used on both slipware and stoneware from 1923, possibly inspired originally from a design seen on a (Chinese) Han Dynasty tomb, but a theme common to the culture of both East and West and having something of William Blake in its visionary and occult symbolism.

The common thread underlying the use of these varying motifs is Leach's creation of a powerful decorative language. By simplying themes or forms to their basic essentials and employing these in the monotone, he thus heightened their symbolic and emotional resonance. There is perhaps an affinity with the Japanese wood block print tradition of Hiroshige and others, much admired by Van Gogh (in turn an artist favoured by the Shirakaba 'Silver Birch' group in Tokyo) who valued their flat tones, bold contours and non-western perspective. Such prints were known to and appreciated by Leach who had trained initially as an etcher and engraver and were collected by his friend and patron Henry Bergen who later donated examples to the British Museum.

1923 slipware charger.

Leach talked about his attitude to decoration in a late interview with David Smith-Greenwood, *A visit with Bernard Leach*, published in Ceramics Monthly in November 1974: 'Now when one speaks of patterns, it needs to be recorded. I think there is practically no pattern-making today. Only in the remnants of folk life and folk culture will you find what I call pattern. It's comparable to metaphors, to poems, to tools, little absolute simplifications of sound, colors, shapes which can be repeated quickly as in music or dance or in poetic couplets. William Blake's are good examples.'

Whatever the inspiration, it is Leach's careful selection of the right decoration for the form, whether on the flat or in the round, that commands attention. Decoration and form were the subjects of much thought and planning and were treated on an equal footing, and many sketches by him survive of pottery with notations on proposed designs, colouration and glaze. This very conscious artistic process is in strong contrast to the approach taken at Mashiko from 1925 by Hamada, and by Michael Cardew at Winchcombe from 1926. Indeed Hamada, who never marked his work after leaving the Leach Pottery and moving to Mashiko, famously commented: 'It took twenty years to forget everything I learned in ten.'

3 A CHRONOLOGICAL ILLUSTRATION OF FORMS

This section is arranged in broadly chronological order and seeks to analyse the forms and styles that predominated in several distinct phases of the early years of the Leach Pottery in the period 1920-1937. Some examples in fabrics other than slipware are included for the sake of completeness and contrast. Additionally, since this study also sets out to trace the impact of our English and Welsh slipware traditions on the Studio Pioneers, examples from Mashiko and Kyoto are included where I have identified a cross-over influence of work by Shoji Hamada and Kawai Kanjiro on subsequent production at the Leach Pottery.

A brief commentary on personal seals

A detailed analysis of marks from examples in museums either dated or of a known date can be found in the appendix. In summary, the first pots from 1921 tend to bear paper labels, possibly because the clay did not easily take an impressed seal. Leach had marked work that he decorated in Japan, usually with a brush, and that calligraphic, cursive quality is also seen on the first impressed BL seal marks employed from 1922-1923. Brushwork, slip-trailed and incised Workshop SI and personal monograms continued to be used freehand, depending on the type of pot and fabric. As time went on, the marking of pots became more formalised, with the SI seal usually complemented by a maker's seal on individual works, although standard forms remained anonymous as to maker – a tradition continued in the later stoneware of the Pottery.

THE FOUNDATION YEARS (1920-1923)

From the surviving examples examined, in the early days brush-decorated low-fired raku style wares seem to have been on an equal footing with conventional earthenwares in the overall output of low-temperature ceramics. This apparent balance may have been skewed by firing failures in the climbing kiln, and raku may well have been glaze fired in a rudimentary kiln (see line engraving of a typical example). The shortage of materials probably meant that pots which did not pass muster were pounded down to grog and used either for kiln materials or to open up throwing materials such as china clay.

This was a period in which the output was primarily of work in the English idiom, with high-status wares slip-trailed in the Toft manner, popular with the Japanese market. As potters new to England and unfamiliar with its ceramic traditions, there was a conscious effort by the founders to investigate and master the techniques and forms of their adopted place of work, with slipware being unknown in Japan. Production went hand in hand with visits to remaining working potteries at Lakes as has already been mentioned, but also Verwood in Dorset: it is believed that Leach went on to see Isaac Button at Soil Hill, Halifax, although Buckley in North Wales remained unvisited and unknown.

The Artificers Guild and the early 'bakings'

The Guild's gallery in Conduit Street, London appears a curious venue for exhibiting ceramics, having a primarily a reputation for displaying metalwork and textiles, and Leach Pottery exhibits researched are primitive and tentative. Leach later recalled that only 10% of early production was of show quality, a reflection of the problems at the St Ives workshop. We illustrate two early slipware examples from the first 'burnings' (firings) in October 1921, at least one of which was exhibited at Conduit Street in 1921. These are from the Bergen gift at the Potteries Museum, Stoke.

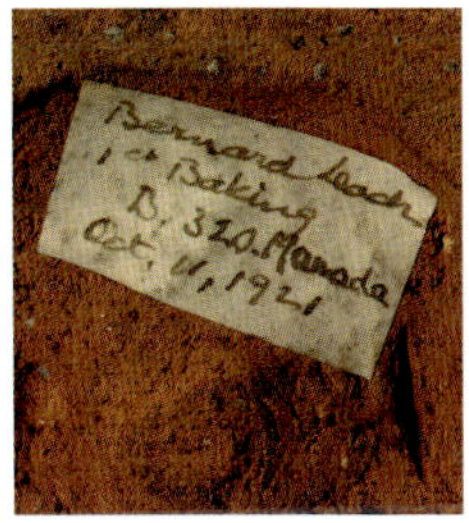

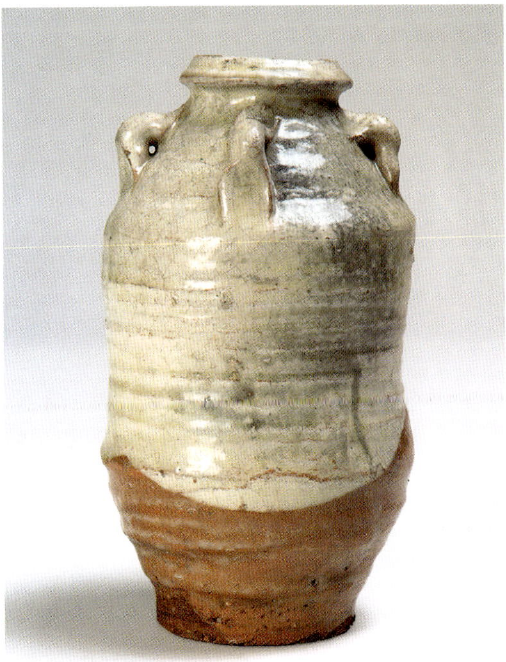

Earthenware bottle by Hamada (1921). Height 17.5cm.

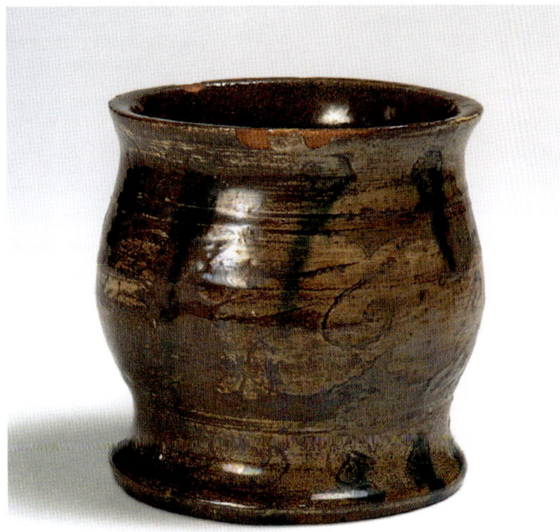

Leach turned and incised slipware jar (1921). Height 12cm.

The Cotswold Gallery

Run by Mrs Finsberg, the wife of an expert on the artist William Turner, this Frith Street gallery specialised in contemporary Cotswold art and furniture. She gave Leach his first one man show in 1922, although we have not been able to identify any specimens purchased on this occasion.

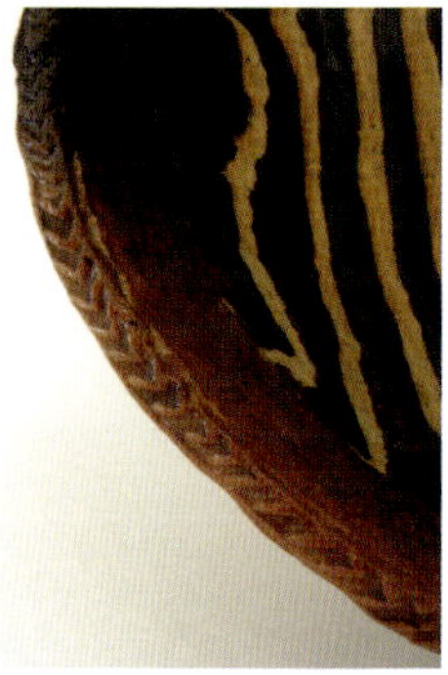

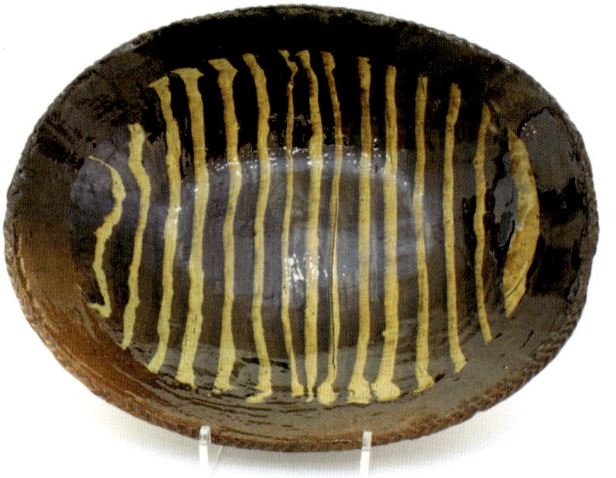

Hump moulded dish and detail (1922). 34 x 28cm.

Neriage and other trial wares of 1922

A number of pots by Hamada have survived, primarily in the Bergen gift at Stoke but also in the Noall gift at The Royal Cornwall Museum, Truro. We illustrate a Neriage (agate) specimen, which appears to have been made by Hamada assembling a series of alternating flat layers of white ball clay and gritty red clay. This striped core was then surrounded by a wide band of one clay type, and the assembled lump was then sliced at right angles giving a number of narrow bats of thin alternating strips of clay, surrounded by a wider border. The flat bat of striped clay was then shaped over a mould, and the finished cut edge protected using a rouletting tool to avoid flaking or chipping. The other Neriage example of mottled appearance uses a similar technique except that the red and white core clays are partially mixed through kneading rather than being made into flat layers. Hamada may have been inspired to produce these Neriage wares by seeing shards from the fields or complete hump-moulded dishes in Noall's collection, decorated simply with white lines of slip, and an example of such 18th and 19th century dishes may be seen in the collection of the Penlee Gallery and Museum, Morrab Gardens, Penzance. The significance to Hamada of his dishes is reflected in the fact that they are all fully marked.

Mottled clay bowl (1922). 6 x 4cm.

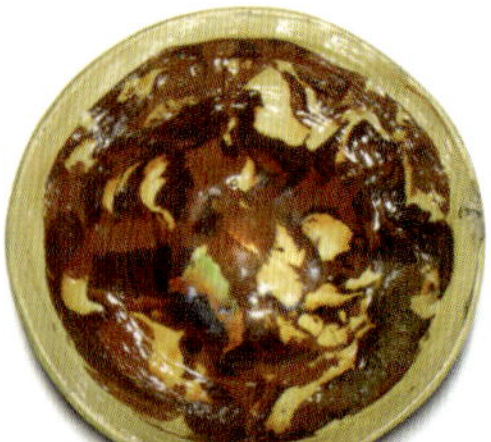

Hare motif dish diameter 20cm.

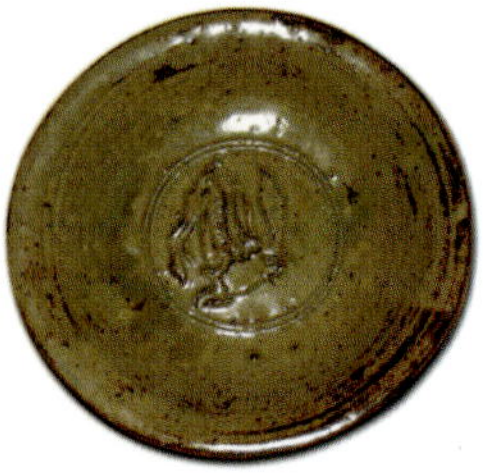

Other early hump-moulded dishes

These two examples from the Bergen gift at the Potteries Museum, Stoke, show different slip treatments of a hare design, a form which is also seen in stoneware under a celadon glaze. Hares were a popular early theme for Leach and are seen in his raku ware in Japan and on other early St Ives slipware. In this instance, the motif has been incised into a fired clay former,

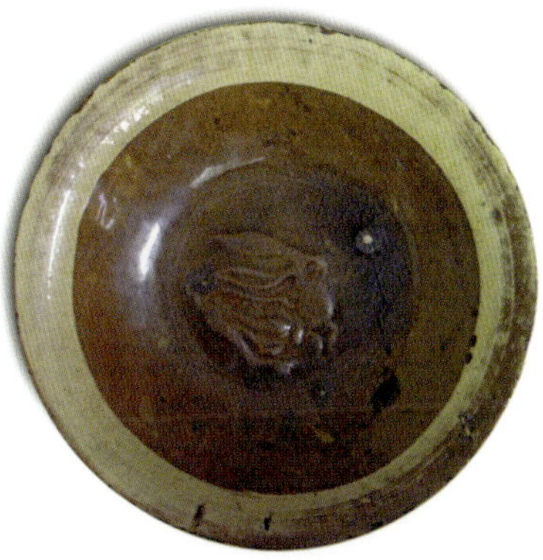

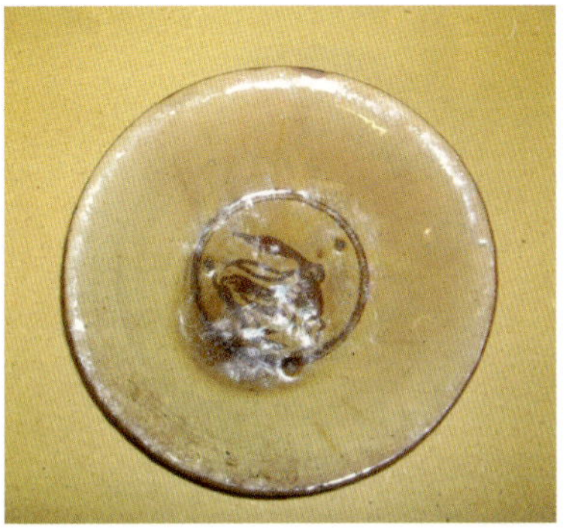

Hare motif dishes all diameter 20cm.

appearing in reverse on the finished moulded dish. The Bergen provenance and simple nature suggest an early date, probably 1922-1923: they bear only a small SI seal.

There are many tales of walks by the two founders through the fields and countryside surrounding St Ives, and of discoveries of shards of moulded slipwares but aside from a few atypical examples by Hamada mentioned above, there is no evidence of the regular production at St Ives of such moulded dishes and bowls until 1929-1930. However, Hamada himself was producing moulded work in stoneware at Mashiko, decorated in the English tradition, by as early as 1925-1926 as is illustrated here.

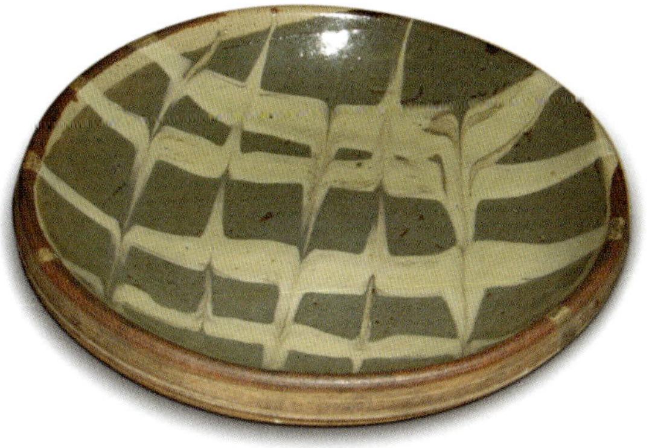

16 x 4cm.

10 x 10cm.

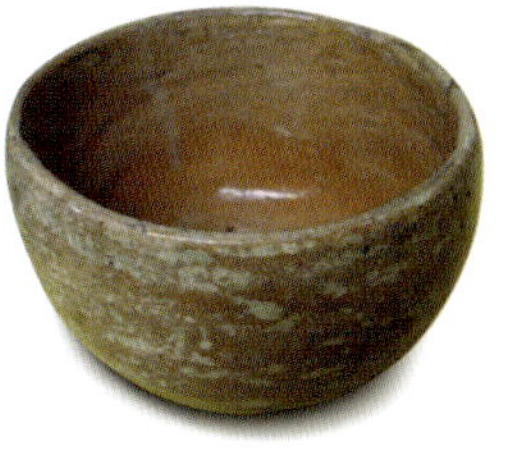

Hamada and Bergen

Henry Bergen paid for pottery classes in 1922. He wrote to Leach in 1924 (Leach Study Archive, Farnham) about wanting to glaze raku style wares thrown by Hamada for him to decorate, but these do not appear to have survived. In the Bergen collection in Stoke are however one or two pinch pots in mottled clay (see illustration), bearing an HB seal, and, though of limited appeal, provide a record of his early visit.

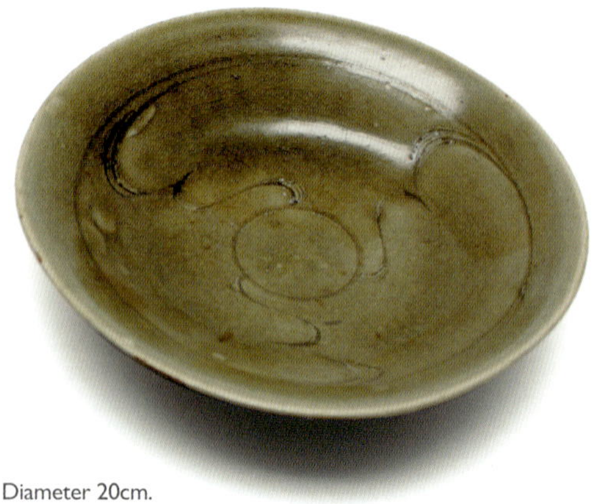

Diameter 20cm.

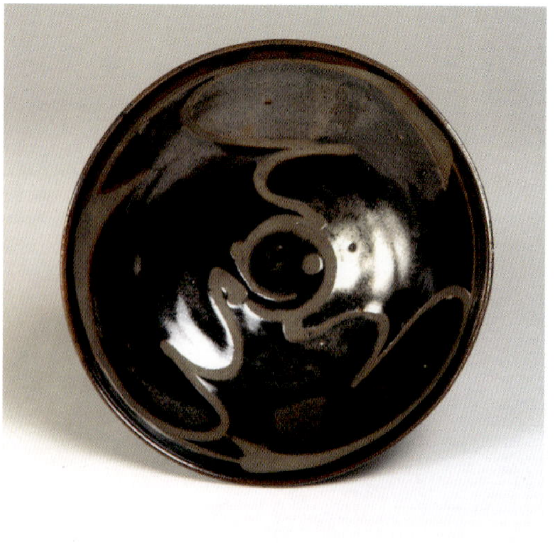

6 x 4cm.

Flaming pearl plate

Diameter 20cm.

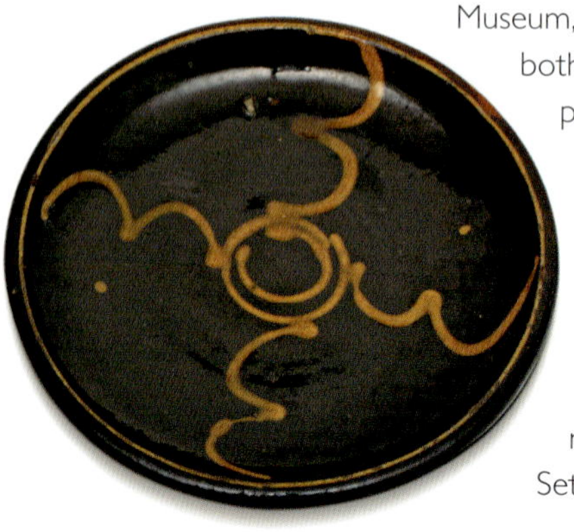

A bowl by Hamada dated to 1922 is held in the collection of the Potteries Museum, Stoke and another in the Southampton Art Gallery, and both are unmarked (see also the 1923 slipware bowl on page 59 and 139). The abstract theme appears to have been inspired by a design from Chinese folklore showing a dragon pursuing a flaming pearl across the sky, and was used by Hamada on other occasions. While also unmarked, the earthenware plate illustrated bears a very similar design in slip trailing, and the fabric and turning of its base are consistent with it having been made at St Ives in 1922, and recalls the turning seen on Seto peasant bowls (see page 15).

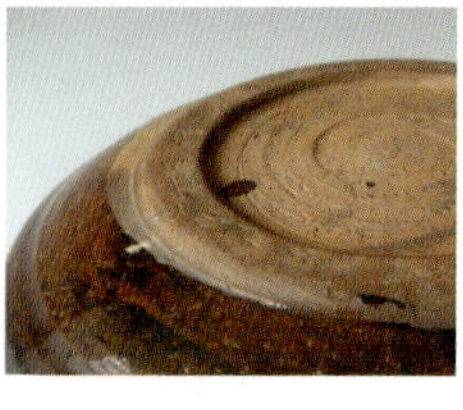

Raku style wares

This is probably an appropriate juncture to discuss raku wares. At this time, raku was a form of low- fired earthenware in which the red-hot pot is removed by tongs from the kiln and allowed to cool rapidly. Subsequently the word has been used to describe a much wider range of wares, to which various treatments have been applied during the cooling. Leach has in the past been credited with introducing oriental raku to the West, although those cream-bodied St Ives pots described as raku which have been researched show no evidence of tong marks and in several instances would have been very difficult to pick up whilst still red-hot.

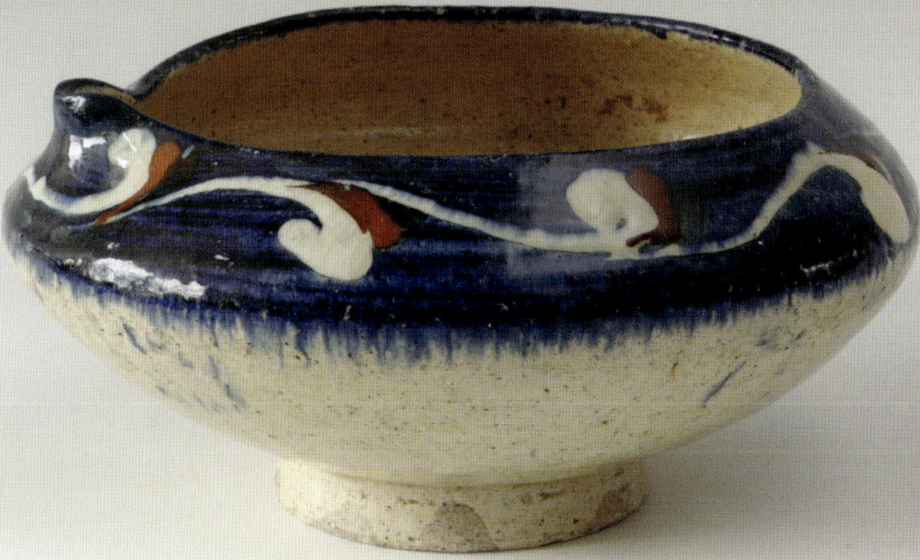

21 x 10.5cm.

For this reason, we have reclassified such St Ives pots as 'low-fired raku style wares': these were probably fired in the cooler upper chamber of a rudimentary igloo shaped kiln, the top of the 1925 Matsu up-draught kiln, or in the top chamber of the main climbing kiln, and allowed to cool normally. It seems likely that true raku wares were however made and fired for weekly demonstration and decoration lessons at the Pottery in the mid to late 1920s, with visitors paying a fee based upon the size of the pot. The coarse nature of the china clay waste primarily used in such raku work would have proved ideal for the thermal shock entailed, and also made this material suitable for higher temperature ceramics.

Emmanuel Cooper, in his biography of Leach, states that the latter did not make such wares at St Ives, and it is true that in *Hamada Potter*, Hamada recalls throwing a quantity of 'raku' in the autumn of 1922 for decoration by Robert Morton Nance (see following section), and may have performed the same service for Leach. However, examples exist bearing both SI and BL seals, probably the best known being a pouring bowl form decorated simply to the rim in contrasting red and white slips on a band of blue brushwork (see illustration).

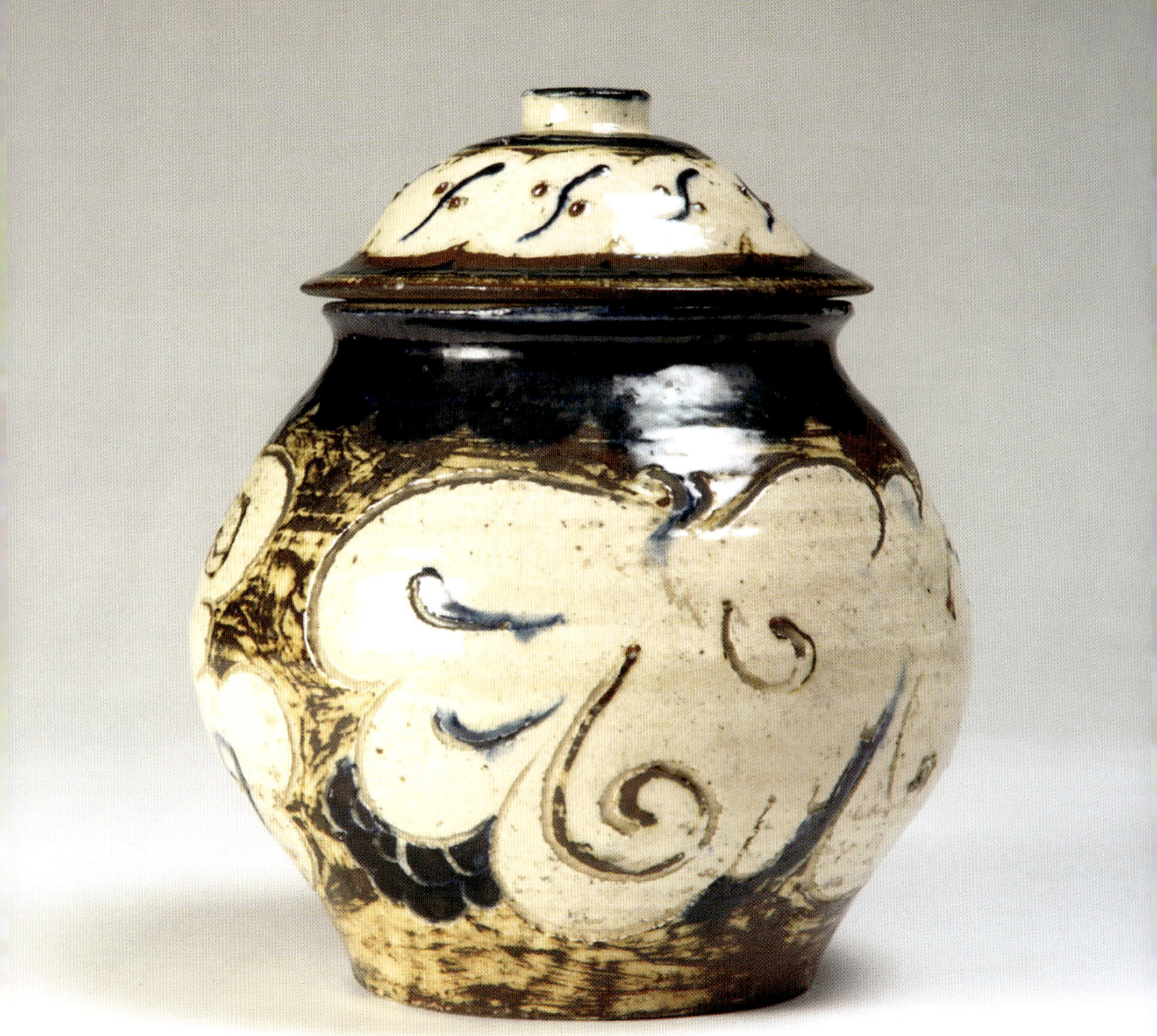

22 x 13cm.

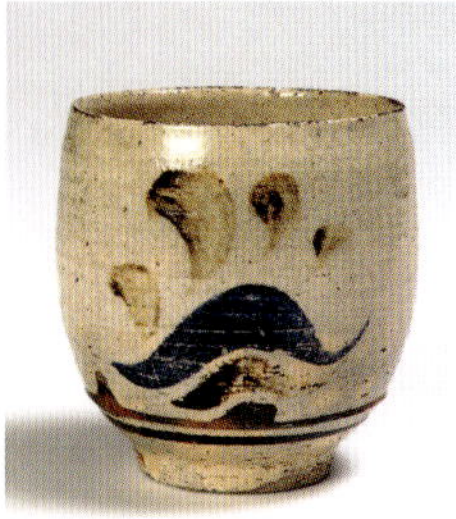

9 x 8cm.

This lidded jar from the Bergen gift at the Potteries Museum, Stoke, harks back to a form seen on several occasions in Leach's raku output whilst in Japan and has a similar cloud-like design. This example is particularly interesting as the lid bears a repeated round stylised design reminiscent of the Yin and Yang emblem (see page 29), achieved by removing a layer of brown slip to leave two brown dots and applying an elongated 'S' in dark blue slip. The brush decorated tea bowl in a similar colouration is also from the Bergen gift, and is again fully marked by Leach.

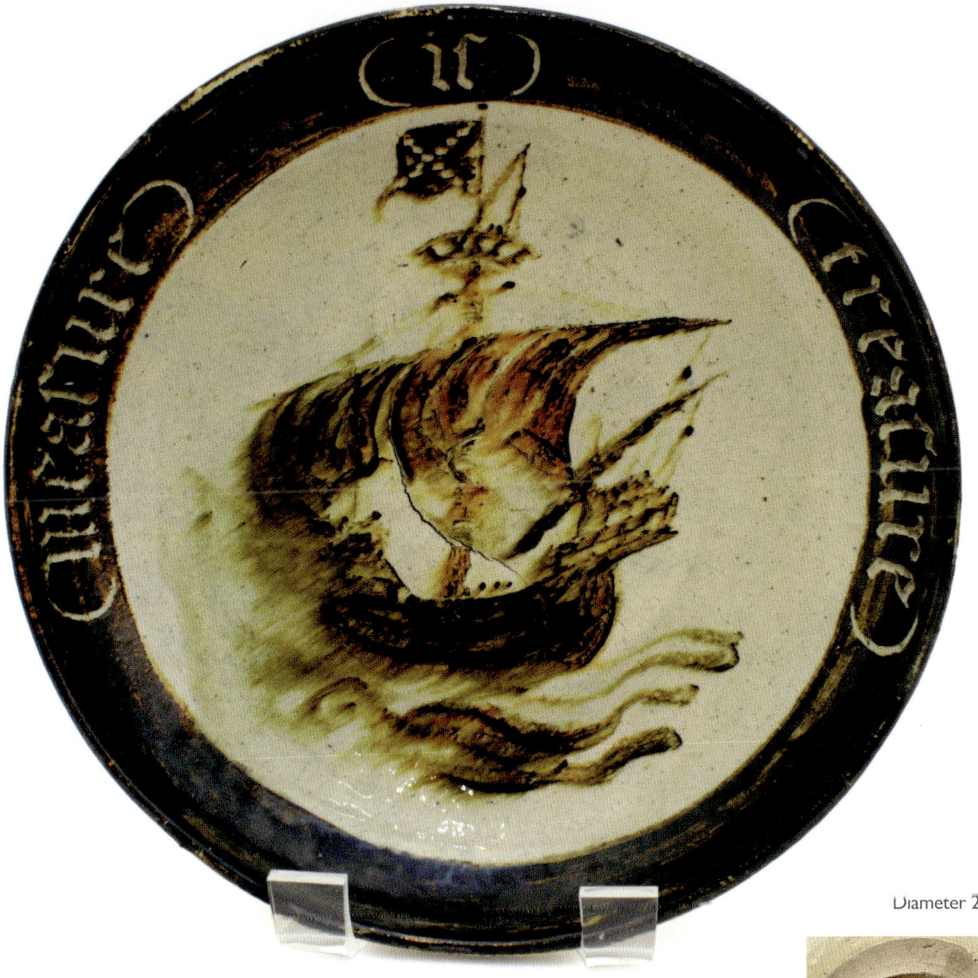

Diameter 29.5cm.

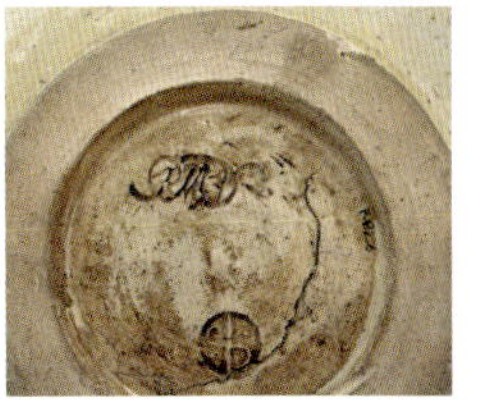

Hamada and Nance

Sadly few pieces have apparently survived from their autumn 1922 collaboration, whether through misfiring or subsequent misadventure. The two examples illustrated both bear only the SI impressed seal and the inscribed cursive initials 'R.M.N.'. The designs used on both reflect separate areas of his wide expertise. The plate showing a galleon in full sail is achieved using brushwork in iron or manganese, and reflects his interest in matters nautical (see page 21). The inscription 'Measure is treasure' is obscure and may be a literary allusion: Nance was very interested in Cornish verse and legend; he composed and published verse and other material on this subject.

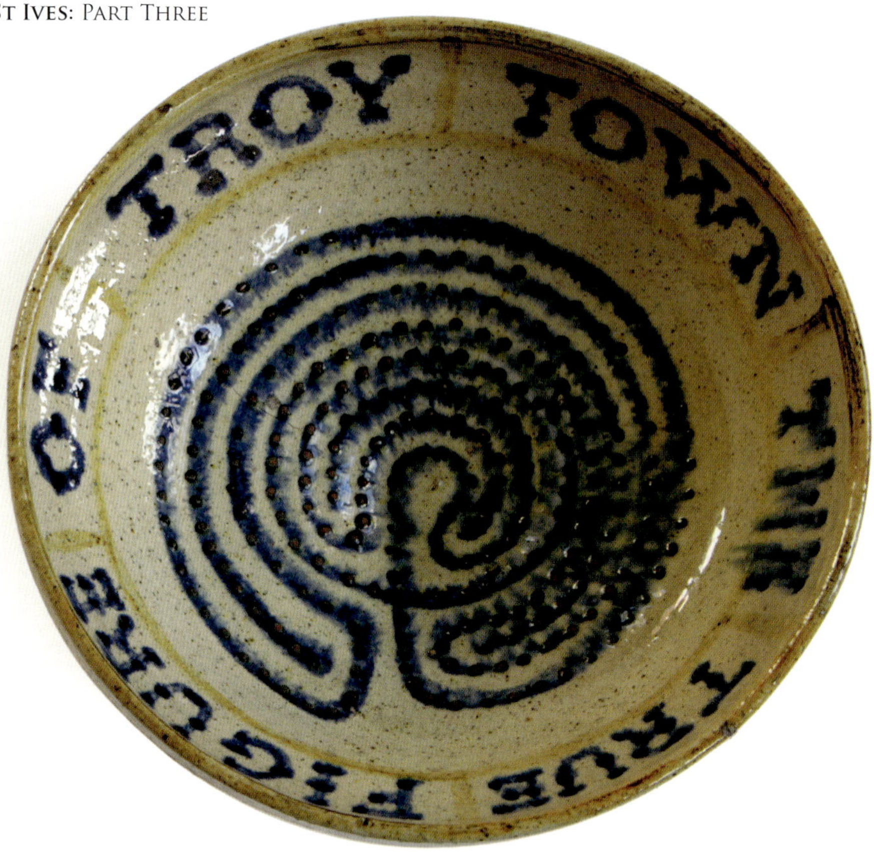

The origins of the deeper bowl are easier to discern. Nance had a long-standing interest in Cornish and West Country archaeology, and in 1913 presented a study of surviving unicursal mazes to the Royal Institution of Cornwall (RIC). Subsequently, he was awarded the Henwood medal by the RIC in 1926 for his 1924 paper *Troy Town*. The unicursal maze at St Agnes in the Scilly Isles, with its design picked out in stones on the hillside, features in the latter study and was the probable inspiration for this bowl. It is decorated using blue (cobalt) slip and with iron brushwork that has dissipated under the lead-rich glaze during firing.

24 x 9cm.

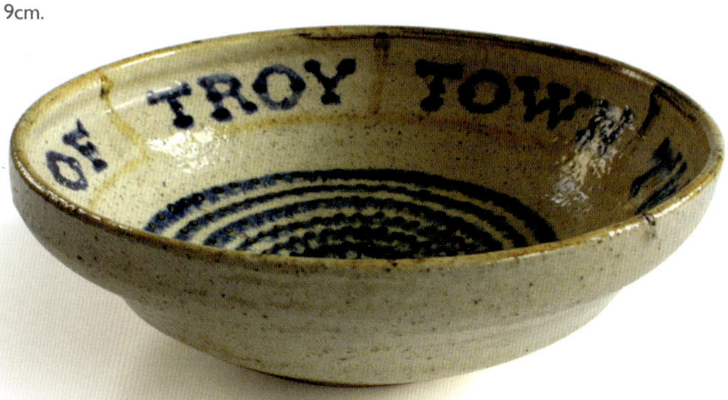

William Blake

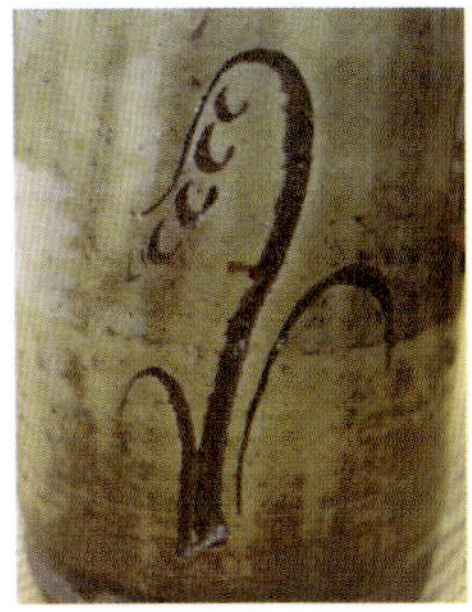

Verse by Blake was the inspiration behind the two Leach pieces illustrated here from 1922-1923, one in conventional slipware and the other raku. The jug form from The Crafts Study Centre, Farnham (CSC) is of red clay with incised decoration and lettering through a white slip under a clear glaze, and bears an impressed SI seal and the monograms WB/BL inscribed to the body near the handle. The three-footed bowl or Koro (incense burner) from a private collection is thrown in a cream-coloured medium, with lettering incised through a band of reddish slip painted on to the white-slipped surface under a clear glaze. It has impressed workshop and personal seals to the underside. Both bear the inscription 'A little flower is the labour of ages'.

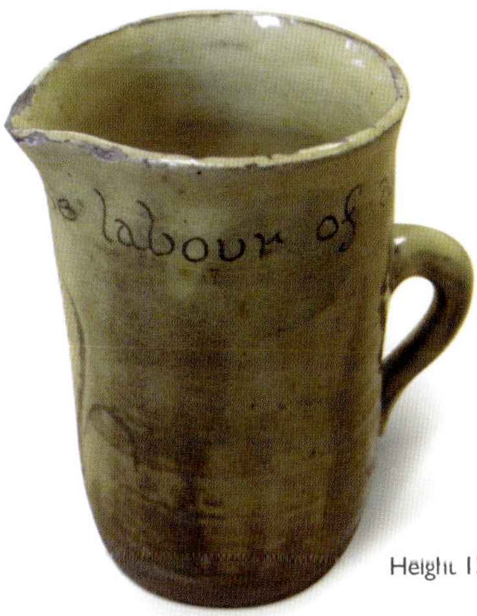

Height 13cm.

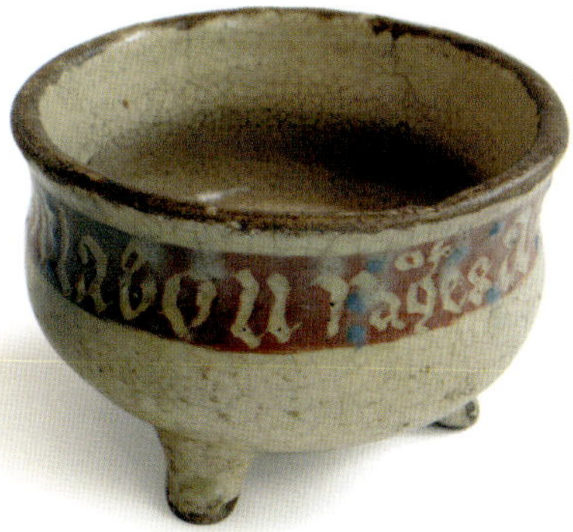

10 x 8cm.

14 x 15cm.

Early standing forms by Leach

The milk jug here from the CSC bears a stylistic quirk in common with an example in the Ohara Museum of Art, Japan which dates from 1922 and shows an early freehand version of the SI workshop emblem incised into its side. They both sit on deep and flared foot rims, which may have been made separately on the wheel then attached to the base. The likelihood of these jugs having been made at about the same time is reinforced by their identical running design border to the rims. The CSC example has incised lettering and decoration through a white slip to an open red body, and small round BL and SI seals inside the foot rim.

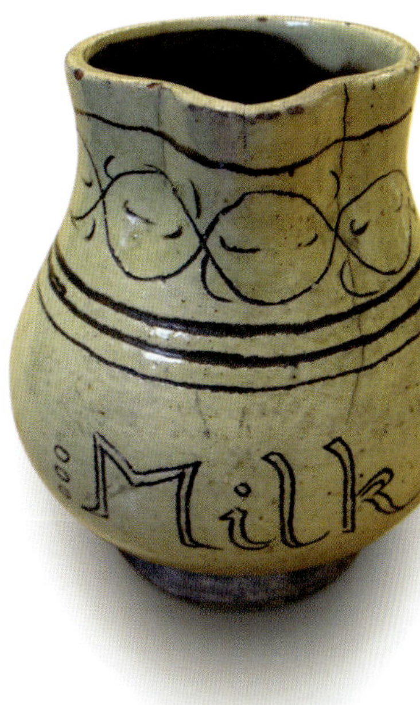

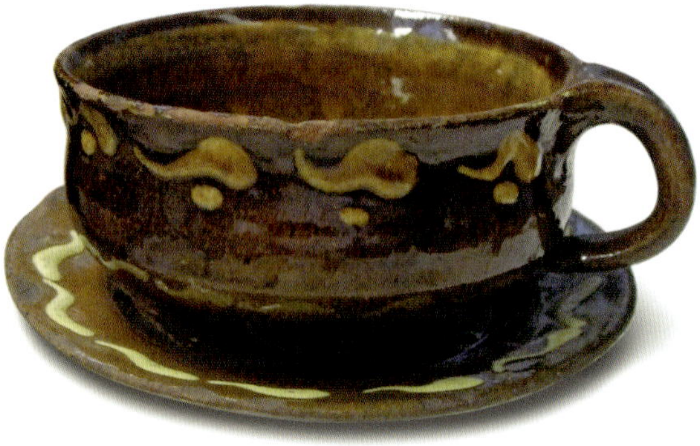

13 x 7cm.

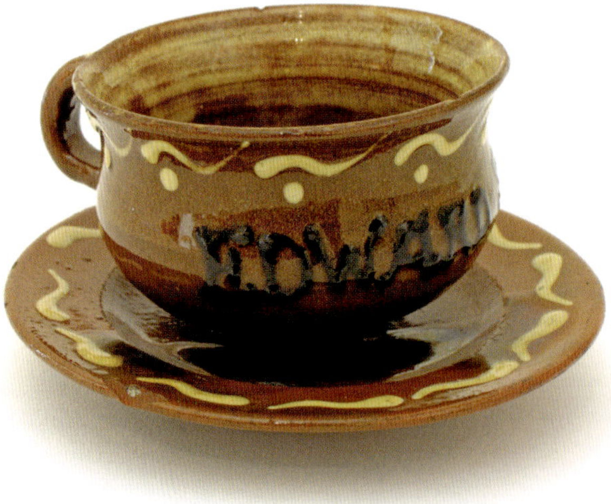

13 x 7cm.

Tea cups and saucers also make an early appearance, and we illustrate here two examples with similar slip-trailed decoration direct to the body under a clear glaze. One, from a private collection, was made for Edward Basset ('Old Bassett'), a retired fisherman who was an early friend of the founders. The other from the collection of the Victoria & Albert Museum (V&A) is otherwise plain. Both bear early circular versions of a BL script seal and the SI monogram.

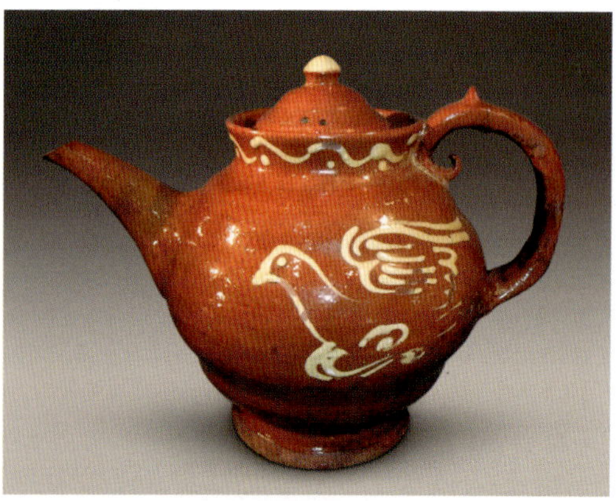

This teapot appears to have been made with the same overall design in mind, and bears identical seals to the tea cups and saucers illustrated. The decoration in white slip of a dove or some other bird may have been inspired by William Blake, judging by a raku plate decorated by Leach while still in Japan in 1917 with a similar bird motif and lettering in slip ('All nature listens silent to him'): it was formerly in the collection of Janet Leach but its whereabouts are currently unknown.

The 1923 shows at the William Paterson Gallery

We now arrive on comparatively firm ground as to date, certainly of when the following example was exhibited. Paterson's in Bond Street, London held shows in April and November 1923 which were primarily associated with Hamada but also included Leach pots. This delightful Hamada bowl now in the V&A is made of red earthenware with incised decoration through a white slip, under a lead glaze stained with a speckling of iron. It bears both personal and workshop seals.

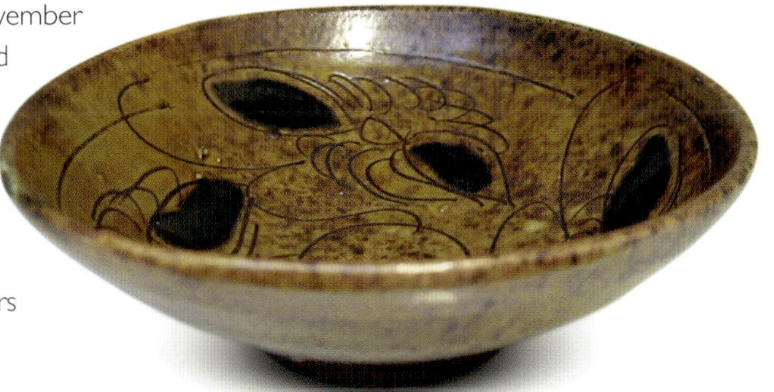

18 x 6.5cm.

Although the provenance for this drug jar by Bernard Leach in the V&A collection is not known, it has a look consistent with the bowl by Hamada. Inscribed with a design of an heraldic lion, and the date 1923, it bears BL and SI seals.

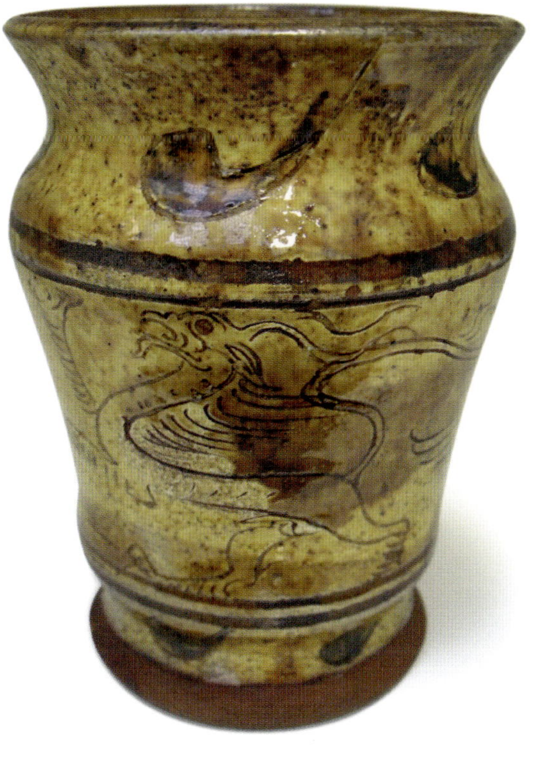

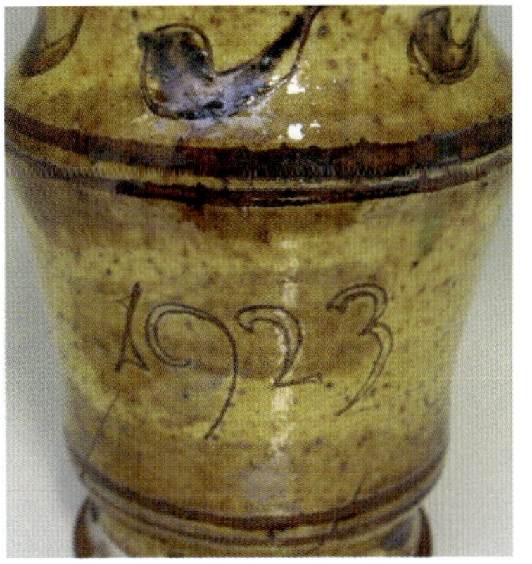

16 x 11.5cm.

British Institute for Industrial Art

The BIIA was established in 1920 by a grant from HM Treasury and was a promoter and exhibiter of good industrial and craft design. It acquired and was given work by Leach from 1923, and its collection of ceramics was subsequently passed to the V&A in 1934. Amongst these were the following two examples again dating from 1923. The first is a lidded jar by Leach with a design in removed and sgraffito slip of a bird in clouds: the design bears comparison with earlier examples, and has workshop and personal seals.

Height 14cm, diameter 15cm.

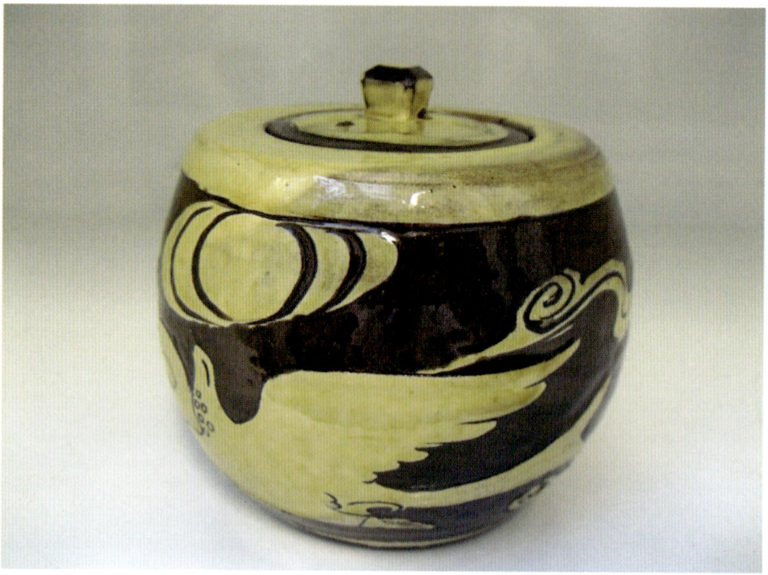

The second is a magnificent large charger with a deep well to the centre, decorated direct to the body with brushed and trailed brown slip under an iron stained lead glaze, the actual fabric being a creamy white medium. It was probably thrown over a wheel head former by Hamada, and its profile bears a strong likeness to the examples by the latter that follow. Leach would have trimmed back the underside to achieve a foot rim and refine the overall line of the finished pot, marking it subsequently in trailed slip with his personal monogram and the date, 1923. In line with other platters of this type, this dish has a rouletted finish to the rim, a departure from the plain cut edge of the 17th-century Toft-school chargers that were a leading influence.

The design is known vernacularly as the 'Tree of Life' and may have been taken from a stone carving on a Han dynasty tomb seen during his time in China in 1917: it is a design theme that recurs in his later work in stoneware. Aside from a horse, deer, snails and fishes, the design also includes the Plough constellation which is depicted on two Bull chargers by

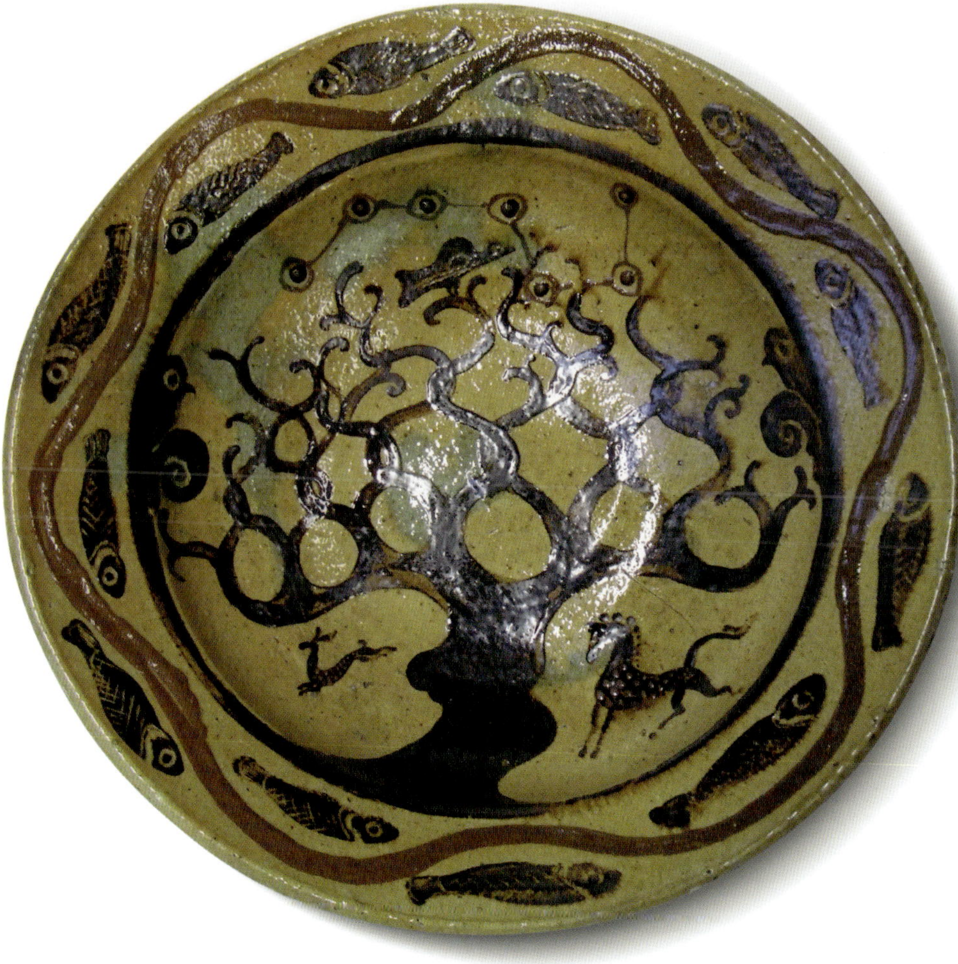

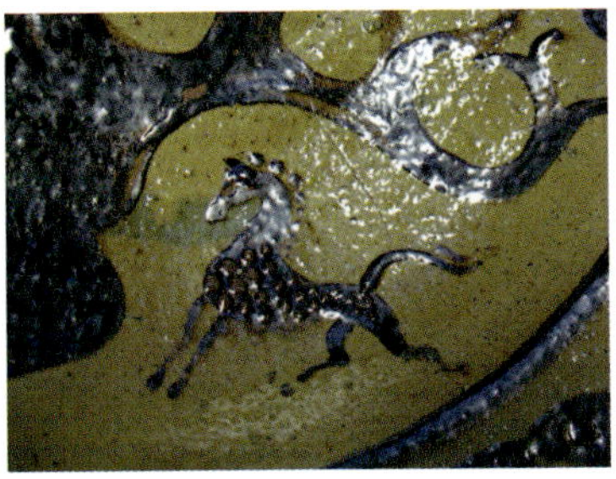

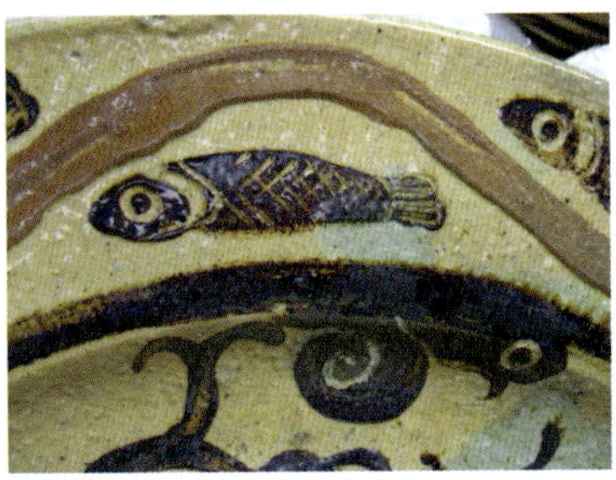

Diameter 42cm, depth 12cm.

Hamada of 1923, and recurs on a later charger by Leach dated 1927 along with other constellation charts, although the significance of these symbols detail is unclear. The labour entailed in such an extensive decorative scheme makes it highly likely that this charger was initially biscuit fired prior to being individually glaze fired in the coolest chamber of the climbing kiln.

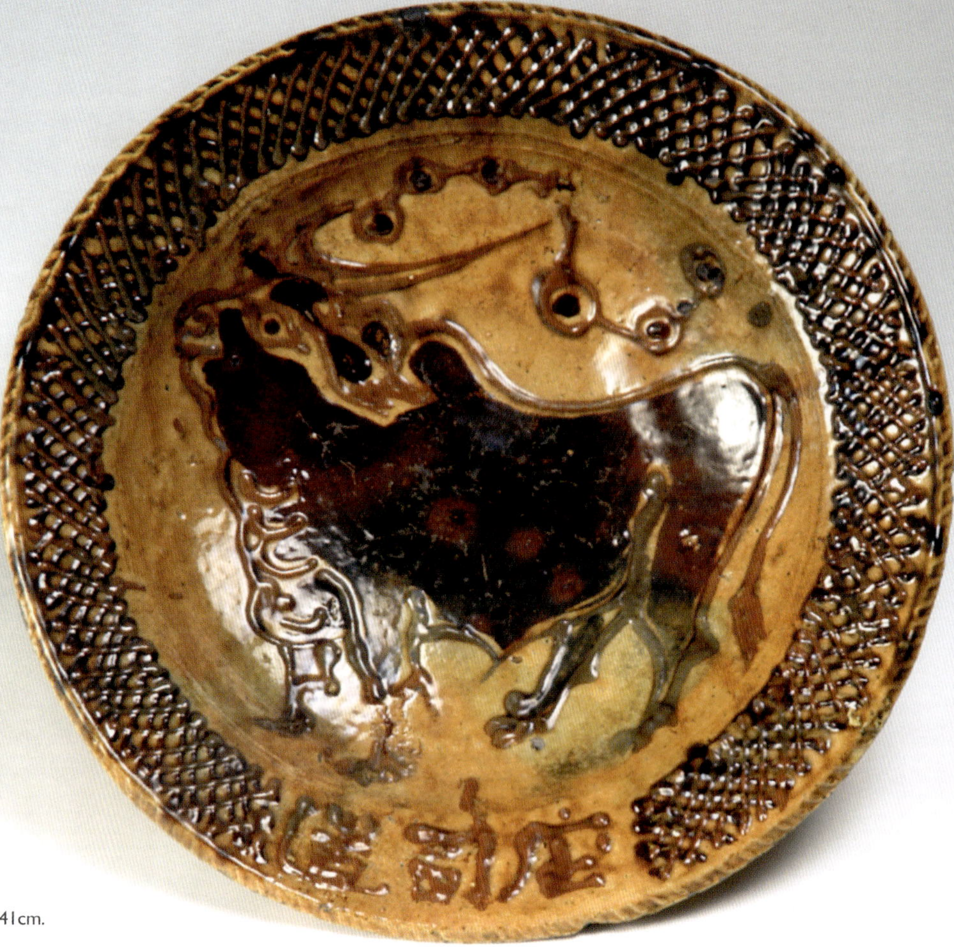

Diameter 41cm.

The Hamada Chargers

These three examples were probably made in 1923, and fired in an up-draught kiln.

Bull design: Two superb examples are illustrated, one from the Potteries Museum, Stoke and the other from a private collection. Both are decorated in dark and light brown trailed and brushed slip, and represent a rare figurative departure for Hamada who otherwise used exclusively stylised abstract or vegetal motifs. Each bears his personal monogram to the front of the chargers in trailed slip, and the trailed SI emblem to the interior of the foot rim. The trellis border is inspired by the chargers of Thomas Toft, although the main motifs of a bull and the plough are not in the English idiom. The throwing medium of each is similar to the Tree of Life charger above, with the overall colouration achieved by the addition of iron oxide to the otherwise clear glaze.

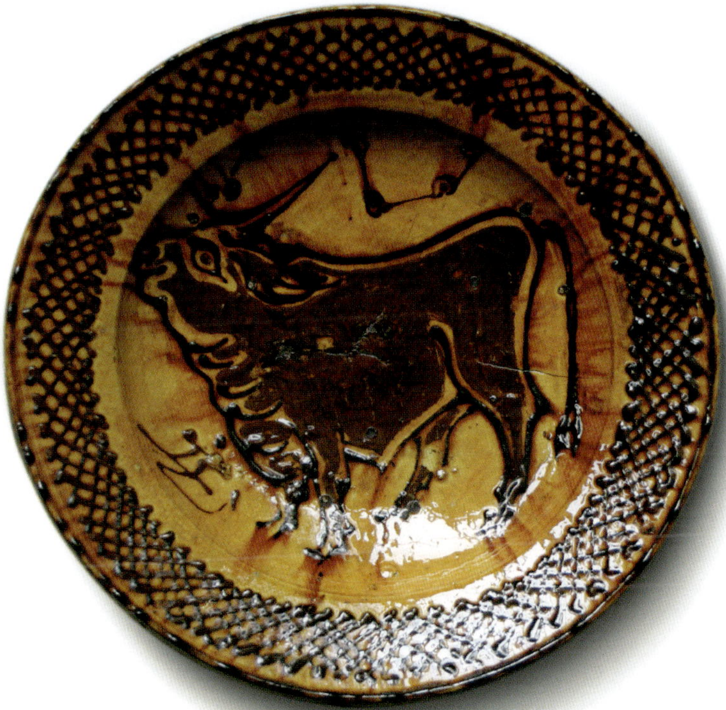

Diameter 45cm.

Sgraffito: This shallow bowl-shaped charger is in the collection of the University of Wales (UW), Aberystwyth, where it has been historically mistakenly described as being made of stoneware. It bears an extensive and sophisticated floral and foliage design achieved using removed and sgraffito slip techniques. The underlying form was thrown from a creamy white medium coated in a manganese brown slip, which when removed provides a strong contrast with the body colour. Hamada used similar techniques in stoneware (see page 43 for a vase from the Potteries Museum, Stoke) which also occur in the Asian ceramic tradition, but this piece shows the tell-tale furze firing characteristics of slipware (see Technical section page 41). Additionally, the movement under the glaze with a 'bleeding' of the manganese background slip is consistent with the effects of the galena glaze that Hamada was known to have used, and the glaze shows chipping and crazing typical of a lower-temperature medium. Lastly, the body clay type is consistent with the previous two Bull chargers. It bears Hamada's personal and the workshop seals.

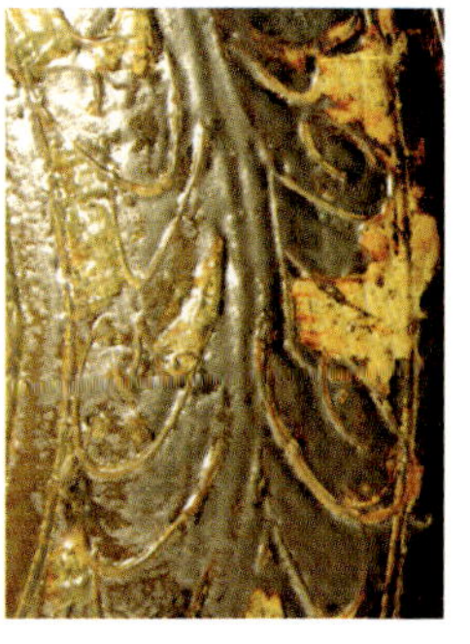

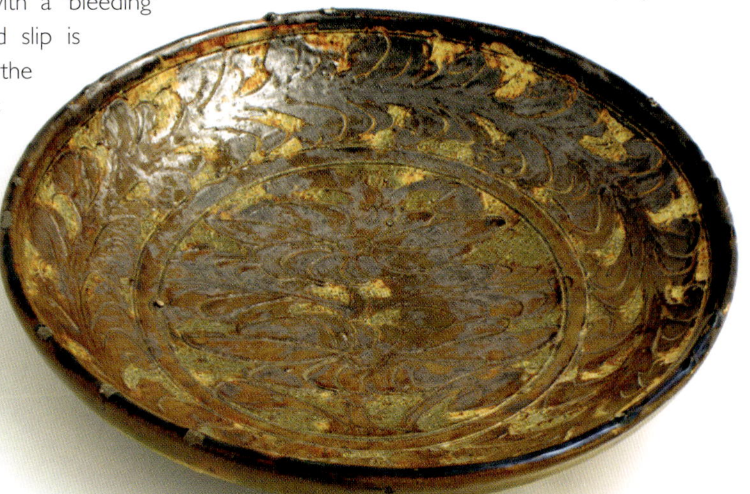

Diameter 39cm, depth 13cm.

THE CARDEWAN PERIOD (1923-1926)

There was an inevitable hiatus in making in between the departure of Hamada for Europe and later to Japan at the end of the year, and Cardew's initial arrival then departure for a holiday in the Mediterranean that coincided with this change of personnel. Additionally, Matsubayashi (Matsu) had already arrived earlier that summer and had started dismantling the failed climbing kiln, and it was probably not until 1924 that there was any finished output from the Leach Pottery. Meanwhile, Cardew was initially put to work making kiln bricks and saggars to assist Matsu, and spent some time being trained by Leach to achieve the style of forms that he admired and wanted to reproduce. Research trips continued, notably to Saunton by Leach in the company of Cardew to visit his family's holiday home and see their collection of Fremington slipwares.

Height 12cm.

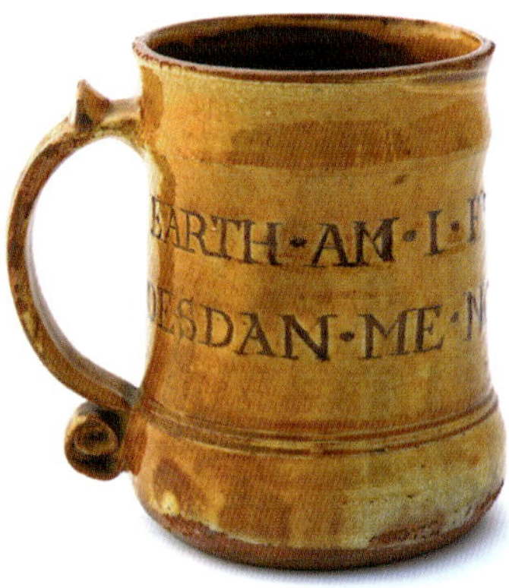

Height 11cm.

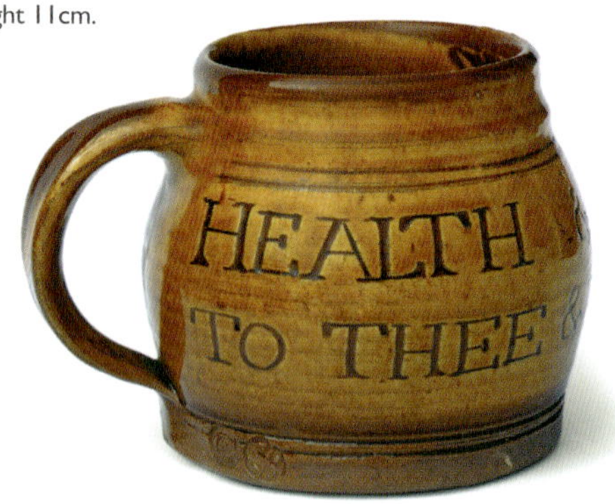

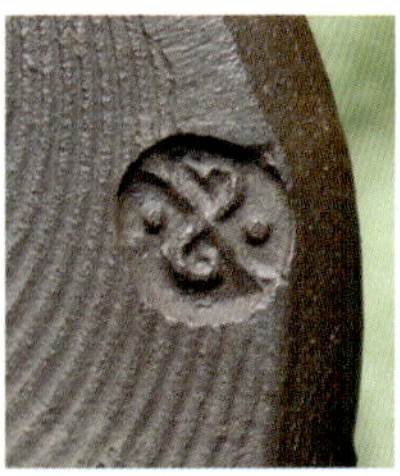

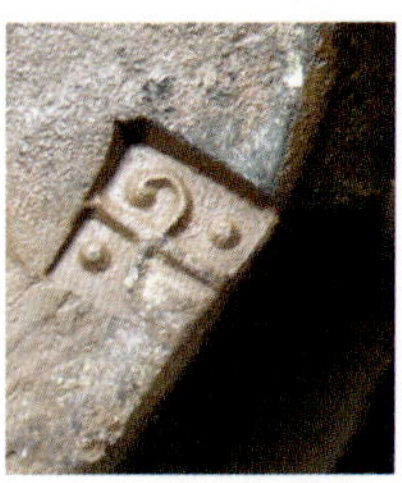

Tourist and commissioned wares

The first identifiable output in this period was a new range of tankards and mugs of varying sizes, all bearing incised decoration either of lettered verses and mottoes or coats of arms. All were thrown from red clay of varying quality, coated with a white slip to provide a strong contrast after decoration using sgraffito. It was a difficult time financially with the loss of Leach's first sponsor, Frances Horne, so urgent ways of raising bread and butter income were important in helping to pay bills. The motto wares were sold to passers-by and the occasional tourist who ventured up Stennack Hill, while pieces bearing shields and the like may have been commissioned by local families and businesses. Some are very well incised implying the hand of Leach whose original training as an etcher and engraver was put to good use. Lettering was usually in the seriffed capitals typical of the alphabets of Johnston and Gill of the Ditchling Craft Guild (see page 23), and while usually in English is sometimes seen in Cornish. The addition of iron oxide

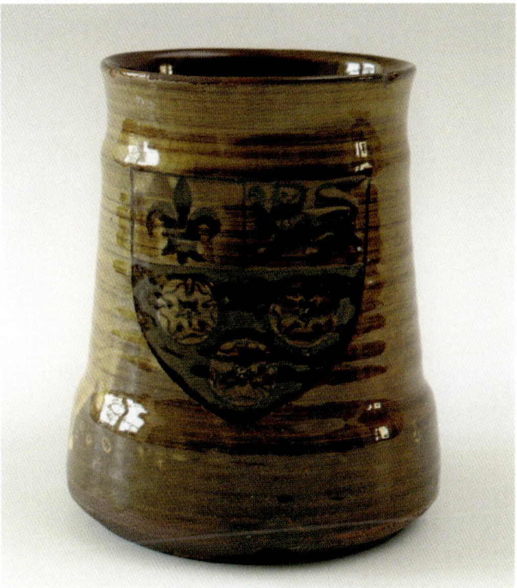

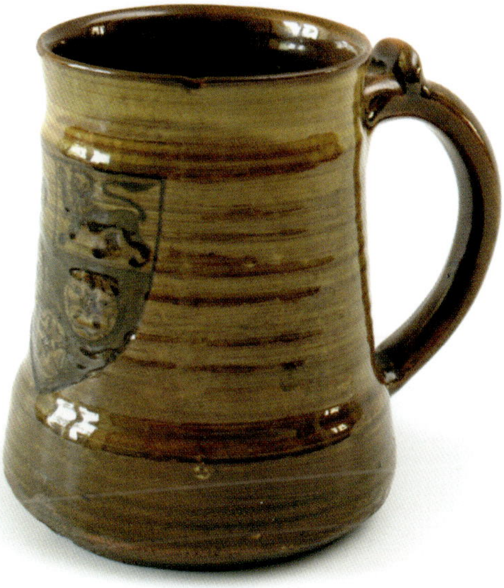

Height 14cm.

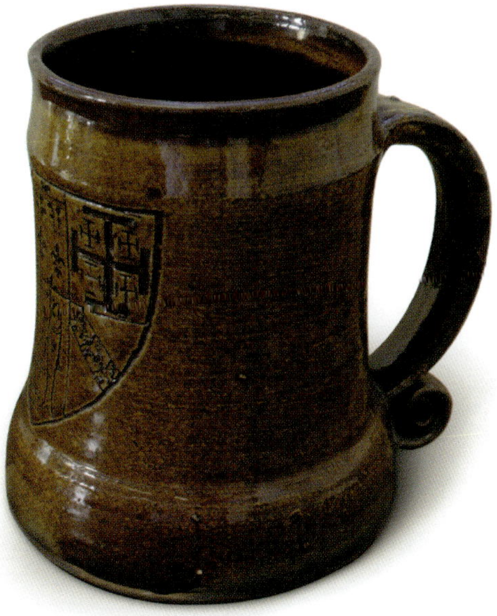

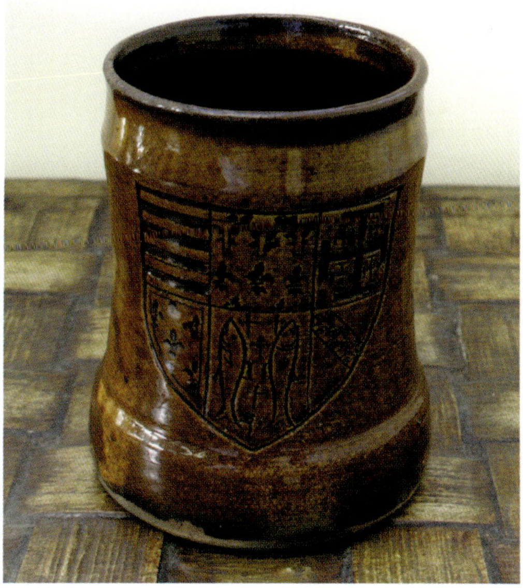

Height 12cm.

to the glaze and poor firing often resulted in a very dark finish, causing them to be nicknamed locally 'Cornish Treacle Wares'. Along with the prototypes that follow, all bear just a round workshop seal with the occasional pot having a small square version (see photographs opposite).

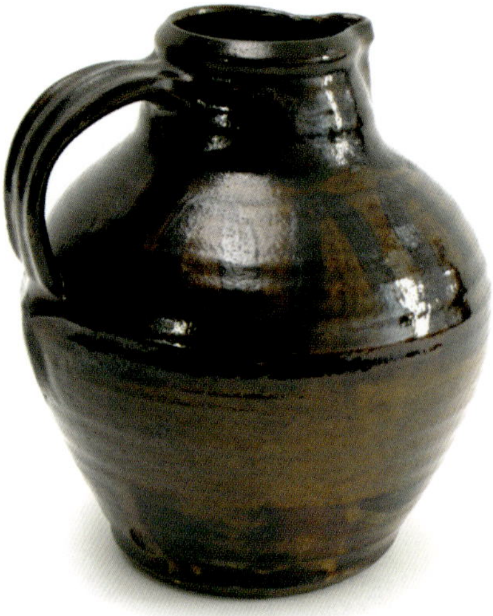

21 x 18cm.

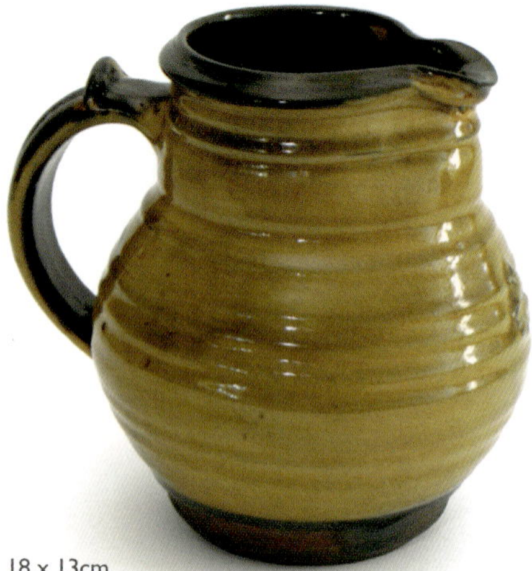

18 x 13cm.

Early Standard Ware Prototypes

It is widely assumed that standardisation of form at the Leach Pottery did not commence until the mid-to late 1930s, but the evidence of the pots is to the contrary, indicating that Leach used early earthenwares as part of a design process. A wide variety of different styles of jugs exist, showing a dark and at times over-fired finish similar to that seen in other pots known to be of this early period, all bearing the workshop seal to the base. Some are almost Rhenish in shape recalling stoneware, some more overtly medieval in inspiration and others look distinctly Devonian in character, the latter trait being seen more and more in Cardew's later St Ives output. A range of

24 x 15cm (right).

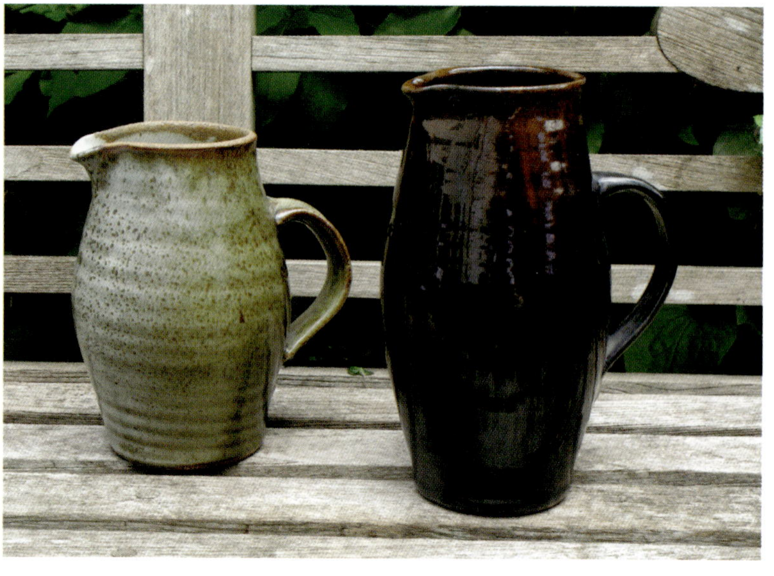

typical forms is illustrated alongside, some bearing simple iron brushwork and others sprigged decoration such as a Fleur de Lys. Also shown is a jug of straighter form alongside a Standard Ware jug in stoneware from the 1960s, for the purpose of comparison.

A range of cider and ale bottles are also seen, usually with iron brushwork, and frequently suffering the same problems of dark glazes and/or over-firing. These should be compared with the Fremington examples on page 24.

22 x 14.5cm.

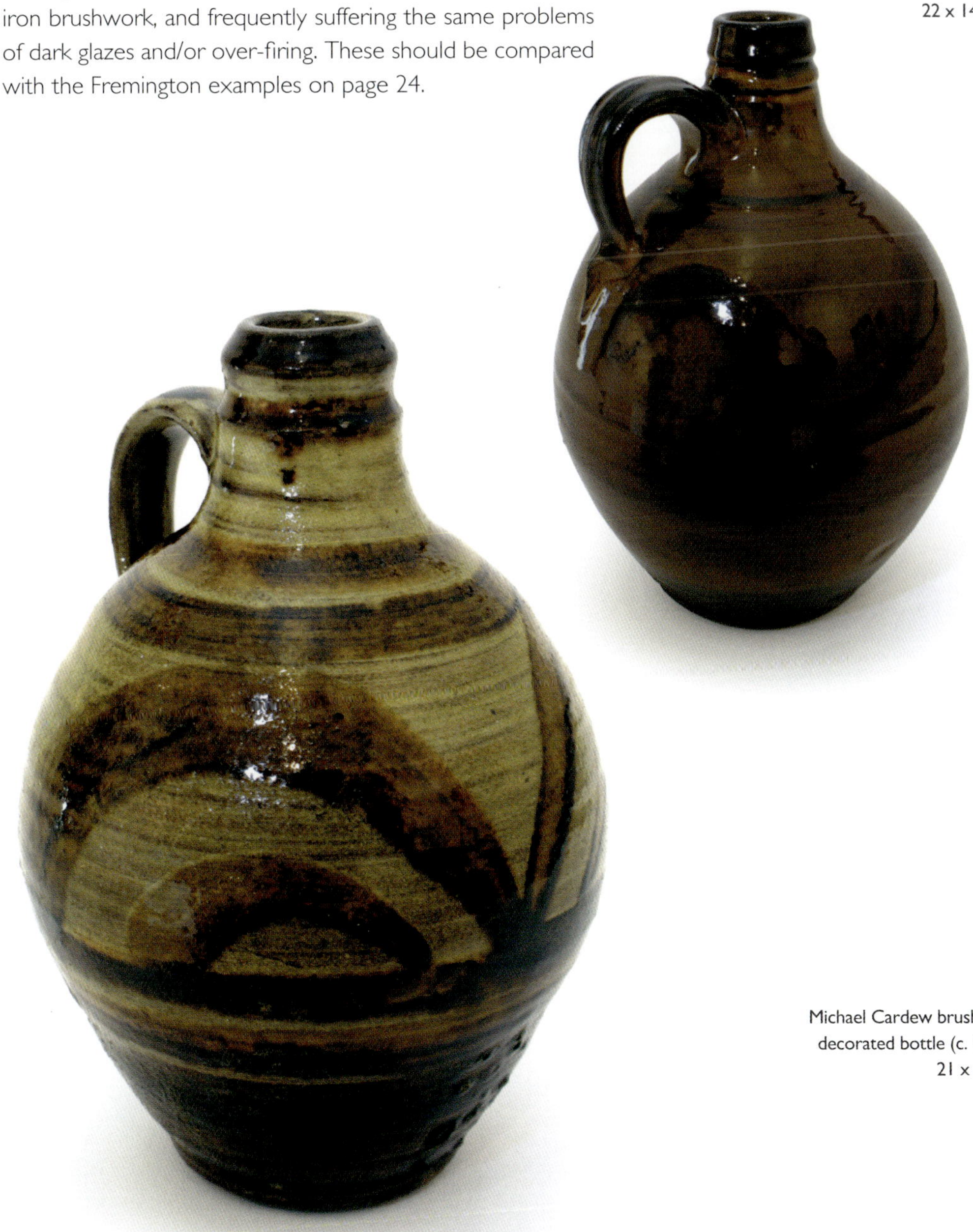

Michael Cardew brushwork decorated bottle (c. 1925). 21 x 13cm.

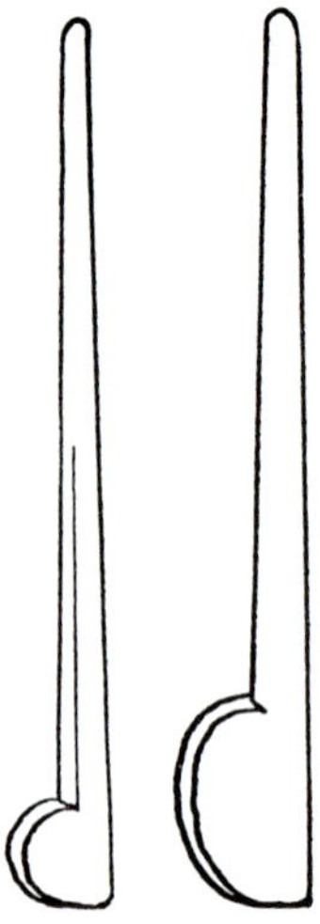

Wooden profiles used in throwing narrow-necked shapes

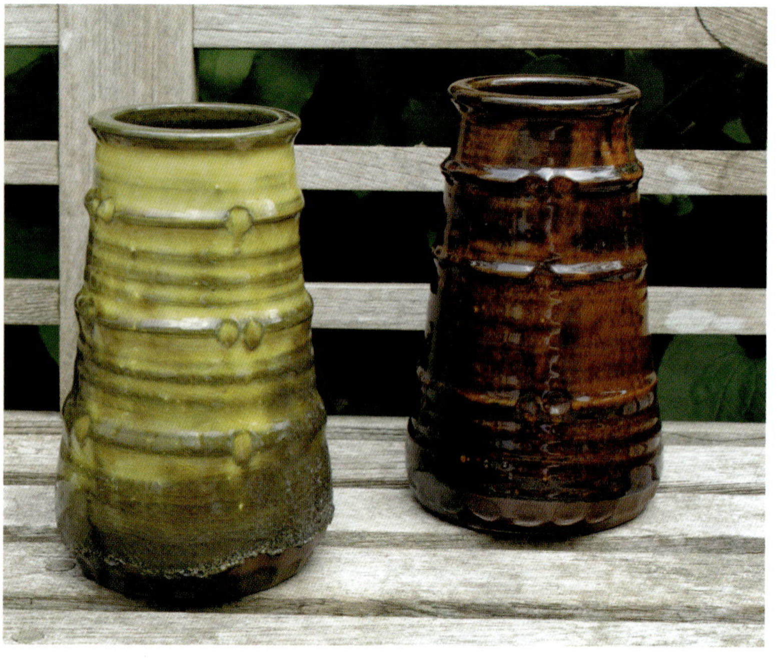

Both 21 x 12cm (max).

Other design trials

At around the same time, Leach threw, or asked Cardew to throw, experimental forms which were then finessed by Leach with detailing to foot, body and rim. That these were regarded primarily as trials despite their individuality is indicated by the absence of a personal seal. The detailing seen on these two examples appears to have been inspired by English medieval wares, with ribbing mimicking the banding on coopered barrels, and thumbing to the base that is typical of a variety of different early jugs. The opinion of David Leach was sought some years ago, who did not claim them as his own but felt that they were very early. A photograph of Leach at work in 1932 on page 31 of *The Art of Bernard Leach* by Carol Hogben shows a finished jug very much in the same idiom. Similar stylistic traits of banding and notching were still in use by both Leach and Hamada in the 1960s, probably achieved using tools similar to those illustrated alongside, from a line engraving in *A potter's book.*

Early Cardew individual wares

It was probably in late 1924 once the new Matsu climbing kiln had settled down, that Cardew began making pieces to his own design, and two are illustrated here. The first is a simple flat-rimmed bowl in the V&A collection, bearing just an incised Fleur de Lys. The other from a private collection is

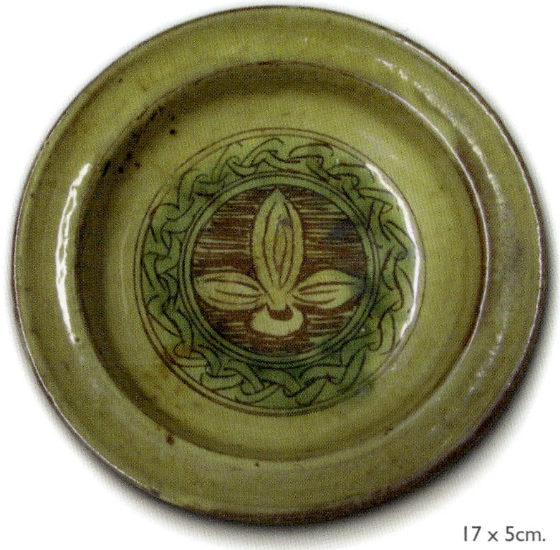

17 x 5cm.

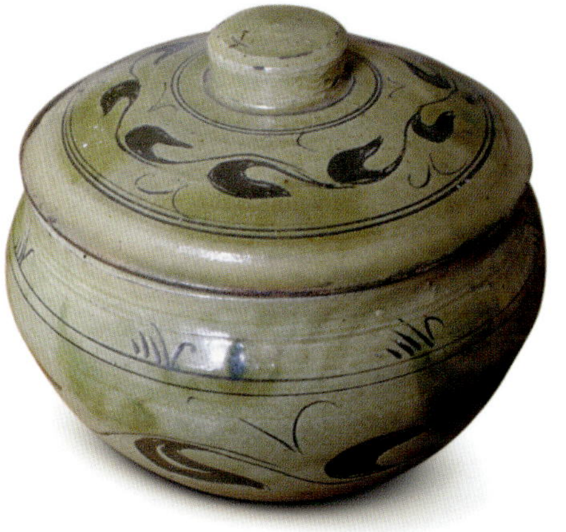

12 x 12cm.

a more ambitious lidded jar with a running decoration incised through a white background slip. Both bear his personal seal (his first personal mark) achieved through the application of his signet ring to the newly thrown pot, which due to its shallow engraving did not always make a clear impression. The round workshop seal is also used.

Wheel Head Chargers

At about this time, the production of large chargers recommenced in earnest, initially fired using the coolest chamber of the rebuilt climbing kiln and later in the new round up-draught slipware and raku kiln completed by Matsu in 1925 (see page 38-39) prior to his departure in 1926. The direction in which the decoration has run and residual marks to the body indicate that these chargers were fired upside down, propped up by kiln stilts to allow the glaze to mature, and residual white spur marks are usually seen. The first designs hark back to Leach's earliest inspirations, with trellis borders of criss-cross slip trailing either in a single or two contrasting colours.

The hare motif: this design features in some of Leach's earliest figurative decoration dating from 1917. It is unusual in that the body colour is reddish, suggesting a mix using a portion of the normal throwing clays employed in standing forms. All the other chargers in the date range 1923-1929 show a creamy-white body with an addition of stiffening grog. The method of marking is also atypical, a simple BL to the underside in a trailed slip colour also used in the border decoration. The hare design is in a dark stained slip painted directly on to the body, with sgraffito detailing, and the same slip is used in the finely trailed trellis border carefully alternated with a contrasting colour. The otherwise clear glaze shows a slight tint reflecting the iron content of the body, some of which was evidently used in the mix.

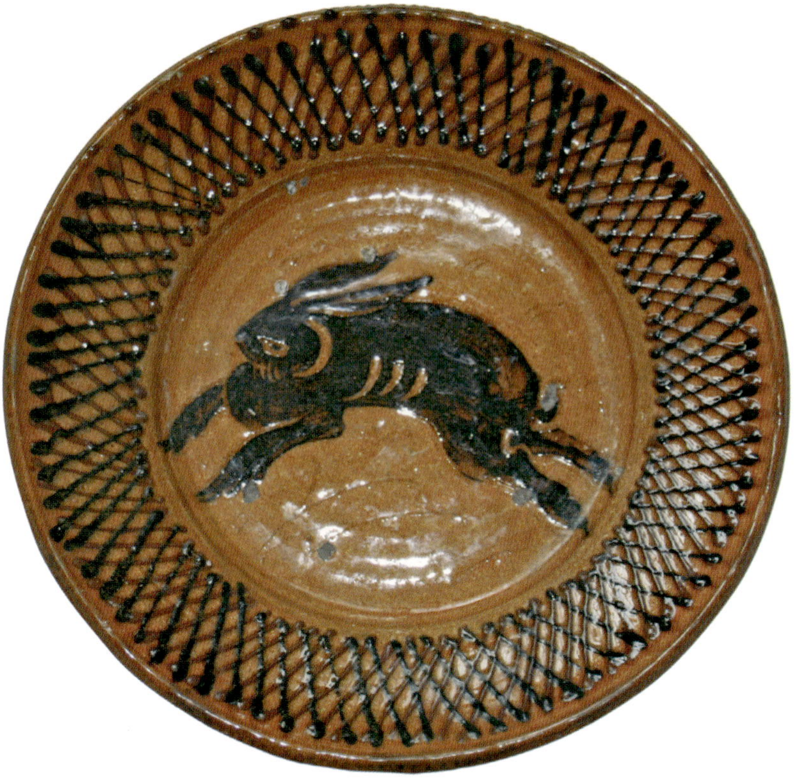

Diameter 44cm.

Diameter 42cm.

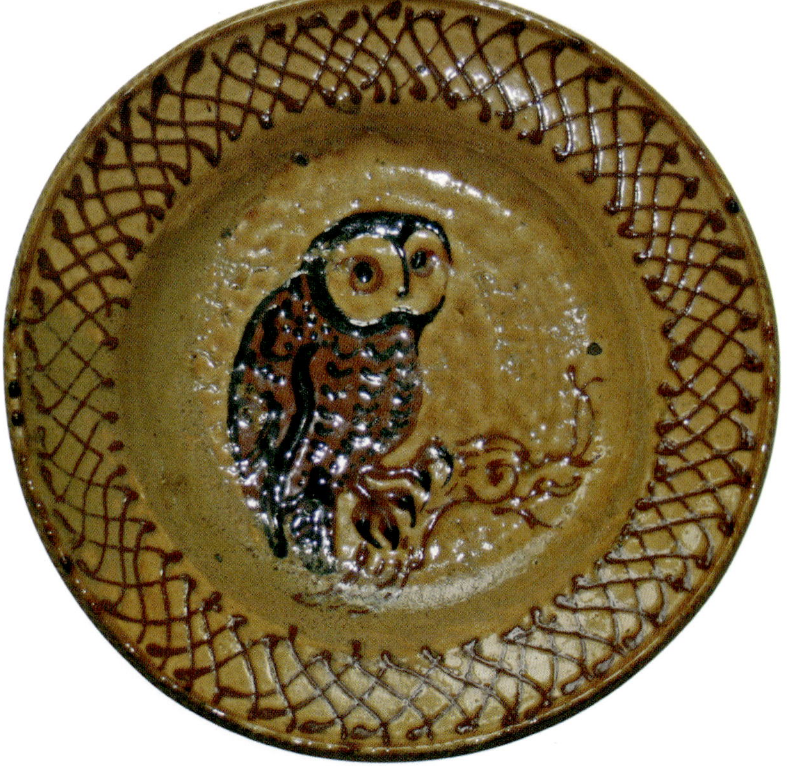

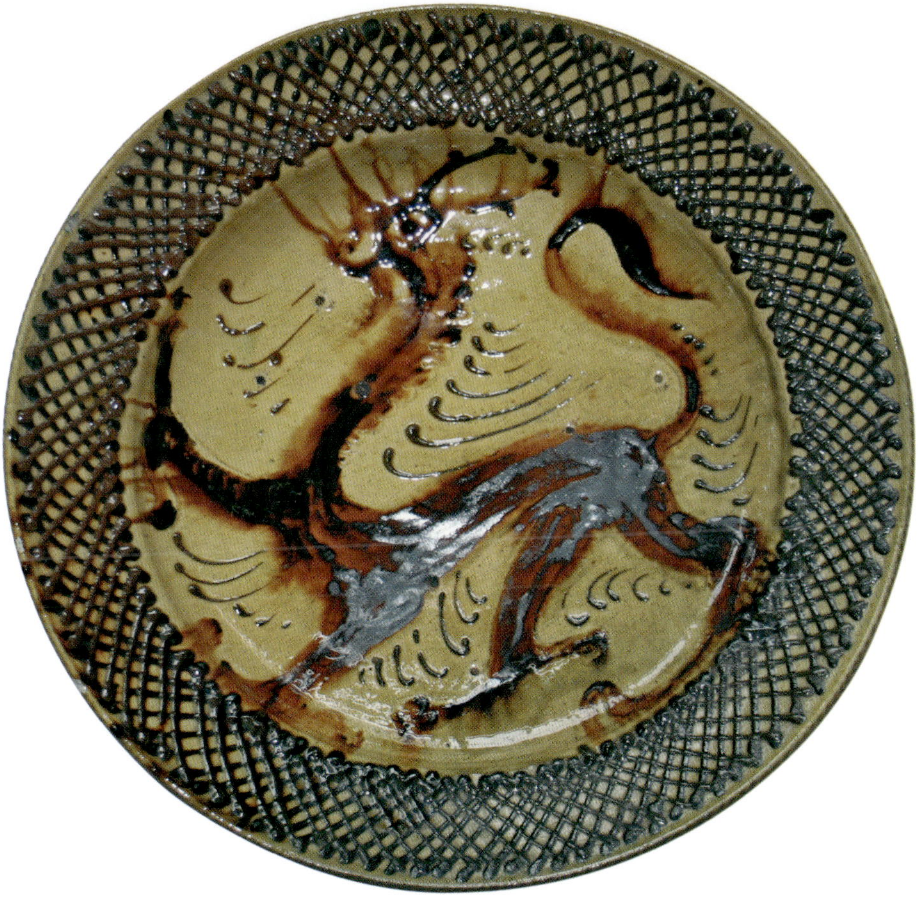

Diameter 48.5cm.

Heraldic griffon: this design which recalls medieval heraldry appears to have been inspired by a Toft school original by Ralph Simpson illustrated in *Quaint Old English Pottery* by Charles J Lomax (plate XI), the source of inspiration for Leach on more than one occasion (see page 59). The decoration uses a rich iron brushwork which has subsequently bled under its lead-rich glaze, together with stained dark slip trailing and bicolour trellis border. It bears the initials BL and date 1925 in trailed and painted slip.

Owl: this simpler design is seen on other media of the mid-1920s, including low-fired tiles (see page 93). Decoration is again direct to the body using painted and trailed slips, with a trellis border in freer style using one of the slips from the main decoration. Dating is difficult in that the trailed BL mark and date has been partially removed, but the style suggests 1926-1929.

Heraldic birds: This little-known charger from 1926 was donated at the time to the Walker Art Gallery, Liverpool by the Contemporary Arts Society.

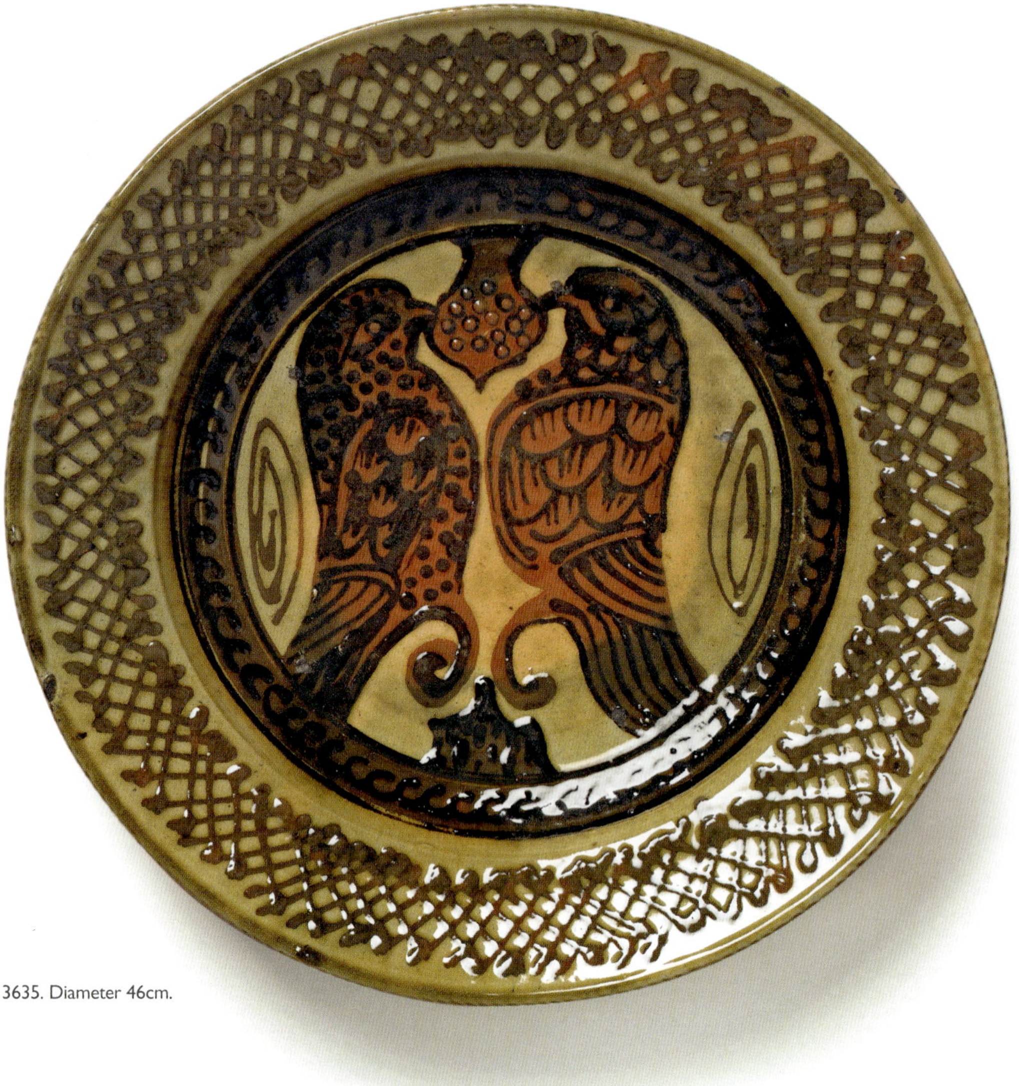

WAG 3635. Diameter 46cm.

It is primarily slip trailed and unusual as a late example in Leach's output employing a Toft-style trellis work border, but showing the development of a more individual style. Notably, Leach has employed as a background motif the horse-eye decoration from Seto peasant dishes. The turned foot rim of this platter bears the date and the BL monogram in the same slip-trailed and brushed colours used in the main decoration.

The Mermaid of Zennor and other chargers: many of these extremely decorative platters were sold to Japanese buyers, and are now in Japanese museums; they are illustrated in some of the excellent Japanese exhibition catalogues of the 1980s and 1990s listed in the bibliography.

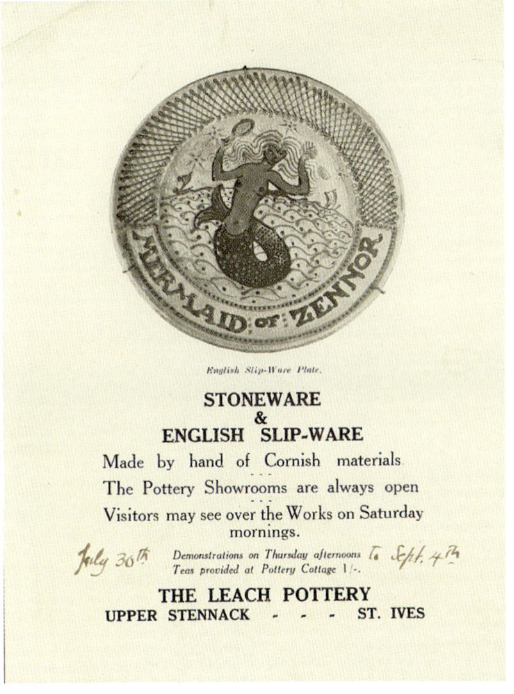

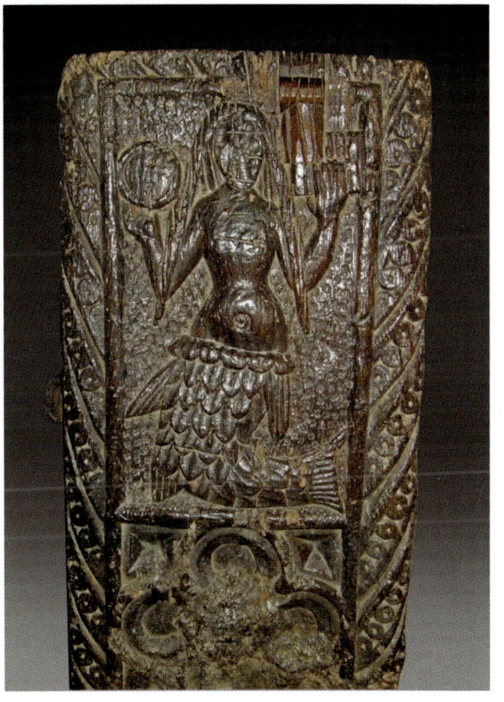

The Mermaid platter (Ohara Museum of Art, Kurashiki) is probably the most famous and was used on publicity material by Leach (see illustration): legend has it that it was inspired by an early pew-end at Zennor church (see photograph) just along the coast from St Ives, but the close similarity to plate VII of *Quaint Old English Pottery* (op cit) implies a different origin. Made in 1925, it may post-date the early Cardew Mermaid and Sea Horse jug in the Noall gift at the Royal Cornwall Museum, Truro (see page 77).

Brush and slip decorated platters

On a smaller scale, these flatter wares seem to have been freely thrown on the wheel by Cardew, prior to the trimming and finishing of their bases and decoration and signing by Leach, when leather hard. We include them at this juncture because of their similarity to the larger and deeper chargers just described from which they appear to be a development, probably dating from 1925-1926. Both off-white and red bodies were used as throwing clays.

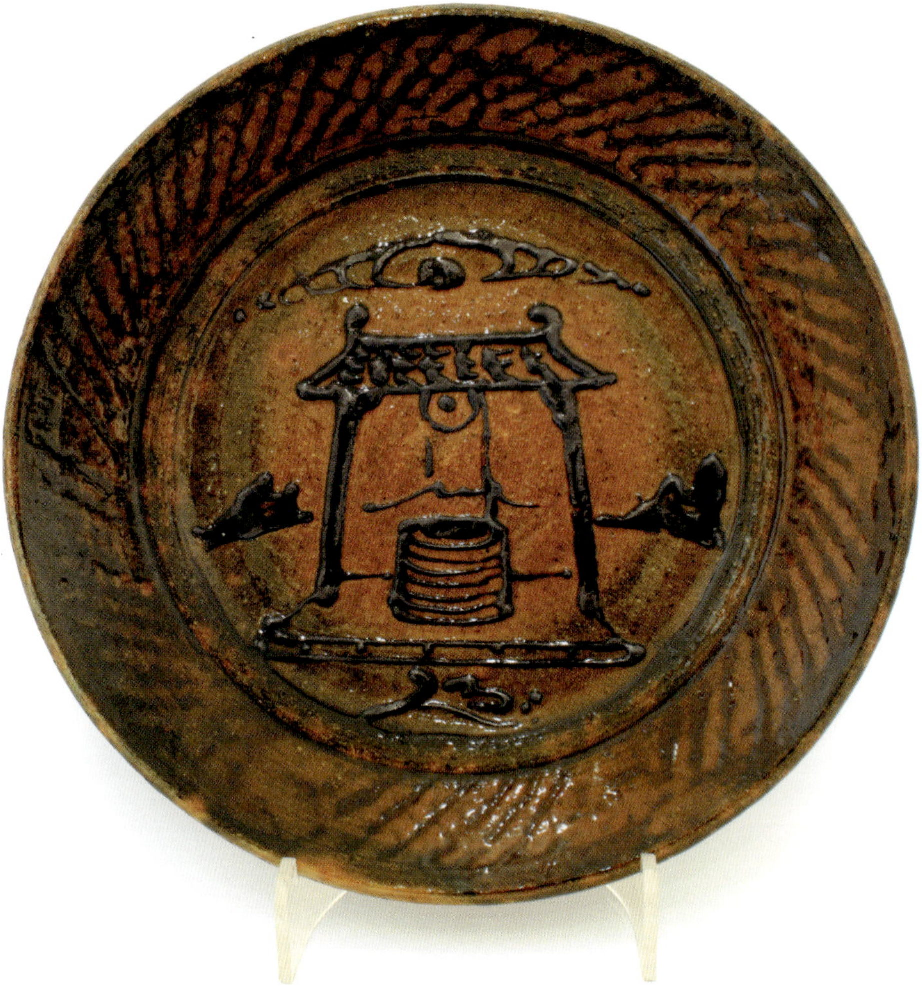

33 x 5.5cm.

Well-head in slip trailing: This well-known platter from the Wingfield Digby collection shows both traditional and symbolic eastern influences. Decorated more simply than its larger predecessors, the iron-rich brown slip used for the main design and trellis border harmonises well with the buff-red body. The elaborate roof over the well and the curved finials to each corner are oriental in style, as are the topographic features, possibly distant hills, on either side and a setting sun seen through clouds above. This landscape recalls Leach's earlier woodcut design for the Shirakaba magazine (see page 15), and anticipates two major chargers from 1929. The platter bears his slip-trailed monogram to the front and foot rim.

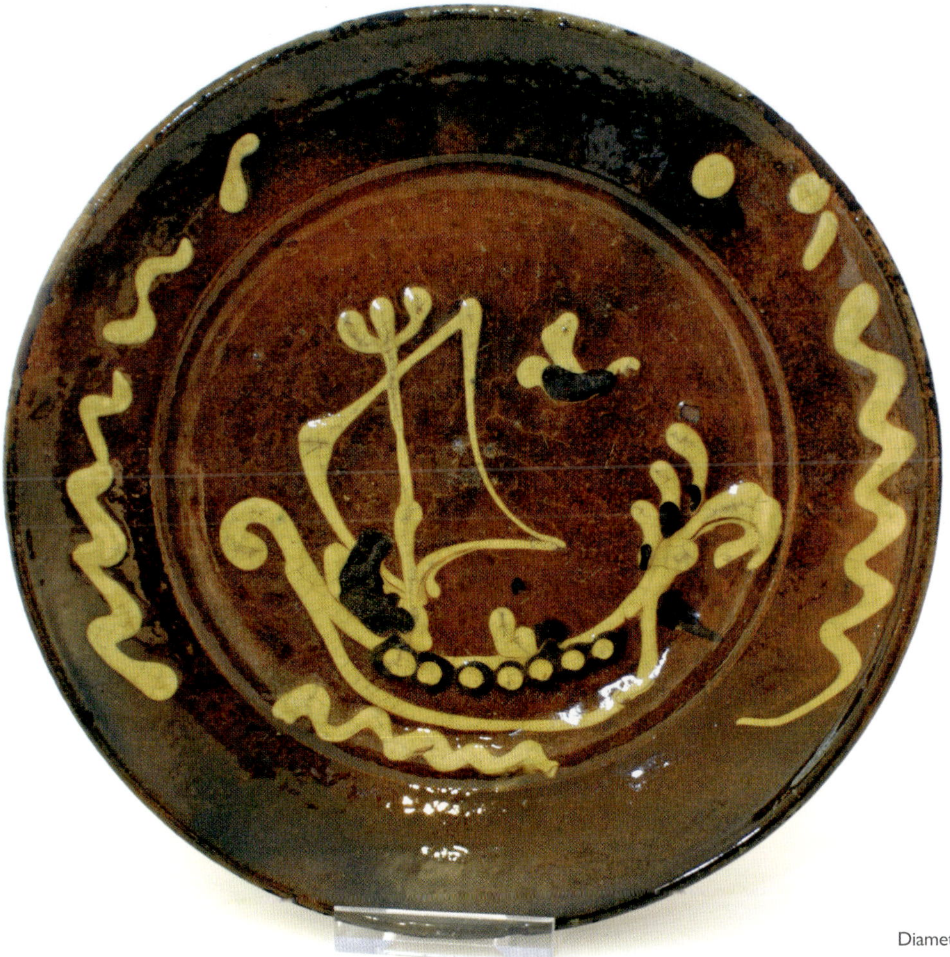

Diameter 23cm.

Galley: This example from a private collection is achieved very simply but is all the better for that. In a change from the last example, Leach has used a white slip to contrast strongly with the red body colour, applying the decoration direct to the thrown surface. The same white slip is used to apply his monogram to the underside. The choice of such a maritime motif has something of the earlier raku dish decorated by Nance in 1922 (see page 55), and Nance's standard work *Sailing ship models* (1924) may have been an indirect inspiration. A brushwork galley was also a favoured Leach design on a new range of stoneware tiles introduced from around 1926.

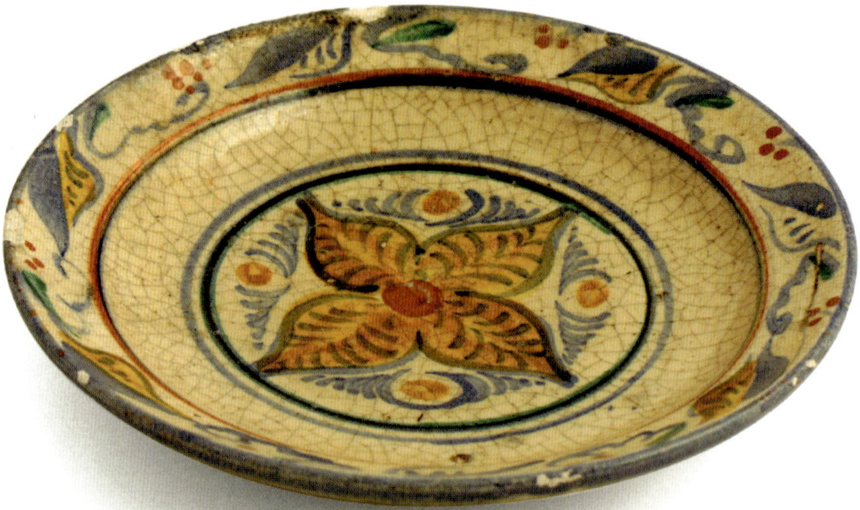

22 x 4cm.

Delft style: This freshly coloured plate, the first of two raku-style examples, is from the collection of UW Aberystwyth. It is dated 1925 and monogrammed to the underside. Leach cleverly employed cream-coloured body clay to achieve the look of delft, which classically has an opaque white glaze over a red body, and painted the delft-inspired design with a brush direct on to the thrown pot.

Brushwork Well-head: This further raku-style pot again uses brushwork applied directly to the body. The basic design in blue (cobalt) is highlighted by contrasting oxide colours, with iron-rich St Erth clay probably used as a red slip in a couple of places. Blue brushwork is also employed for the BL monogram to the centre of the turned foot rim. It has been suggested by some that this design is a reference to the holy wells seen in and around Cornwall. These springs, venerated since pre-Christian times, are, however, very plain, sometimes marked at most by a simple Celtic wayside cross. The inspiration for this design is in line with the earlier example from the Wingfield Digby collection.

Diameter 21cm.

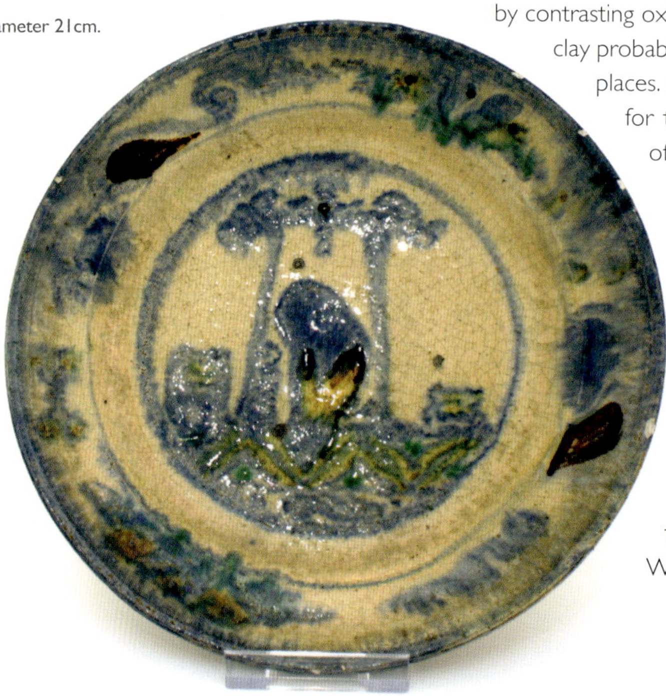

Cornwall and the West Country again

These highly decorative platters and chargers were at the top end of production in the mid-1920s. As an adjunct to the tourist and commissioned wares described on pages 64-65, Cardew started to throw larger forms by early 1925, sometimes as presentation pieces to friends and on other occasions as trial pieces to develop his skills. These were increasingly decorated by him rather than by Leach alone.

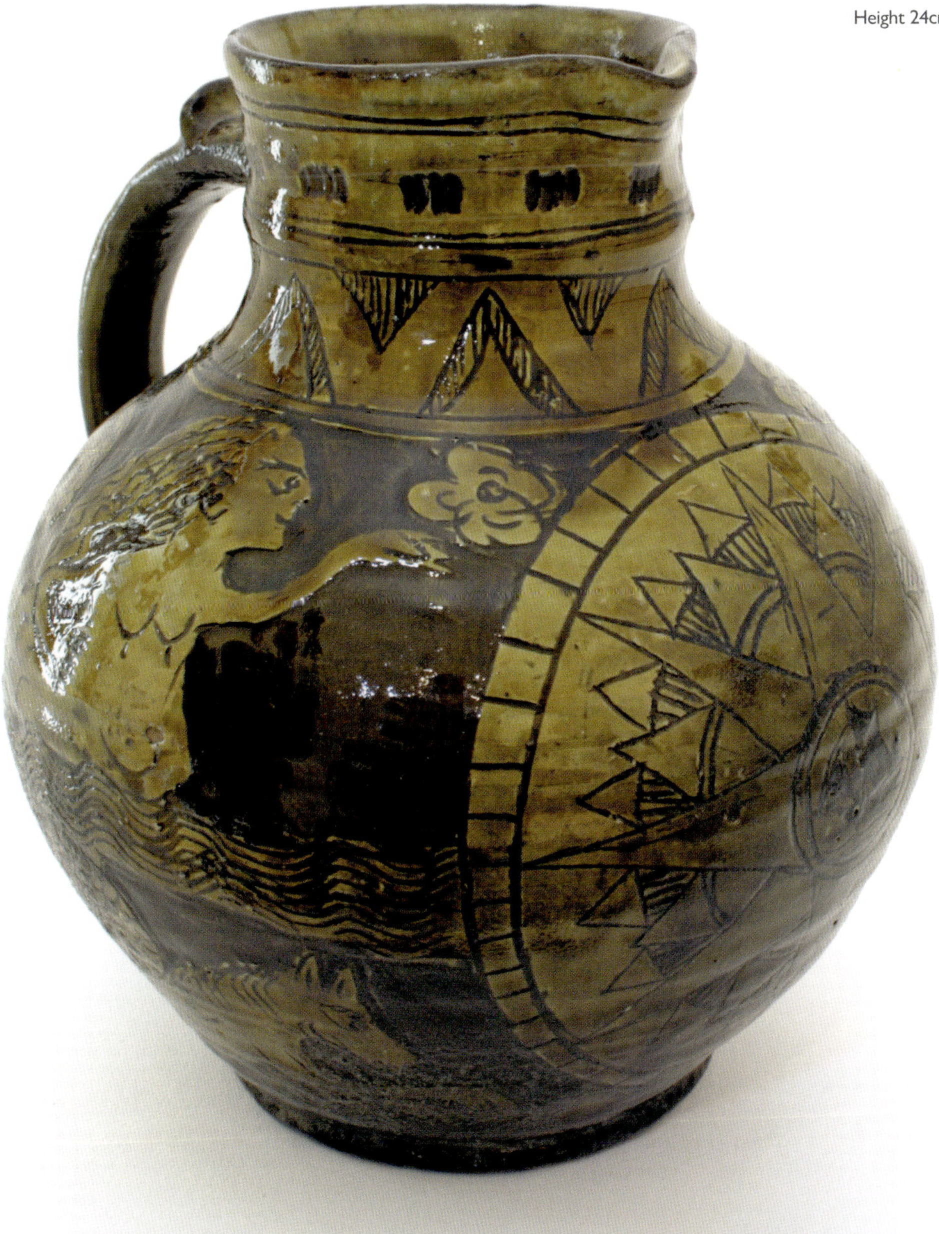

Height 24cm, width 20cm.

The Mermaid and seahorse jug: This superb pot from the Noall gift at the Royal Cornwall Museum, Truro (RCM) is referred to in the North Devon tradition as a 'Ships Jug' and is a faithful copy of an 18th-century example in the collection of the Royal Albert Memorial Museum, Exeter which Cardew clearly saw and admired. It was an ambitious piece for him to attempt at this early stage, both in terms of size and the elaborate sgraffito decoration. The original is glazed conventionally and pale straw in colouration whereas the unusual selection of green (copper) may have been a reflection of Cardew's 1924 visit to Saunton with Leach, where they would have seen EB Fishley pieces glazed in his famous copper oxide finish. It bears an SI and Cardew's signet ring seal, and is also incised MAC near the handle, following the North Devon style.

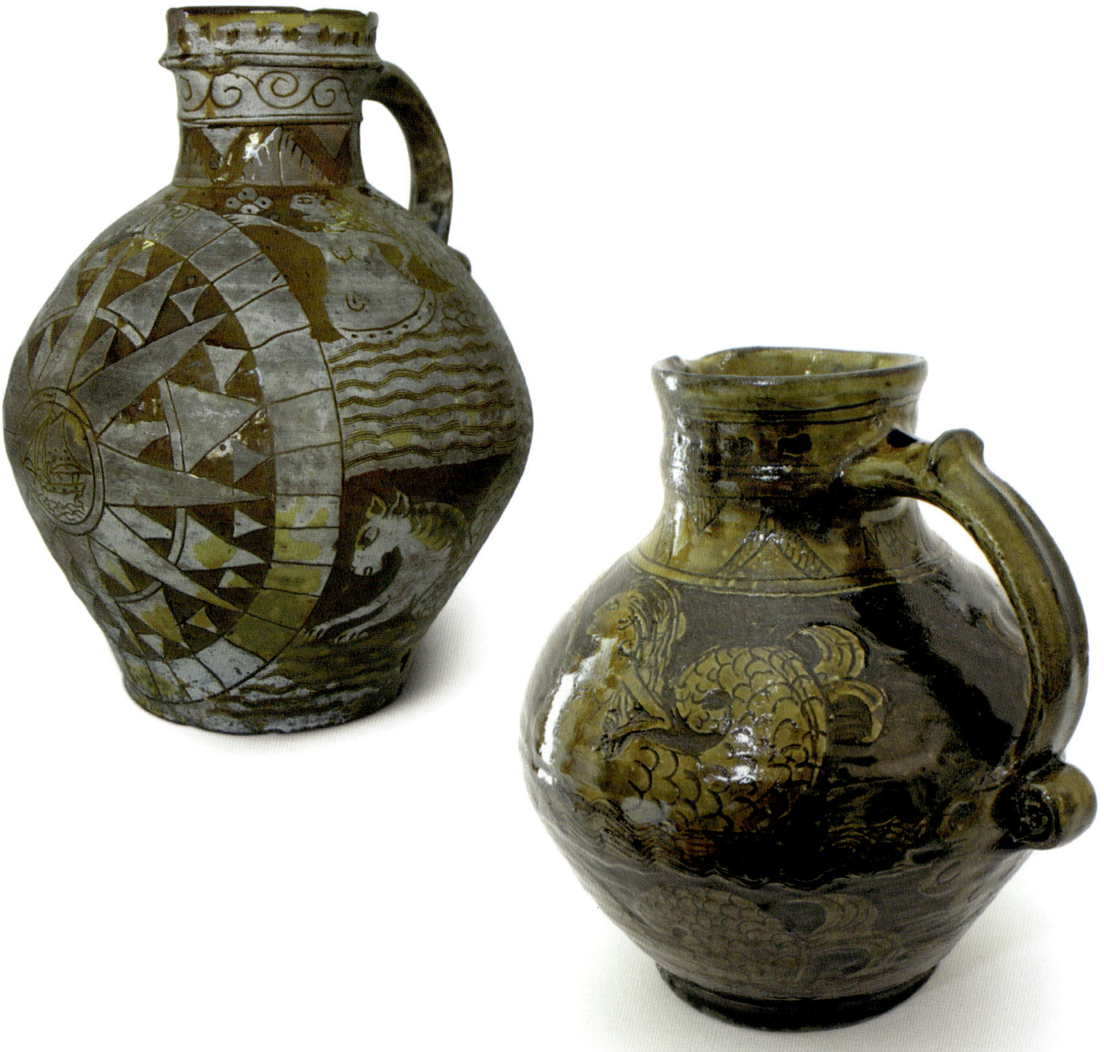

Cornish jugs for Robert Morton Nance: Subsequently, Cardew made this large jug decorated in sgraffito with a verse in English and Cornish and a curious motif of two intertwined snakes. Its dark colour may reflect the preference of Leach to add iron oxide to the glaze mix, and in line with many Leach Pottery standing forms of this period, the base has been over-fired. This effect is seen on pots thought to have been fired in an upper chamber of the 1924 climbing kiln, before the round slipware kiln of 1925

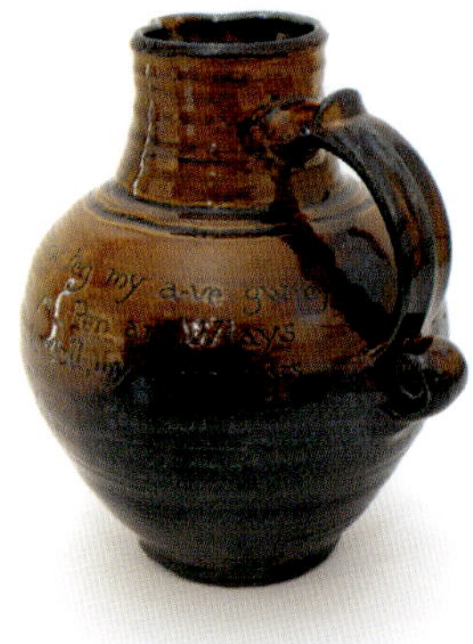

Height 24.5cm, width 19.5cm.

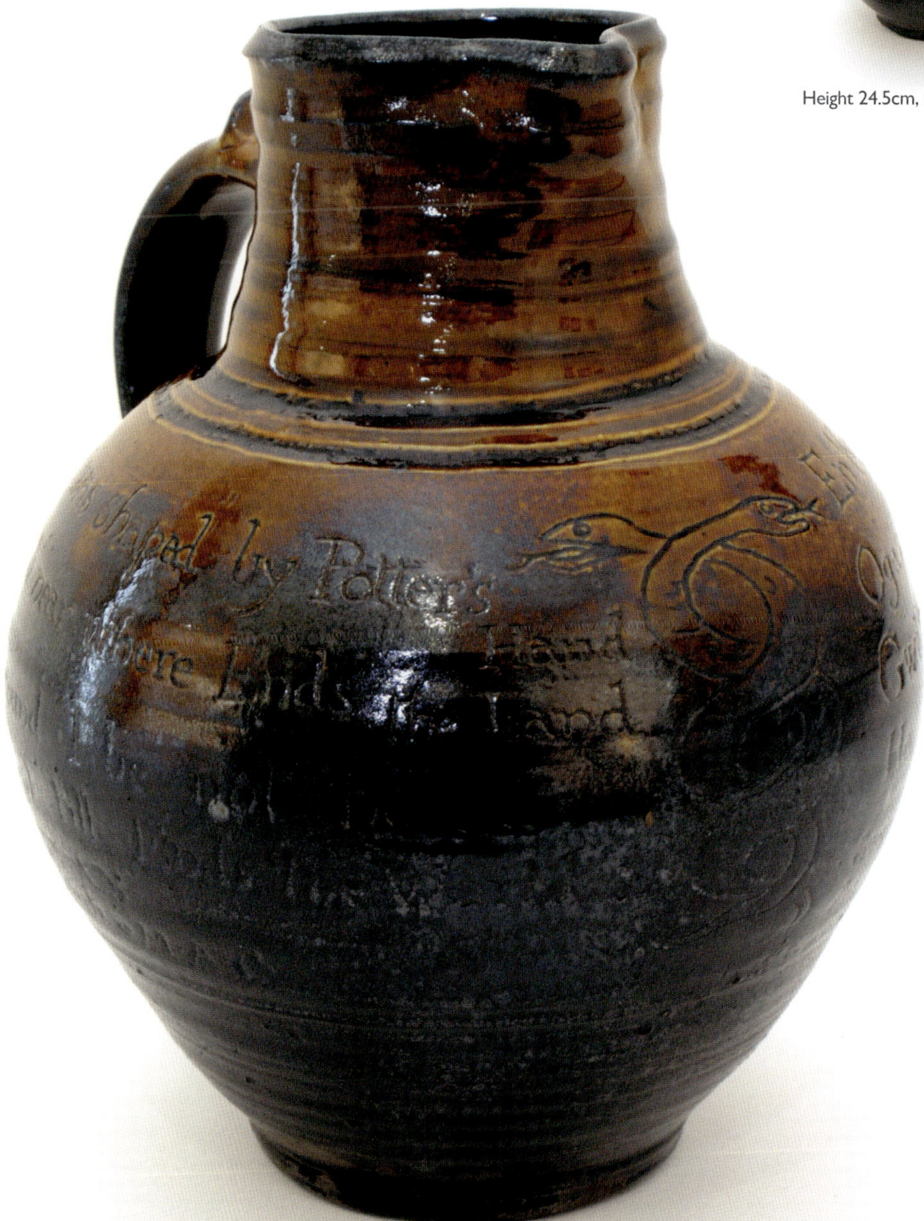

was completed, and may be because secondary stoking was used in the base of these upper chambers, immediately below the kiln shelving, to raise heat levels sufficiently to finish the glazes. It bears Cardew's early personal seal and the standard SI emblem. In strong contrast aesthetically is this example from 1925, probably fired in the new kiln; it relies on iron-rich clay in the glaze to colour the final finish. This bulbous tankard is incised in Cornish, bears a dedication 'rag (to) R.M.N.', and bears the same seals as the previous Nance piece. Cardew made a further tankard incised in Cornish for his friend in the early days at Winchcombe (see page 23).

Height 16cm, width 14cm.

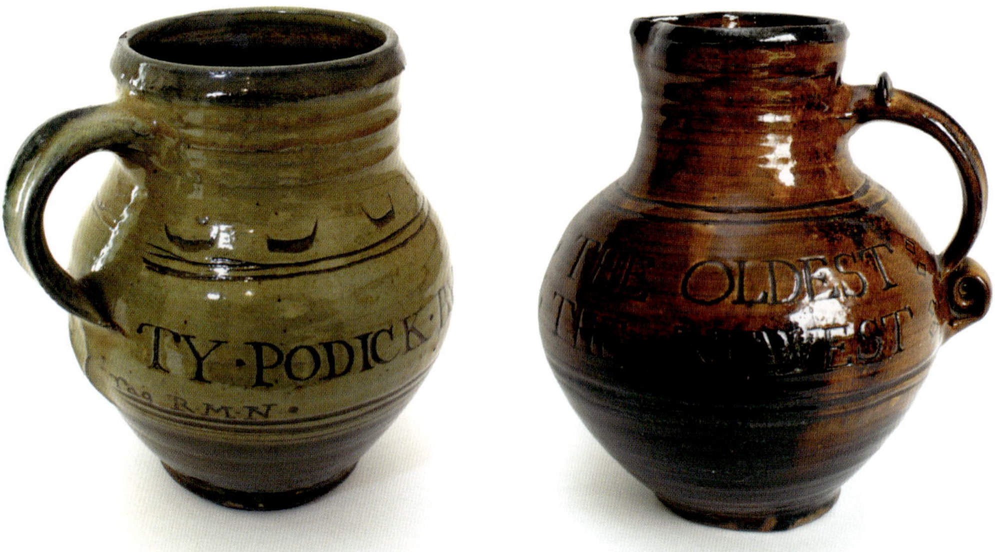

A musical interlude: Cardew was a keen clarinettist and he played with the Penzance Orchestral Society on several occasions in the 1920s. I am indebted to Margaret Williams for her research into the Society, and her entertaining book *The food of love* (2007) which records an important collaboration between the Society and Cardew in 1929 that we will return to later. Cardew became friendly with Walter Barnes, the founder and conductor of the Society orchestra, and made this scroll-handled jug for him as a presentation, probably in 1925. The inscription 'The best wine is the oldest...The best water is the newest' is believed to be a reference to a piece by Mozart. The jug bears his formal MC and the workshop seals.

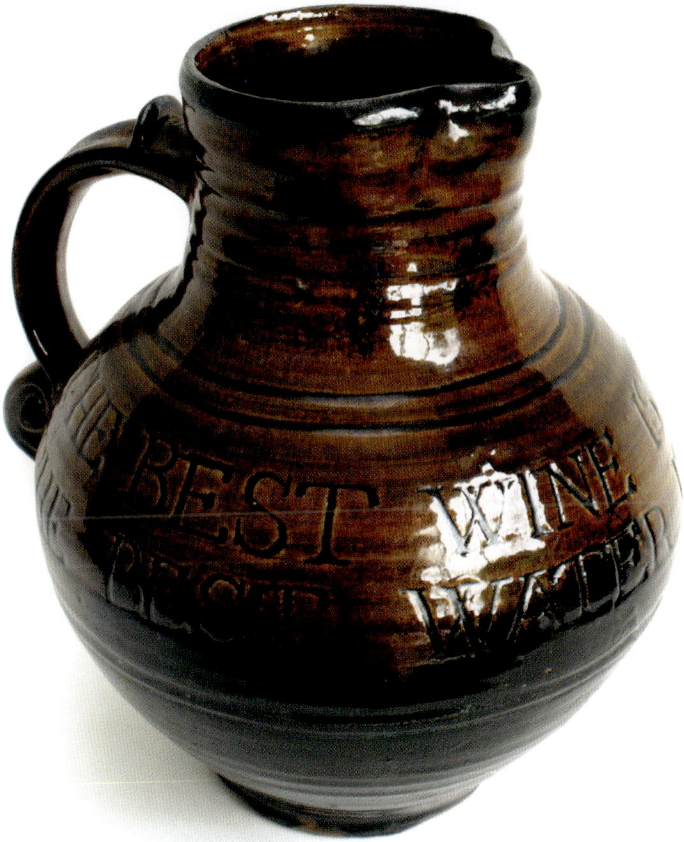

Height 22cm, width 18cm.

Later sgraffito wares: The establishment of a new kiln, while not without problems, improved the overall finish and output of standing forms in 1925-1926. Slight under-firing seemed to have become an issue (see Technical notes on pages 39-40), although this unusual pair of tankards from a private collection, dated 1925 and bearing the initials BL to the side and the workshop seal, came out well.

Largest 11 x 9cm.

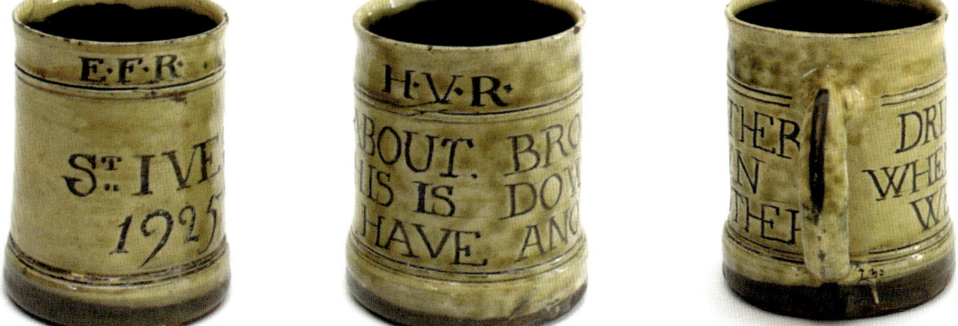

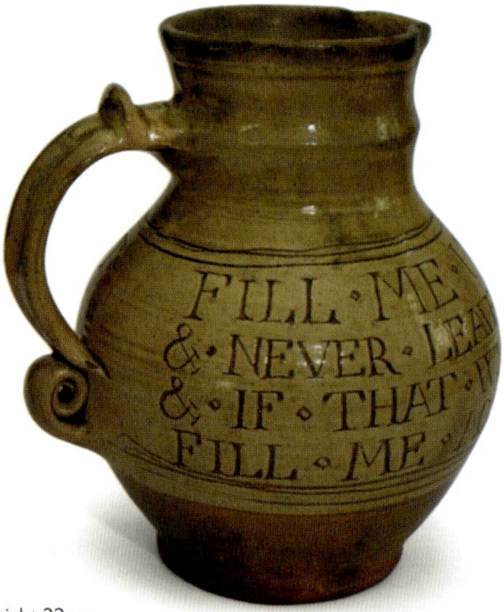

Height 22cm.

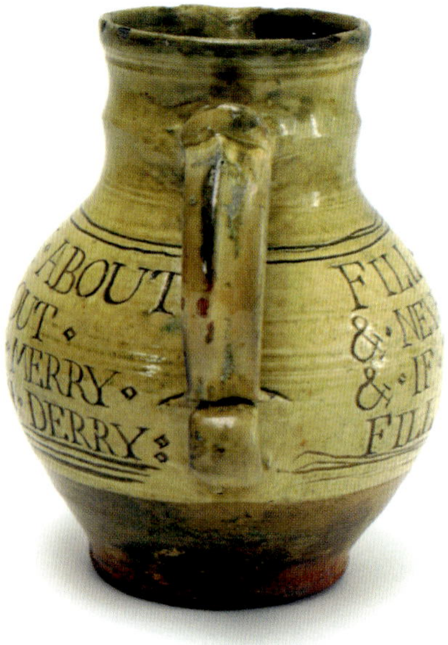

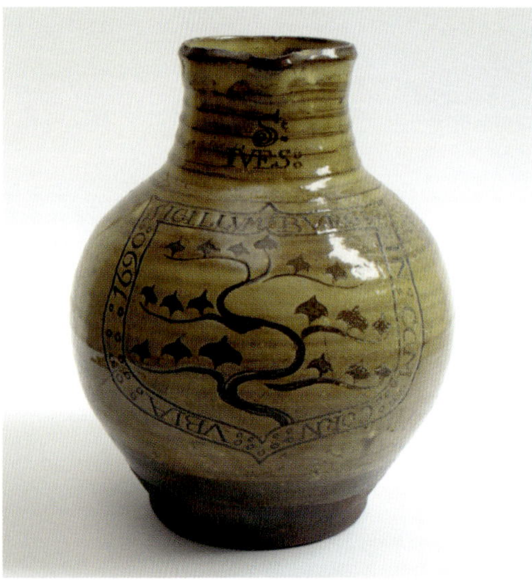

Larger jugs with scroll handles increasingly in the North Devon idiom were produced, and these two examples are fairly typical although plainer examples are sometimes seen. The first bears a rhyme in Gill-style seriffed capitals 'Fill me up & drink about & never leave till all is out...& if that will not make you merry fill me again and sing down derry'. The last example in this group is a large harvest jug bearing the ancient shield of the town of St Ives. Both of these are from private collections and bear Cardew's personal and the workshop seals, with the latter also incised with Leach's monogram and the date 1926 reflecting his role as decorator.

Cardew's ghost

Cardew departed later that year to set up his own workshop at the old Greet Pottery near Winchcombe in Gloucestershire, but kept in regular touch with Leach, collaborating with him on exhibitions in London at the New Handworkers' Gallery in the early 1930s. There was also a significant reunion in 1929 with shared demonstrations which affected subsequent output at both their workshops, and also glaze trials using a Japanese raku finish. Before his departure, Cardew also appears to have thrown a number of chargers, probably then biscuit fired for later decoration.

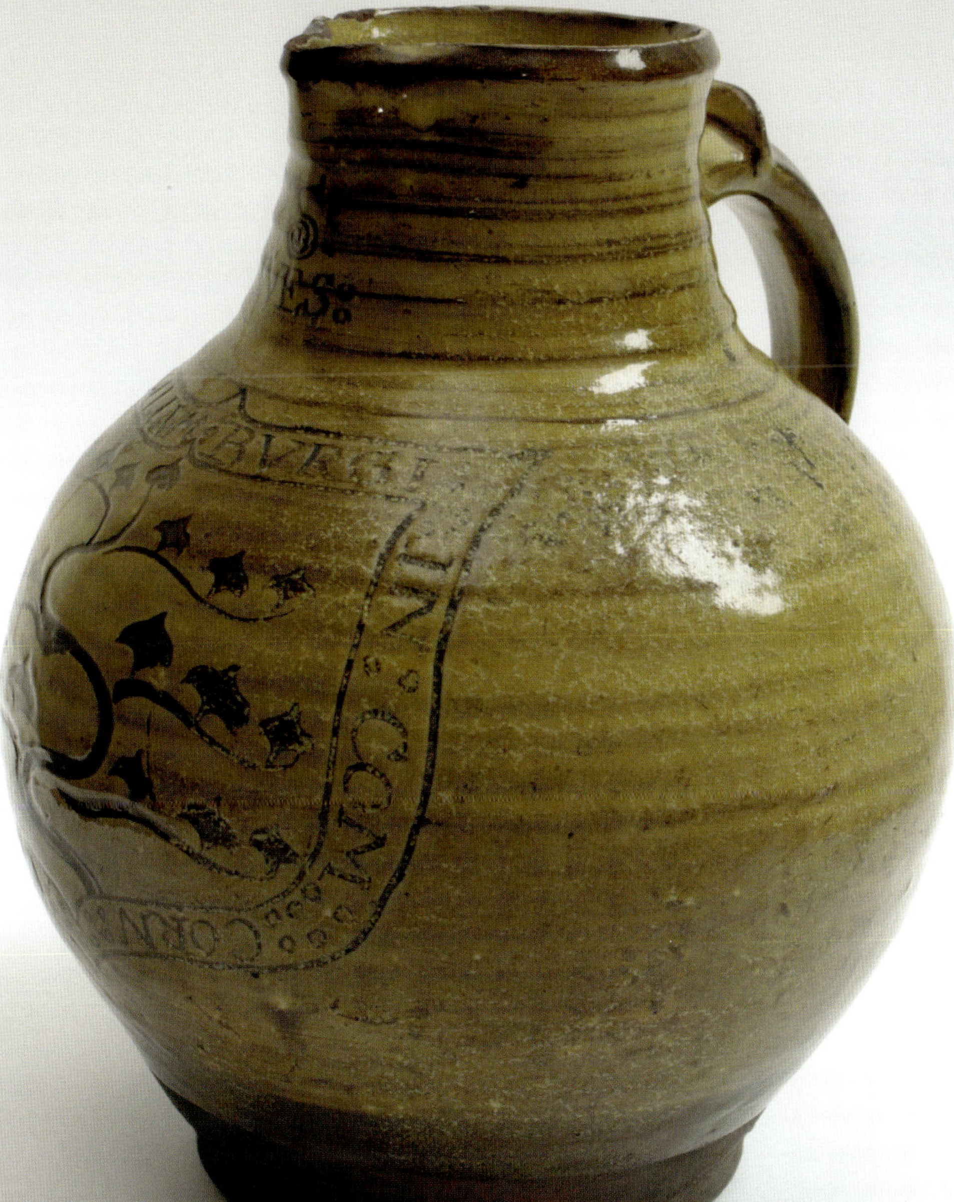

Height 27cm, width 20cm (maximum).

Late brushwork and other chargers

There is a small but distinctive group of chargers of similar size to the earlier Toft-inspired examples, but with iron brushwork rather than trailed slip as the predominant method of decoration. Some mild kiln warping is seen on examples from 1923-1926, a reflection of the problems potters face in firing all flat wares, magnified by the size of these chargers and their wide rims. The warping of these versions is generally more severe, and spur mark scars to the foot rim side of these pots imply that they were stacked in small groups, one on top of another. It may be that a shortage of fuel or the loss of the experience of Cardew led to a misjudgement on the part of Leach, leading him unwisely to abandon the previous practice of firing these singly on the kiln shelves (see technical section page 39 for detailed coverage of kiln issues).

37 x 7cm.

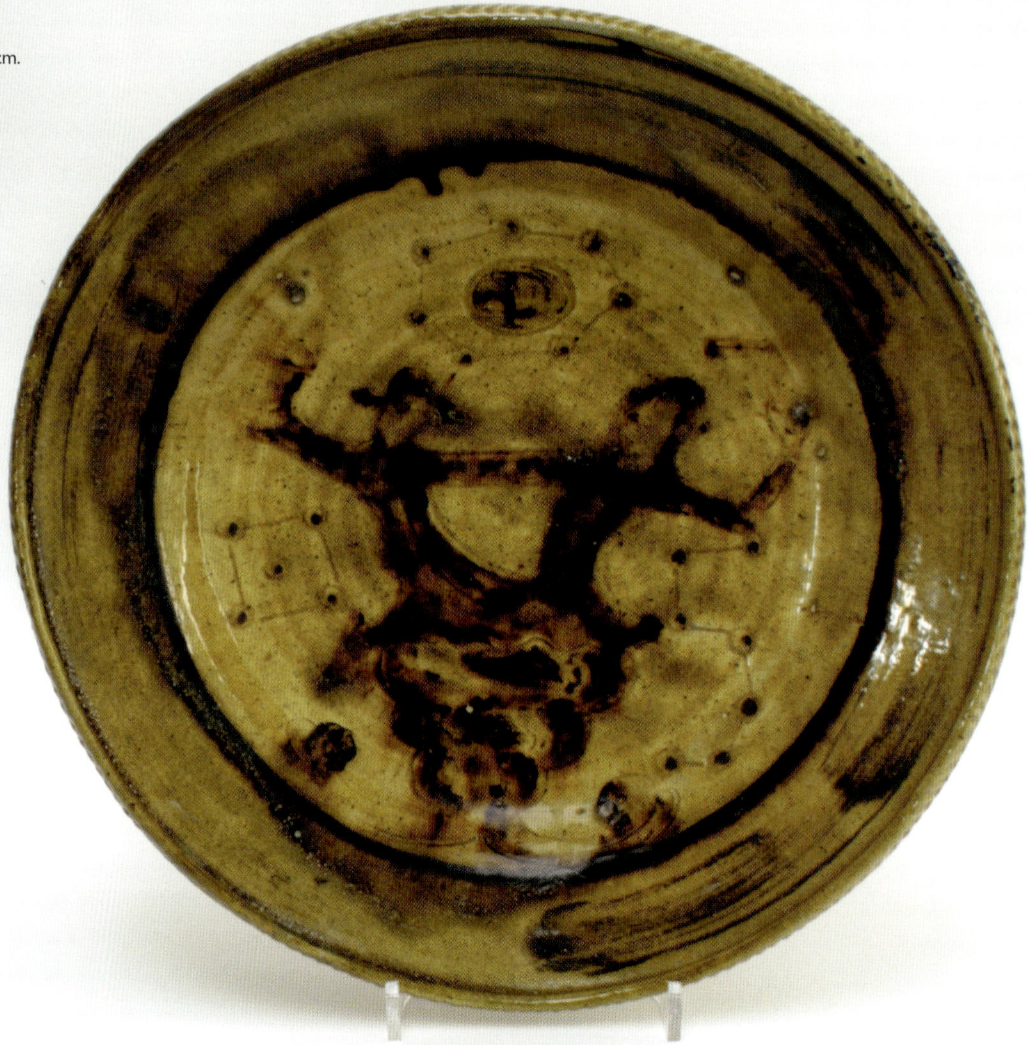

Gemini (the Twins): This curious design in brushwork from a private collection is intriguing, depicting two figures linking arms, one with a bush hat similar to one worn by his son David in Scout uniform. The background has incised constellations, including the ubiquitous Plough, and also Gemini, hence the title I have given it. The oval symbol over their heads remains unidentified. There is a BL monogram in the foot rim and the date 1927, using a dark brown slip also employed for a circular border to the main design.

Shadow Puppet: This example from the Craft Study Centre, Farnham has had a hard life, and shows kiln warping and mild firing cracks. The central design appears to have been inspired by the shadow puppets of Bali. The background motifs are difficult to identify. It is undated but bears a BL monogram in slip trailing.

Diameter 52cm.

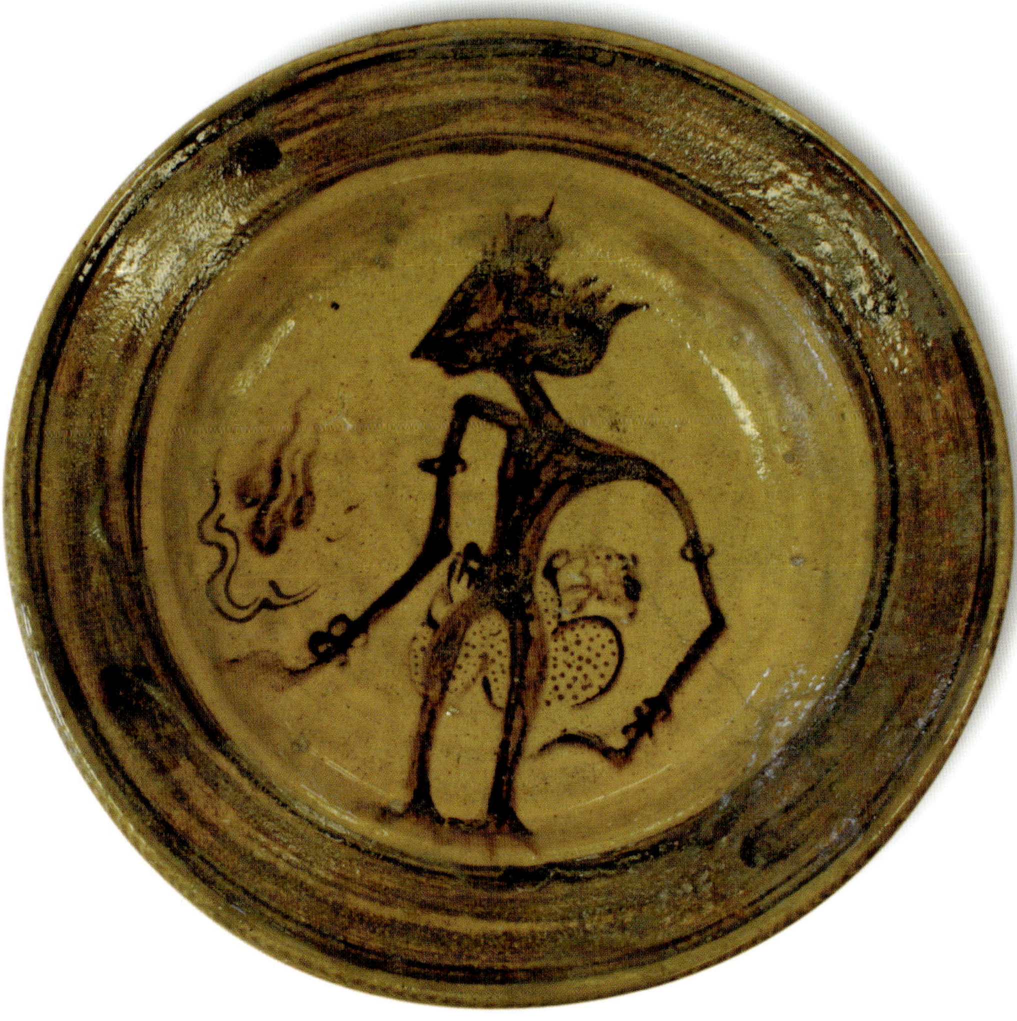

JAPAN AND THE RETURN OF HAMADA (1926-1930)

To Mashiko and Kyoto

Mention has been made earlier of Hamada's interest in and passion for hump-moulded English and Welsh dishes with freehand and abstract slip decoration. Indeed, much of the proceeds of his second very successful selling show at the William Paterson Gallery in autumn 1923 were spent by him acquiring such dishes and various textiles to take back with him to Japan. Kawai Kanjiro in Tokyo acted as a poste restante for his purchases during his travels in Europe before returning home, and in *Hamada Potter*, Hamada recounts the impression on his friend of seeing ten of these dishes made, which led Kawai to make his own hump and thrown versions in stoneware, very much in the same 'English' spirit.

The passion for the English tradition evident at the Leach Pottery in the first years had by 1926 moved primarily to Mashiko, Kyoto and Winchcombe. That it was rekindled to some extent from the late 1920s was arguably due to the continuing enthusiasm in the intervening period of Hamada, Kawai Kanjiro and Cardew, with the first two following a Midlands and Northern inspiration, and with Cardew at Winchcombe reviving the traditions of North Devon and the Fishley dynasty as we will now recount.

Kawai peasant style bowl with una-no-me decoration. 17 x 4.5cm.

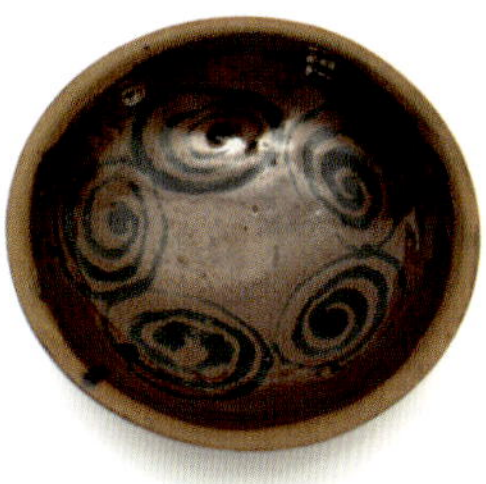

The efforts of Hamada and Kawai were strongly fostered by the collector the Rev Milner White, who purchased Hamada's peasant-style bowls from Paterson's, Old Bond Street in 1926 and 1929 and Kawai's from the Beaux Arts Gallery, New Bond Street in 1929. These stonewares were essentially hybrids, having the form of the Japanese peasant wares from Seto, but decorated using glaze and slip trailing in the decorative style of the earthenwares of Buckley, North Wales and the English Midlands. Both hump-moulded and free-thrown versions were made.

The peasant style wares of Hamada

In *Hamada Potter*, the latter writes: 'One can think of many ways of decorating a pot with one or two contrasting slips. The English 'medieval' (sic) slipware dishes are an outstanding example of slip trailing....My glazing and decorating experience is parallel to that of calligraphy...A good calligrapher is really writing properly when he is writing from the upper arm, nearest to the heart...No matter how the script is formed – sometimes he even makes mistakes – reading it produces a good feeling.' It is heartfelt spontaneity too that characterises the free nature of Hamada's decoration of the pieces illustrated, and he was to produce a similar set of peasant-style wares as late as the 1960s.

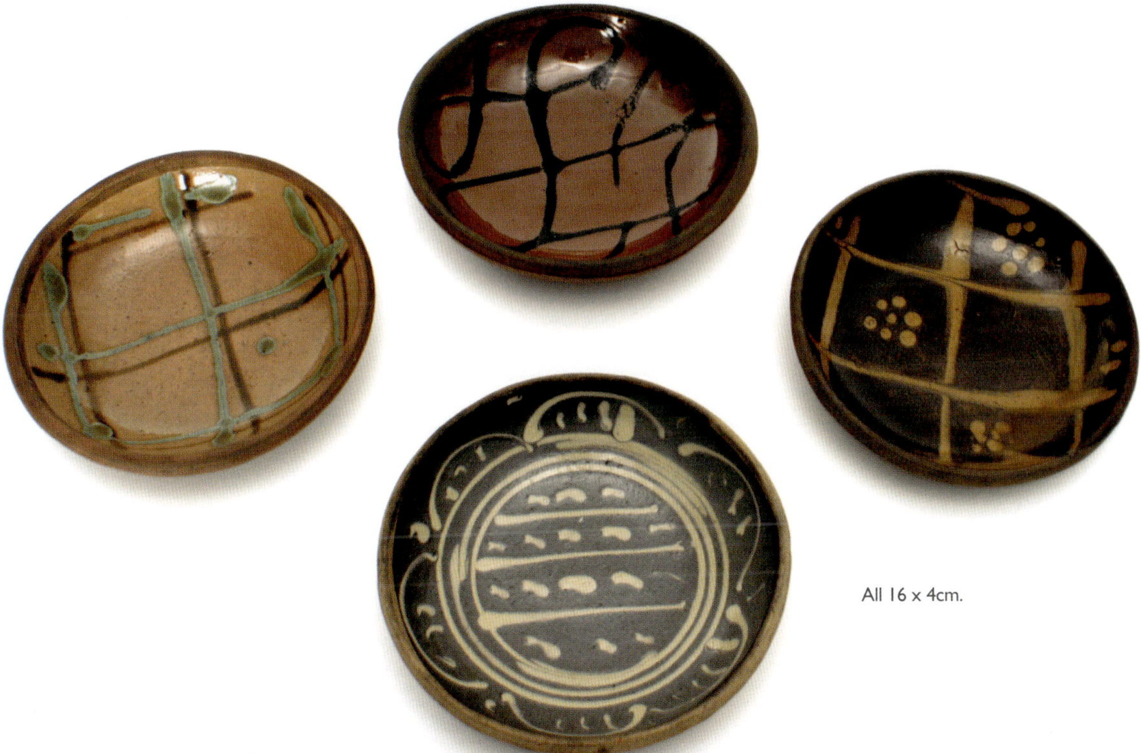

All 16 x 4cm.

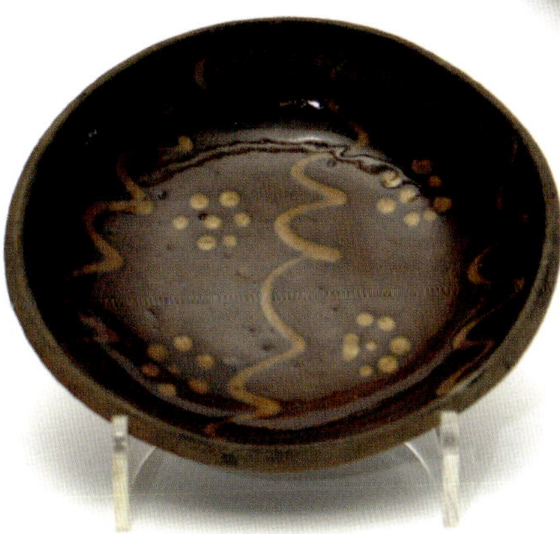

Diameter 16cm.

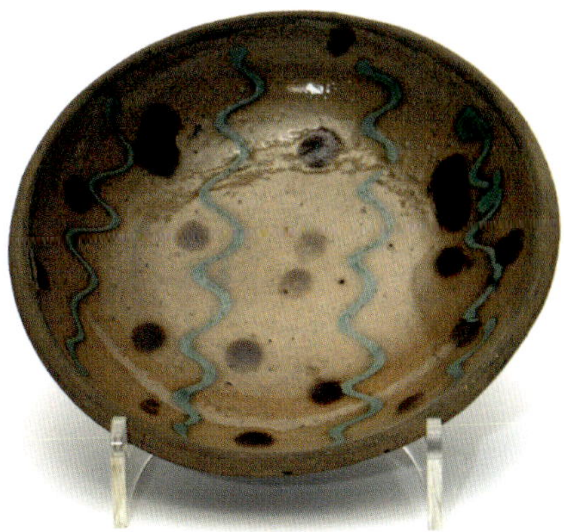

Diameter 16cm.

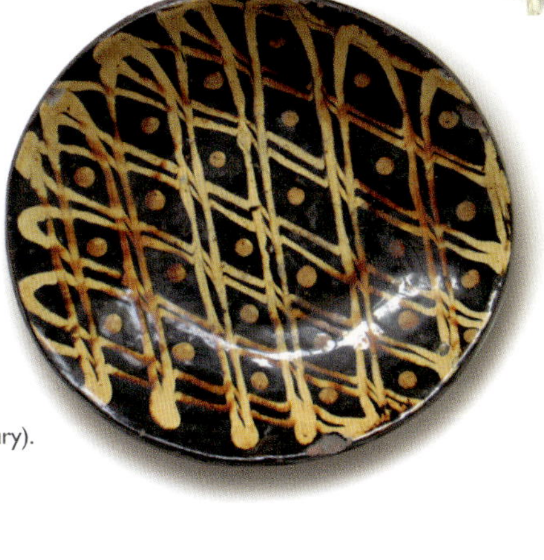

Buckley slip trailed dish (19th century).
Diameter 25cm.

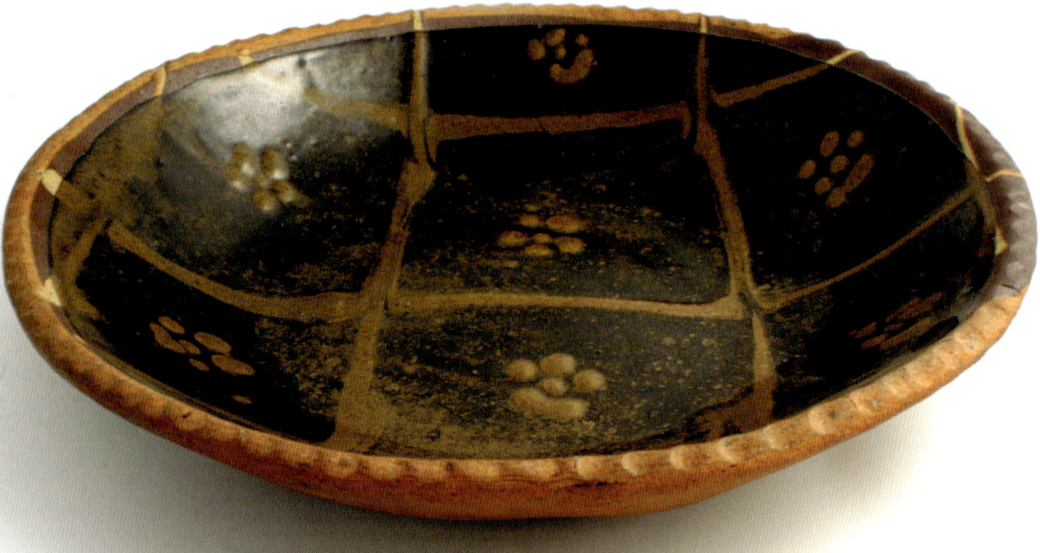

Diameter 35cm.

He was probably not aware of the true age of the wares that he admired and collected, namely 18th and 19th century rather than medieval, but they were nevertheless representative of a timeless tradition, handed down over the centuries. They are often referred to generically as 'Staffordshire' although some of those that Hamada most valued, judging from his own output, were from the Buckley area of North Wales and pre-dated Staffordshire. Examples from both traditions are shown, for the purposes of comparison.

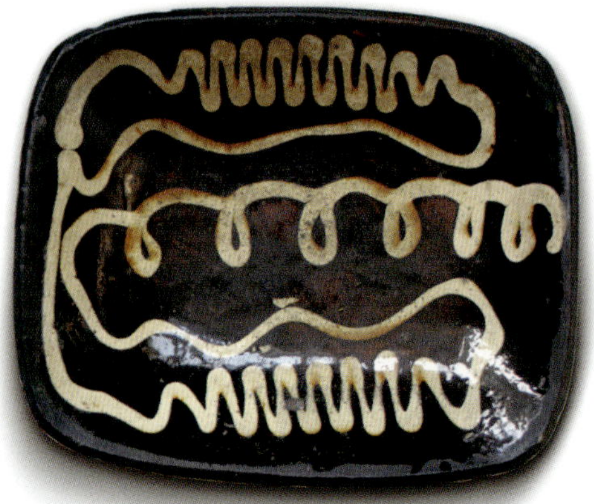

Length 36cm.

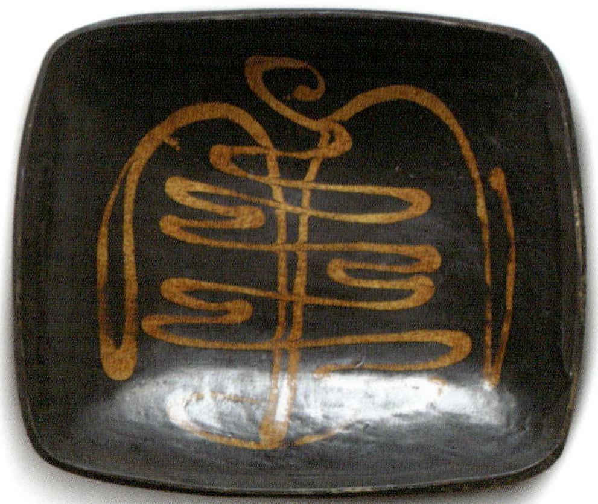

43 x 37 x 7.5cm.

The peasant style wares of Kawai

Kawai had tried his hand at such English and Welsh slipware designs in the mid-1920s although the Milner White examples illustrated here are somewhat later. There are subtle differences in style from Hamada, with the Kyoto wares having less freedom and spontaneity; they are not exactly contrived but have a strong sense of formal pattern and design closer to a Leachian aesthetic. The classic Midlands slipware design, the 'Boney Pie', believed to represent the remains of a carved chicken, appears to have been one of the inspirations (see illustration for the purposes of comparison).

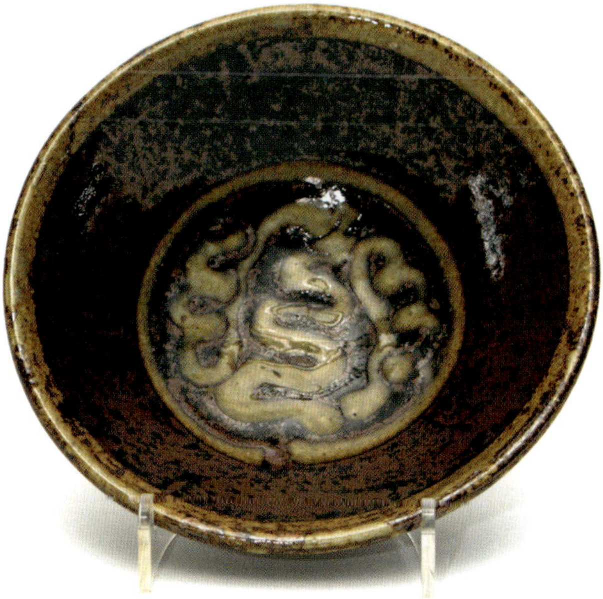

Diameter 20cm.

Inlaid and wax resist decorated red-ware dish by Kawai.

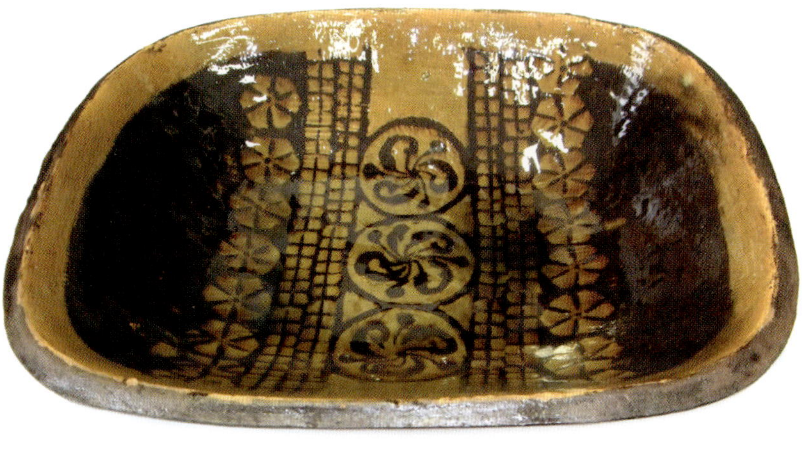

19 x 6cm.

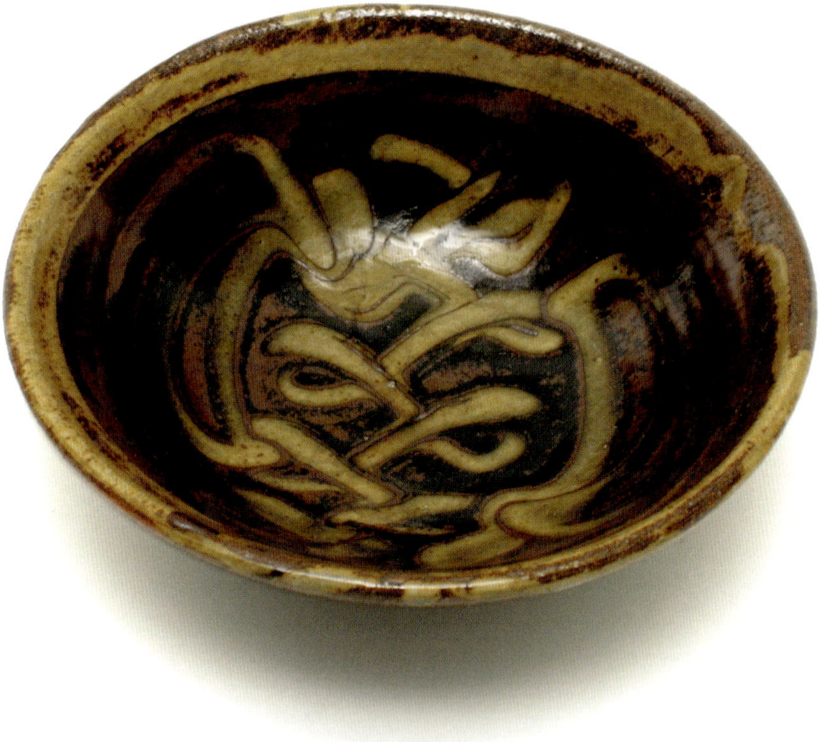

Diameter 20cm.

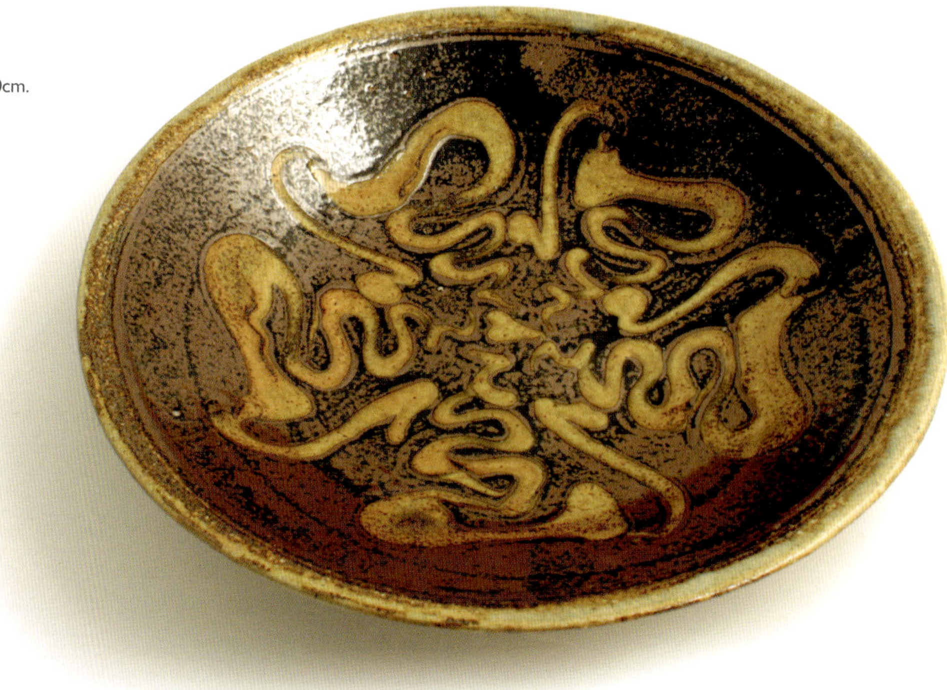

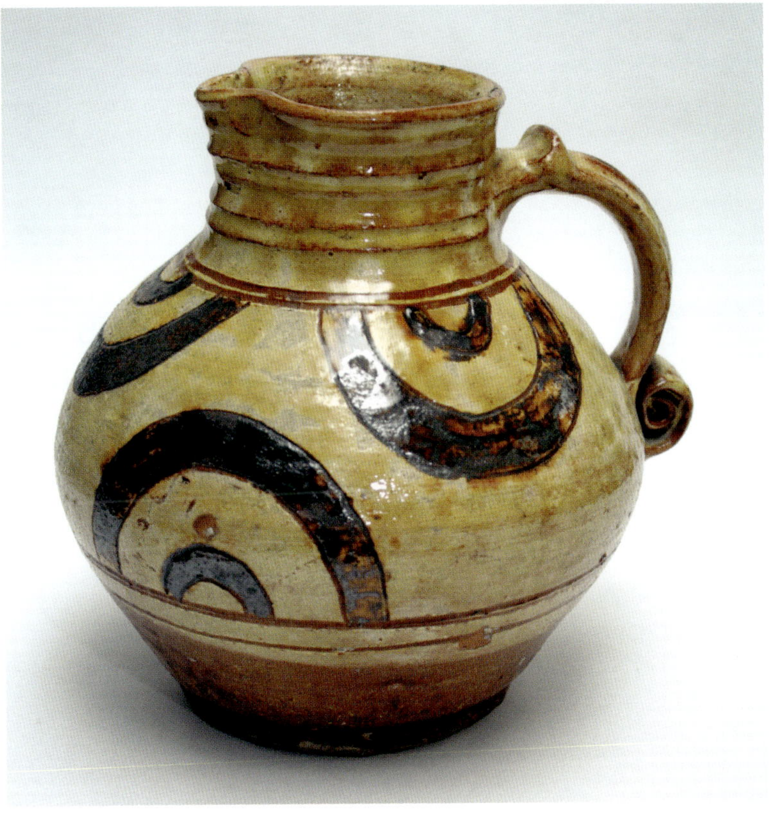

Height 22cm.

Cardew at Winchcombe

This is not the place for an extensive account of Cardew's exploits in Gloucestershire from 1926, and readers wishing to learn more are directed to our 2007 title, *Michael Cardew and the West Country Slipware Tradition*. But, in summary, his early time at Winchcombe was given over to the recreation of a traditional slipware Pottery with a wide range of coarse earthenwares at the low end, and glazed and decorative wares as the acme, co-fired in a traditional bottle kiln as homage to the Fremington workshop of EB Fishley. Of the decorated wares, the twin initial bases were full-blooded Devon form and Sung-influenced pots on a smaller scale, continuing on from the individual wares made by him at St Ives. Jugs, lidded jars and bowls predominated, and two are illustrated here.

Height 12cm, width 10cm.

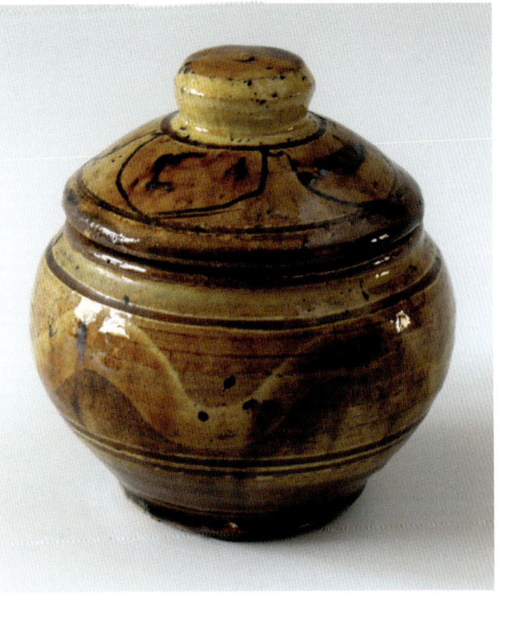

Tiles and trauma

In St Ives, Leach had lost the services of Cardew and was primarily reliant on the help of Art College graduates with very much less ability on the wheel. The period 1927-1931 was a time of growing operating losses, with a need to generate a steady income to pay the bills. Instead of motto jugs and tankards, the two sources of income to augment the fees from paying pupil/helpers were raku decorating classes held on Thursday afternoons in summer, and the development of a range of decorative tiles. Leach had developed an interest in interior design when in Japan, and produced a range of furnishings in an Anglo-Oriental style which were exhibited in the period immediately after WW1. A 1928 Leach Pottery leaflet 'offers 3 x 3 and 4 x 4 (inch) hand-made and painted tiles in both wares, at a cost, which works out per fireplace of 50 to 150 tiles, of £5 to £10'.

Tiles were a natural extension of this interiors theme, were easily produced and provided an excellent decorative medium for the artist manqué. Some are illustrated here alongside earlier one-off low-fired examples dating from 1925-1926, although full production probably did not commence until 1927. The great majority in stoneware appear to have been made in a tile press incorporating four SI seals – unfortunately reversed when the mould for the backs was made from fireclay slipped with china clay to provide a level surface ready for brushwork decoration primarily in black (manganese),

Large kiln shelf 'tile' with brushwork decoration by Leach, monogrammed and dated 1925. 29 x 23 x 4cm.

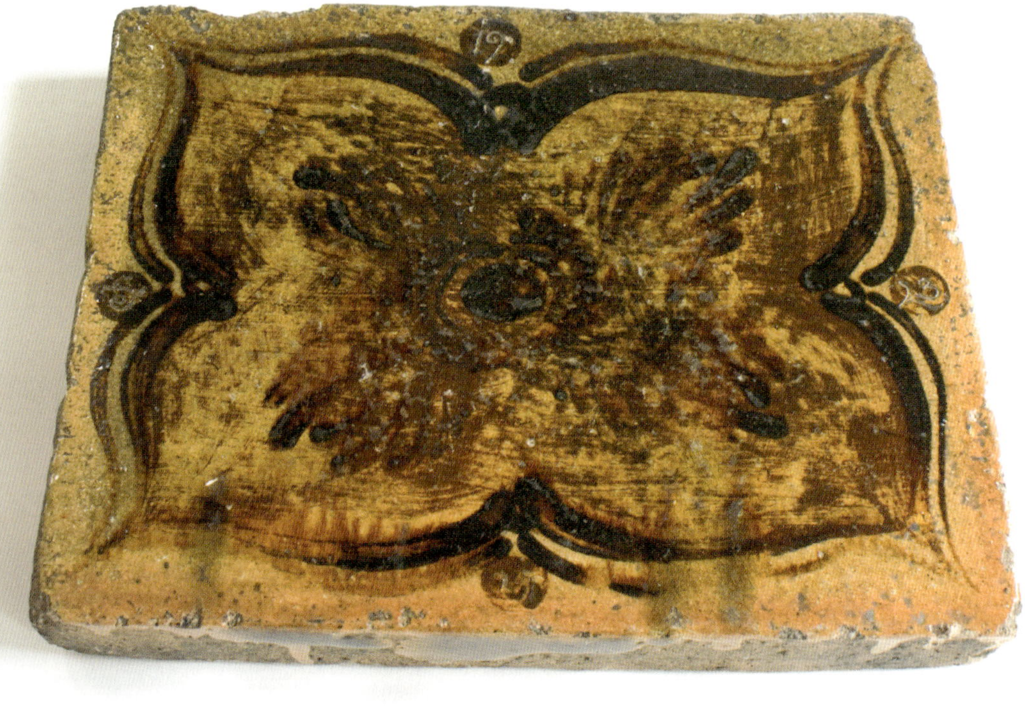

brown (iron) and blue (cobalt). These have a delightful sketch-like quality, and play to Leach's strengths as an artist with a representational rather than abstract eye.

From examples acquired by Milner White in 1927-1929, probably the most avid collector in this period, the only other products in this period were on a small scale, probably thrown by Leach on a Japanese wheel. They ranged from vases and lidded pots to a tea service from 1927. A larger overall scale of production was achieved by uniting tiles into large framed panels of a single pictorial scene or a decorative scheme, and magnificent examples may be seen in the collection of the York Art Gallery and Museum.

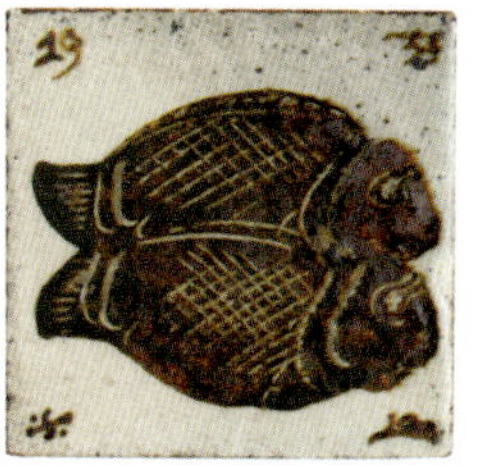

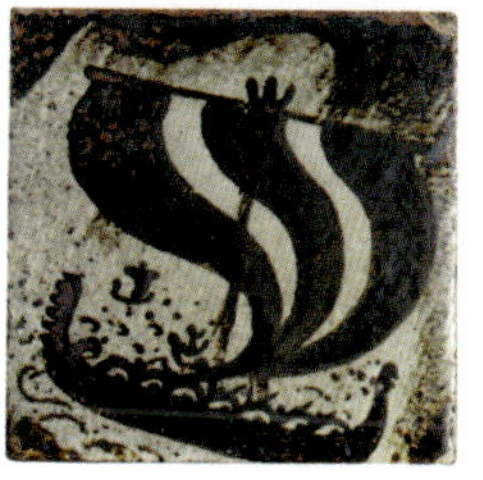

10 x 10cm.

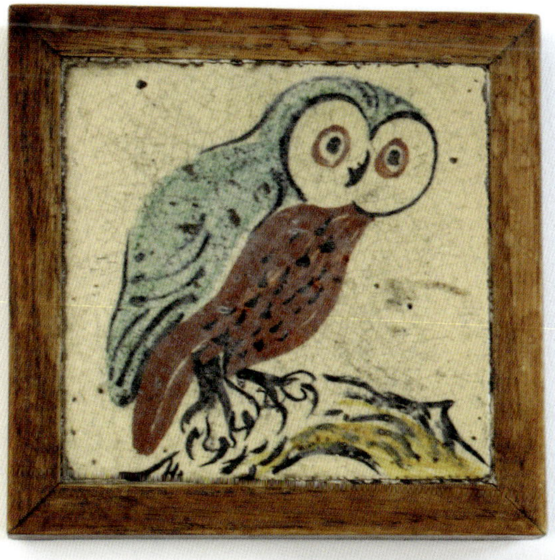

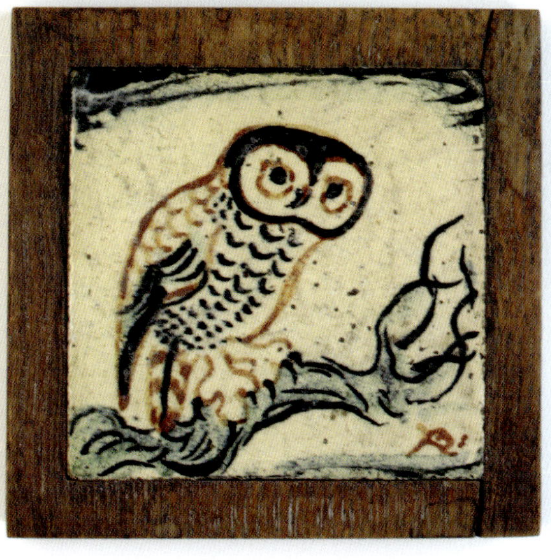

10 x 10cm.

The return of Hamada

It was the return of Hamada to St Ives, accompanied by Yanagi, which was the catalyst for a return to making slipware at the Leach Pottery. They arrived in 1929 for a 4-month stay, and some time was spent in Paris as the guests of Henry Bergen, with visits to see Gill and the Ditchling community as well as Cardew at Winchcombe. Hamada stayed with Leach at St Ives, and it seems very likely that their discussions of the past spurred a revisiting of their earlier collaborations, particularly on the following chargers decorated by Leach.

Diameter 45cm.

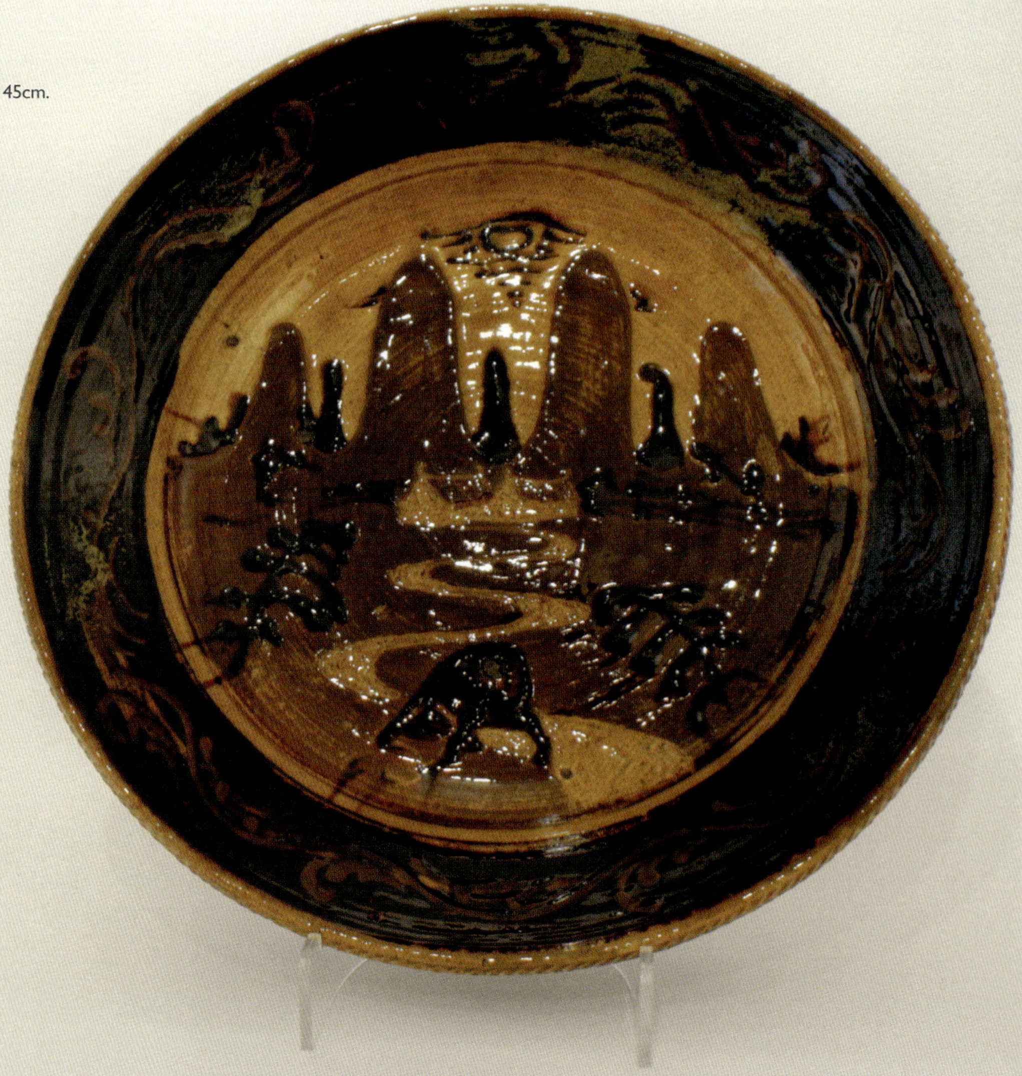

The late Landscape chargers

After a break of three years, another group of large chargers emerged in 1929 with a similar shape and fabric to earlier examples but a more matured and sophisticated aesthetic. For want of a better term I have coined the one above, reflecting the uniting of a variety of symbolic elements and motifs. Two are illustrated here, one from the Noall gift at the RCM and the other from the Elmhirst collection, now housed at High Cross House, Dartington, Devon, where it is listed as 'Hills in China'.

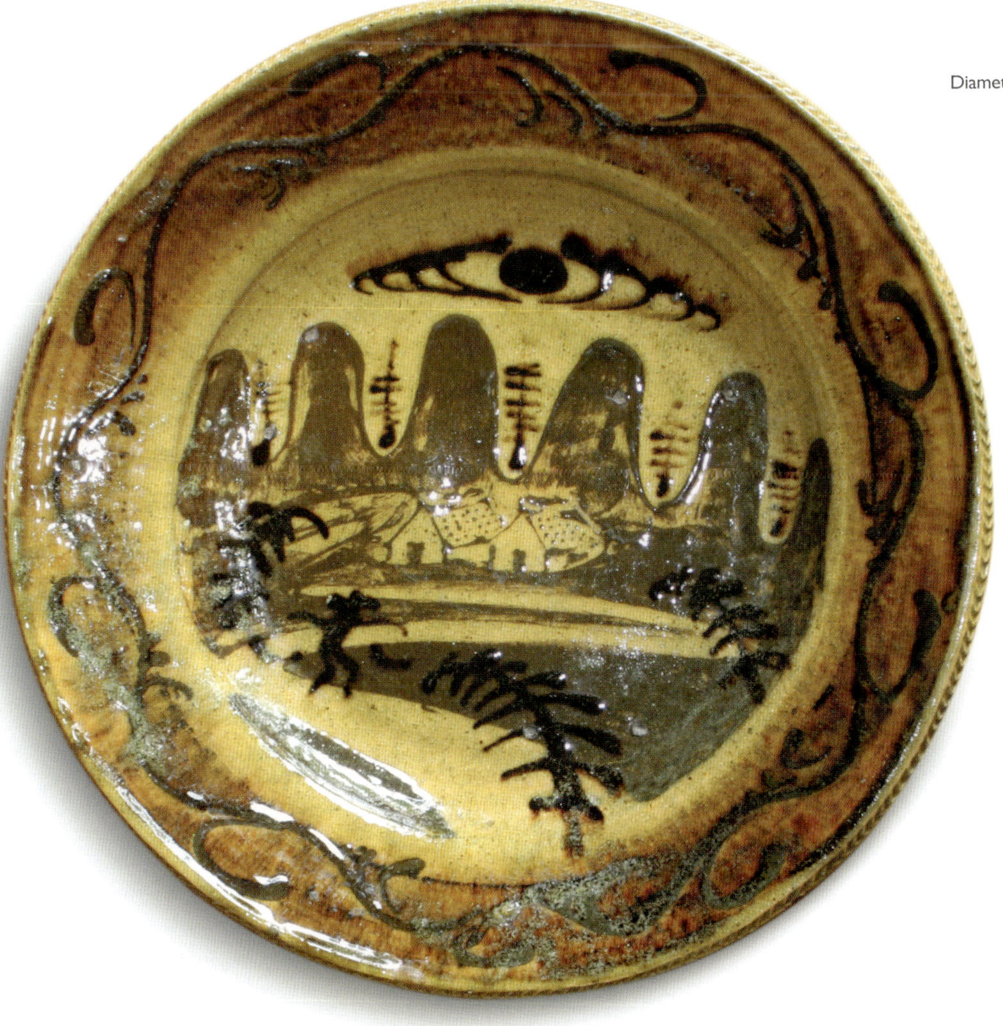

Diameter 51.5cm.

One commentator has suggested the influence of William Blake in these works, but, while the latter was an undoubted influence on Leach, a closer parallel is with the visionary pastoral landscapes of Blake's follower and near contemporary, Samuel Palmer. The poet, dramatist and art scholar, Laurence Binyon, was a devotee and revivalist of the work of Blake and in 1925 produced a lavishly illustrated large format book, *The followers of William Blake*, featuring some 30 examples of Palmer's work, many from the V&A and British Museum. A major exhibition of Palmer's work was held in the 1920s, and it is implausible that Leach was not aware of the work of a fellow artist who also specialised in etchings as a medium. Palmer developed a series of symbolic motifs – the lonely tower, the high cloud- which appear consistently in his works in different media, and the parallels appear self-evident, even if not a conscious homage.

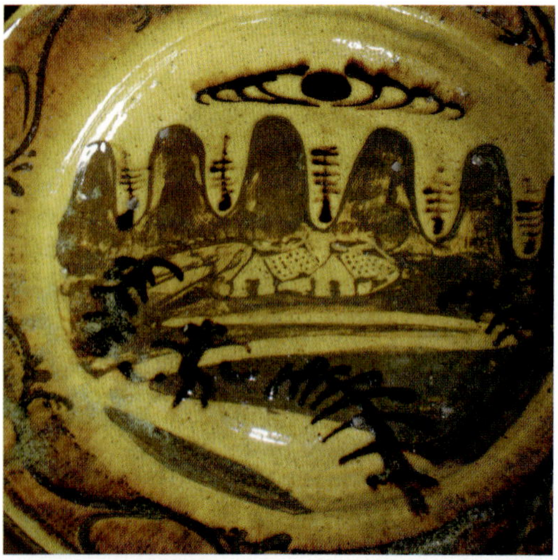

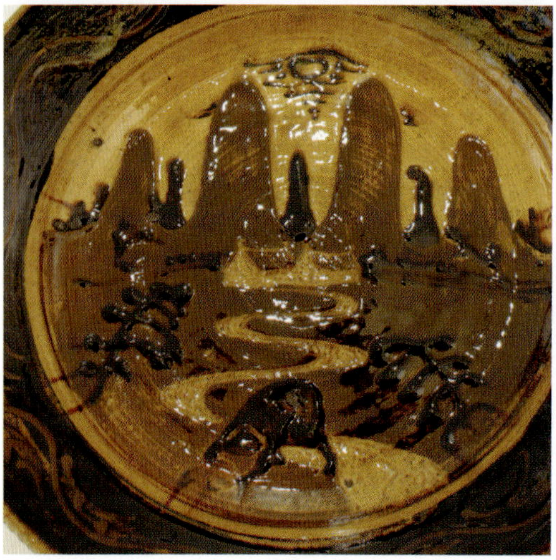

Whatever the inspiration, the achievement is inspired, a late high-water mark in the use of slipware at the Leach Pottery, employing all Leach's skills in the application of designs from a wide variety of sources, and employing the full range of slip techniques and colours. Virtually all the symbolic devices of Leach are present – the winding path, the high village, the distant mountains, the setting sun and the pilgrim- with the feeling of a virtual landscape reinforced by the inclusion of a stylised representation of fir trees taken from the Chinese decorative idiom. That the two were partner pieces is suggested by the use of complementary but different running designs to the rim border, framing the compositions – one slip-trailed and the other relying on combing. Both have the same cream body fabric seen in 1923-1926 examples, and are trimmed to the underside with slip-trailed monograms, one just with the BL monogram and the other also dated 1929.

Brushwork and glazes at Winchcombe

The country workshop ethos re-established by Cardew at Winchcombe from 1929 was one predicated on the use of materials sourced locally wherever possible. Comparatively little is recounted about their visit to Winchcombe by Hamada or Leach, although Sidney Tustin

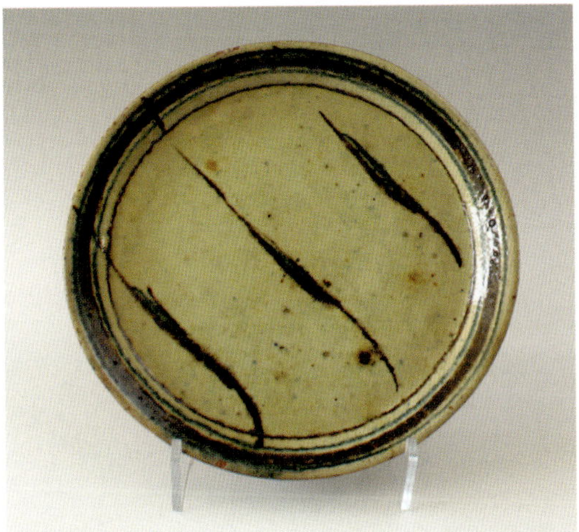

Diameter 27cm.

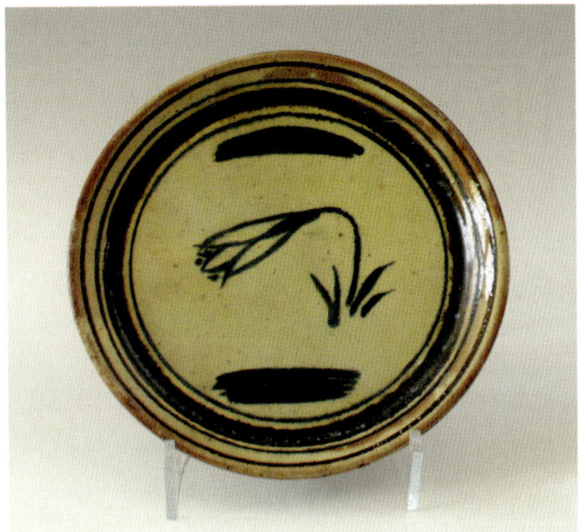

Diameter 24cm.

(1913-2005) still remembered it fondly when I interviewed him in 2005 for *Sid Tustin, Winchcombe potter*, in particular Hamada's demonstrations of decorating plates thrown by him (Tustin). The Winchcombe plates illustrated are atypical as to decoration, finishing and firing, with brushed oxides of cobalt (blue) and manganese (purplish brown) then in extensive use by Leach at St Ives, but previously unknown at Winchcombe. The distinctive glassy glaze employed showing a network of fine surface crazing, and the freshness of colouration imply that an atypical finish was used – very probably a white lead-based raku glaze mix to a recipe by Kenzan I also employed by Leach on St Ives raku style pots of the 1920s .

Although somewhat out of context but with a strong St Ives and Cornish connection, this plate of similar form to the brushwork examples is known to have been thrown and decorated by Cardew in 1929, possibly during the visit of Leach for the latter to take back with him to Cornwall for delivery to Walter Barnes. It commemorates the first performance that year by Barnes and the Penzance Orchestral Society of a previously unknown piece by Mozart, a *Concertante Quartette* for four wind instruments and orchestra. Cardew had discovered the manuscript for this piece in a library while studying at Exeter College, Oxford, and played the clarinet at the performance in Penzance as one of the four soloists. He had also made presentation pieces for Barnes during his time at St Ives (see page 80).

Diameter 26.5cm.

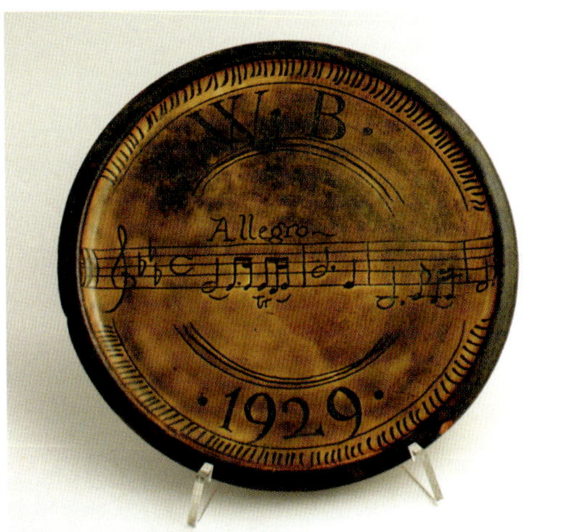

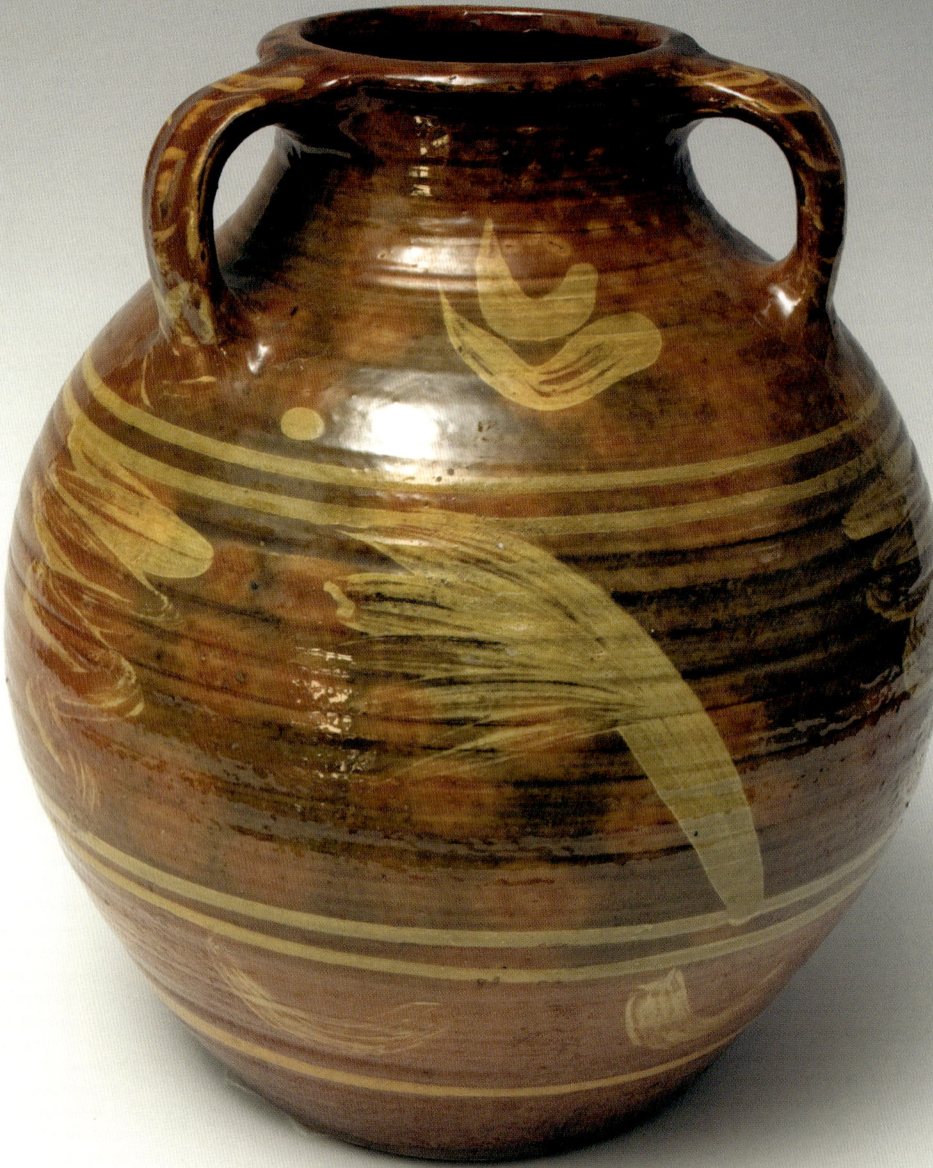

34 x 25cm.

Subsequently, in the first few years of the 1930s, Cardew employed manganese on decorated wares both to stain slips and for brushwork: while manganese slips are a classic component in the Northern hump-moulded wares, their use at Winchcombe produced rather dull results visually. On a more positive note, Cardew's brushwork at Winchcombe was perceptibly improved from this time, as is demonstrated by this large handled jar from around 1930 in the broad oriental tradition (private collection).

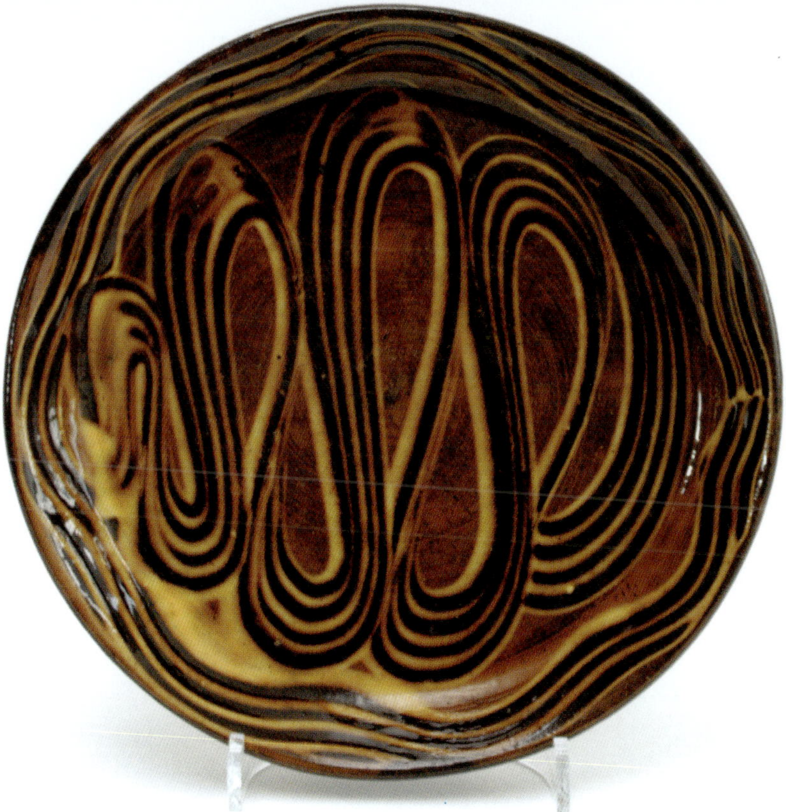

Diameter 23cm.

Fremington wares and combed decoration

The influences were probably not just one way. By the late 1920s, Cardew had started to develop a range of standard forms thrown jointly by Elijah Comfort and himself, including plates, bowls and stew-pots, all relying primarily on simple combing through the slip for their decoration. Cardew was very practised in this technique, absorbed from the Fremington ovalled dishes of his childhood, and had perfected this skill as early as 1925 as this St Ives platter eloquently evidences. A photo of Winchcombe standard wares of the late 1920s is shown alongside for comparison. Combing was to be adopted as a decorative technique by Leach in the early 1930s, as the subsequent section reveals.

Diameter of casserole 22cm.

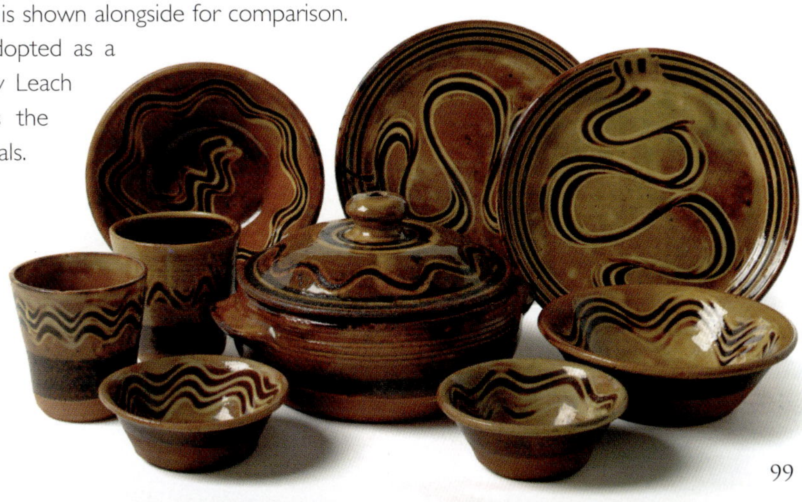

DARTINGTON, STOKE AND ST IVES: (1930-1937)

The development of hump-moulded wares at the Leach Pottery

Diameter 32cm.

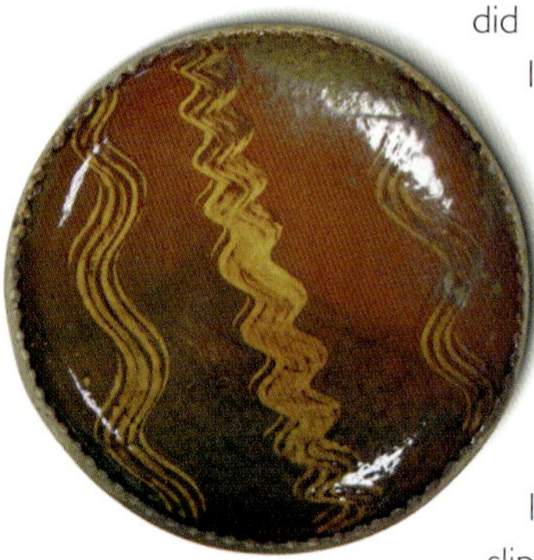

The shared view of commentators in both Britain and Japan is that Leach did not commence making hump-moulded dishes until around 1929-1930, and these two examples employing combing for the first time in Leach's decorative output are possibly some of the earliest. The first, a smaller round version from the CSC appears almost a trial piece for this very well-known oblong dish, retained and treasured by Leach until his death and now in a private collection. A basket-weave effect has been cleverly achieved, probably by using a kidney with a notched edge on one side and the other smooth, combed backwards and forwards through a secondary layer of red slip (probably St Erth clay) to reveal a white background slip. Both these dishes bear only the SI workshop seal, the size of mark varied in line with the piece. Leach is also known to have had a hand in making a few thrown and ovalled combed pie dishes in the Fremington manner, and the one illustrated bears a small oblong script seal that Leach is known to have used in the 1930s, both at St Ives and later at Dartington.

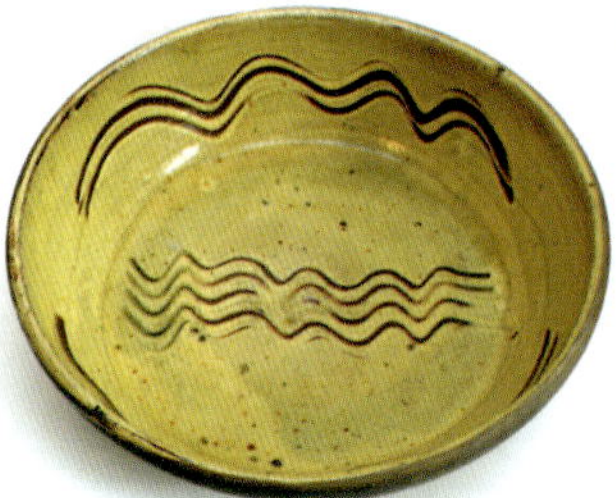

25 x 21 x 8cm.

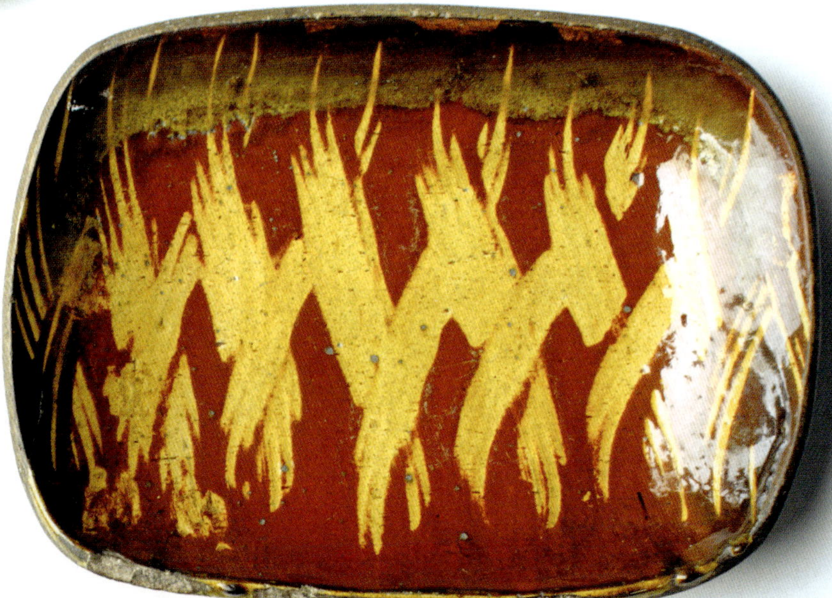

Length 41cm.

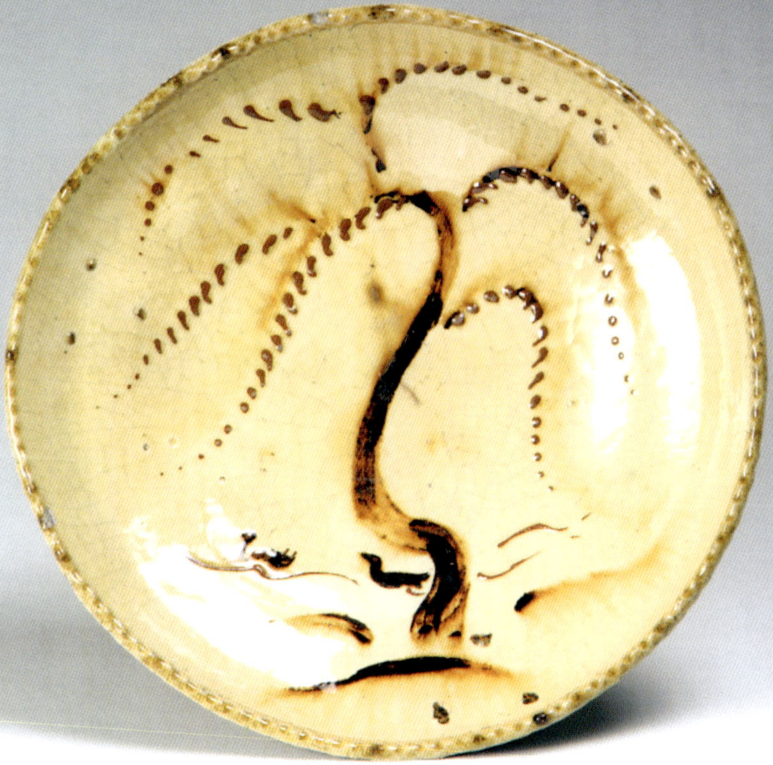

Diameter 33cm.

This further moulded dish from the Potteries Museum, Stoke again bears the 1930s BL seal and relies on a very light creamy white clay mix not dissimilar to one used for raku and some other early earthenwares. The brushwork and slip-trailed design of a weeping willow tree near water with ducks in the background appears to have been applied direct to the body under a clear, lead-rich glaze, as indicated by the slight bleeding of the decoration.

30 x 5cm.

As a complete contrast, this example in the V&A, moulded from a buffish clay, relies entirely on a dark, probably manganese-stained background slip for its colouration. Leach has subsequently delicately trailed white slip to achieve a similar image of a willow, carefully feathering some of the lines to suggest branches. The upper surface has then been glazed with an iron oxide rich finish, darkened slightly by the presence of the rich background slip. It is listed by Oliver Watson as dating from 1932, and bears older style round personal and workshop seals, still to hand for ready use.

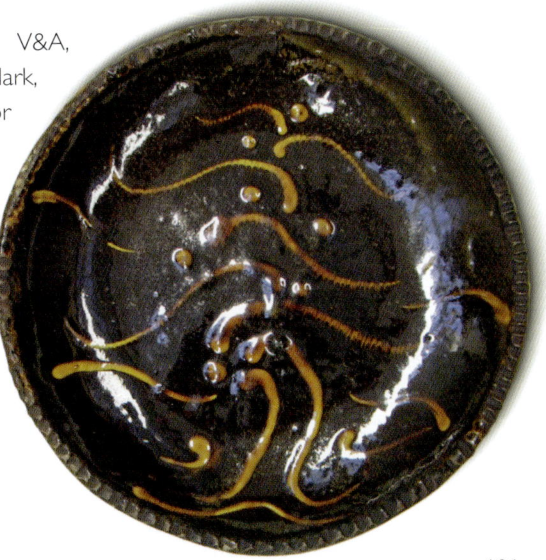

The Dartington workshop and the Elmhirsts

After accumulating a record working loss of £901 in 1931, Leach finally accepted the offer of Leonard and Dorothy Elmhirst to establish himself on their estate in Devon. He set up a small experimental pottery in 1931 to develop traditional slipware techniques, with a larger building completed nearby at Shinners Bridge in 1933. Leach had earlier recruited Bernard Forrester, a former modeller at Minton, and Forrester and Harry Davis were sent down to work at St Ives by 1933, with their wages paid by the Elmhirsts. Although there had been an original proposal to move operations completely to Devon from Cornwall, Leach's benefactors provided £3,000 to finance experiments in stoneware at St Ives from 1937. The Elmhirsts also supported him personally in the late 1930s, and Leach was based at Dartington during the finalisation of the text of A potter's book.

In the first years that Leach was based at Dartington (c.1931-1934), he developed a design for a small tea service as well as other table-wares and individual pieces, probably in conjunction with his son David (see below). Most of these ceramics are characterised by the employment of a black, possibly manganese, slip used to cover the entire pot surface, both glazed and unglazed. All bear just the small oblong version of his script seal and no workshop mark. A number of pots are also seen from time to time bearing a simple impressed 'D' for the Elmhirst-funded workshop and such wares are difficult to attribute as to maker and decorator.

15 x 2.6cm.

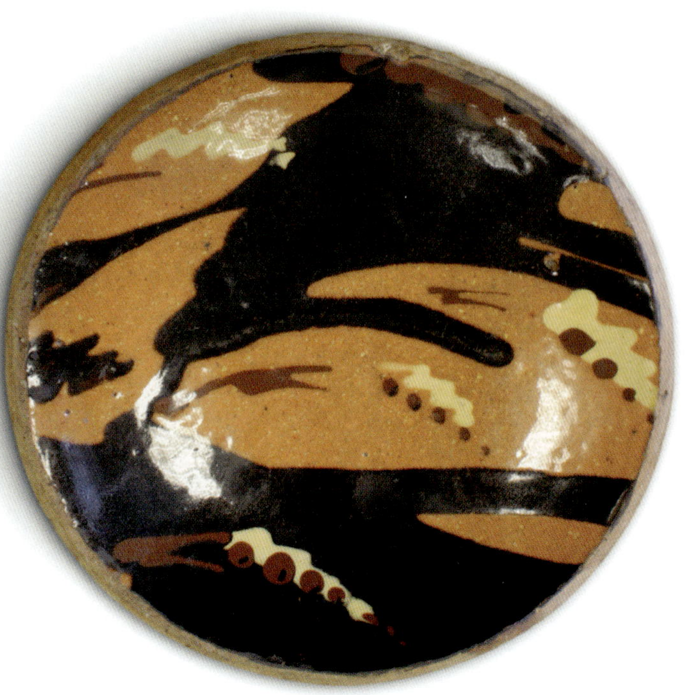

Individual Dartington wares

The majority of the hump-moulded dishes that are ascribed to Leach's time at Dartington in 1932-1934 and in 1936 are distinctively different in style from his previous output, with the use of a more abstract rather than representational approach to design.

Of the two we illustrate, the first has some common ground in its decorative treatment with the larger hump-moulded dish of willow tree design in the collection of the V&A (see above). The other of similar size and finish shows a stylised oak leaf, and both use white slip for decoration over a dark (probably manganese) background slip under an amber glaze, and bear a small oblong script BL seal.

These two further examples, ascribed to Dartington through type, marking (with a small BL script seal) and current ownership, both rely on an intricate use of overlays of contrasting slip colours for their impact. The first example in the High Cross House collection at Dartington has a

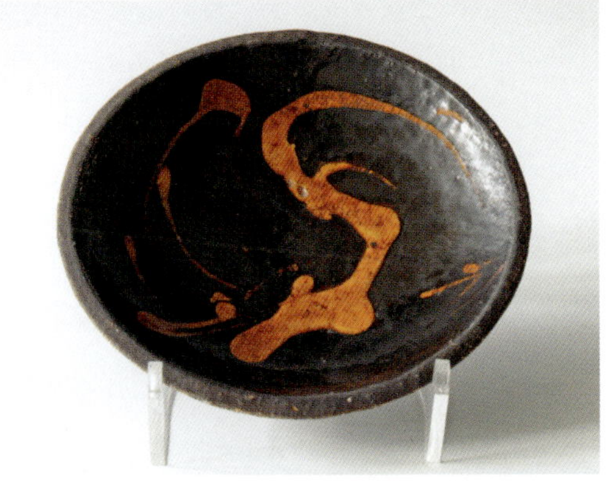

Both 15 x 3cm.

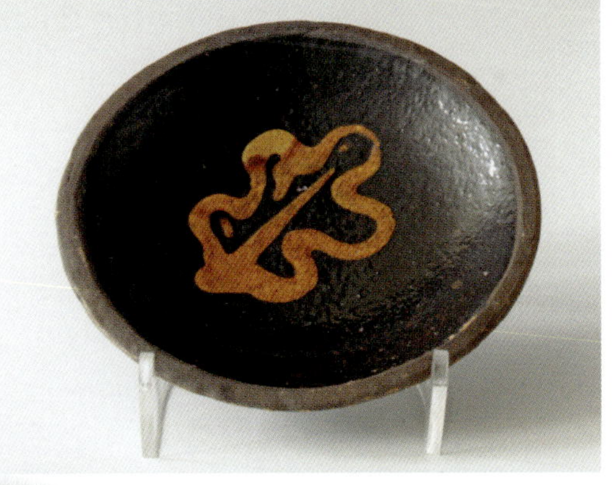

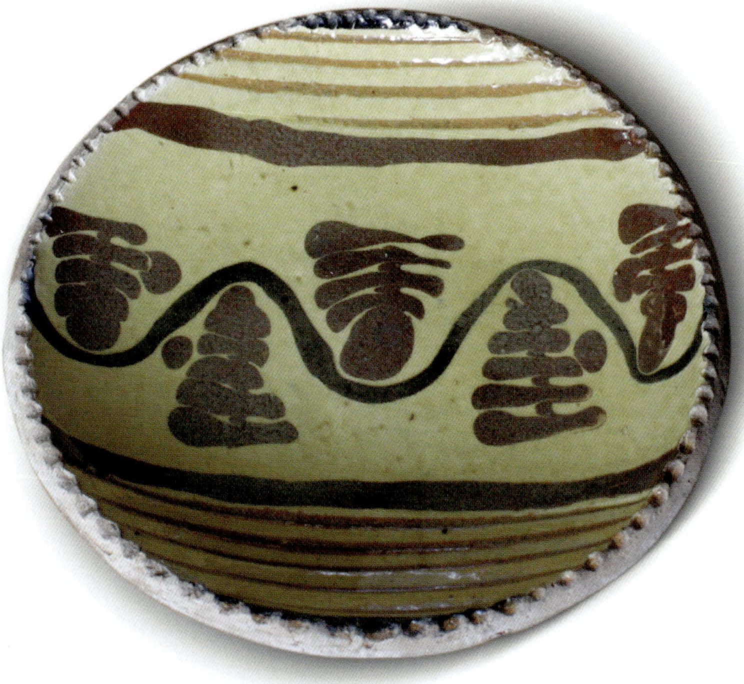

20 x 3cm.

familiar Leachian design of mountains and stylised fir trees although expressed atypically as a pattern. The slips in the centre of the design have been applied quickly while still fluid, leading to a softening of the motifs. It should be compared with a more conventional version of the same theme on the later and larger 'paper resist' oblong dish of 1937 on page 110 .

Broadly similar slip colours are used on the CSC dish on page 102, which probably employs wax resist on a body otherwise coated in black slip (note that the dish edge has been trimmed back which has the effect of disguising the method). The buff slightly granular body colour reserved by the resist technique has then been overlaid with trailed designs in cream and pale brown slip. The decidedly abstract decorative treatment used on this dish is very unusual in comparison with other known work by Bernard.

9 x 9cm.

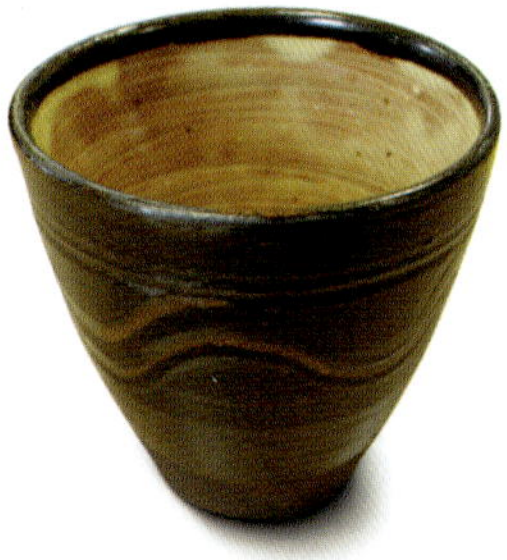

Dartington functional wares

The same dark background slip and small BL script seal was used on the following examples of functional wares, all ascribed to the Dartington workshop. This cup and saucer is part of a small coffee set comprising a pot with side handle, milk and cream jugs (see design sketch), the residue of which is held at the CSC. The cup, unusually for Dartington wares, has a clean base revealing a buff fabric. A thin black slip covers the majority of the surfaces of both cup and saucer, with a simple white spot decoration applied under an iron-rich amber glaze. The beaker has the same background slip, but deep combing of the background slip through to the body for its embellishment. All bear the small personal seal of 1930-1934, and are believed to have been made using clay from North Devon.

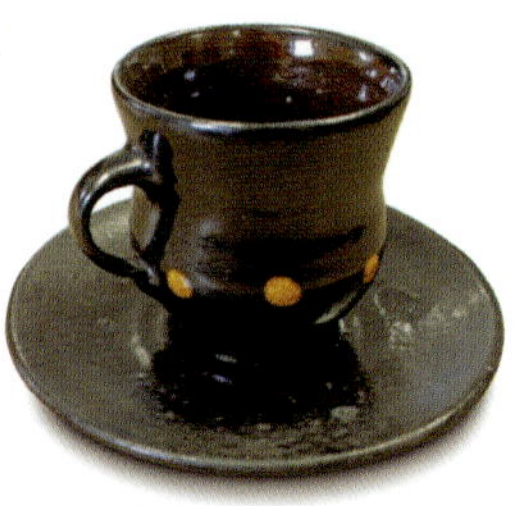

11.5 x 7cm.

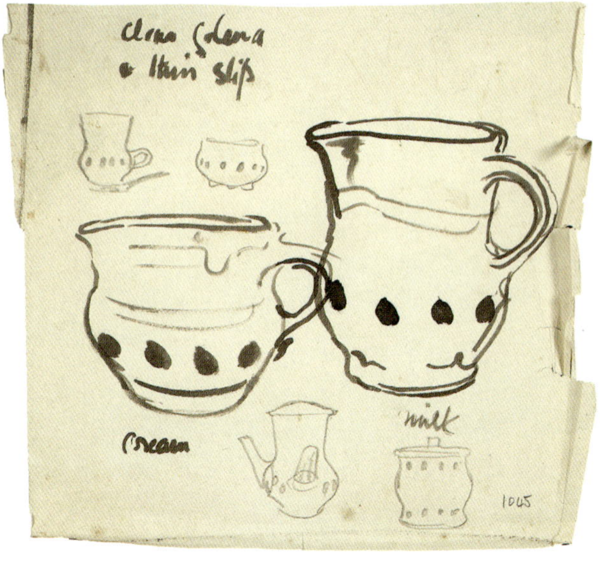

Robin 'Dicon' Nance

Dicon had commenced an apprenticeship with Leach by 1925, and his practical contribution to the development of the 'Leach wheel' has already been highlighted. His skills in woodcraft had first been developed in working at his father Robert's arm in the early 1920s in the making of models of sailing ships. Aside from the prosaic role of making frames for decorated St Ives tiles, Nance also showed his engineering skills in building a water-driven stamping mill for pounding grog in 1927 (see Emmanuel Cooper, *Bernard Leach, Life and Work*, illustrations facing p 206). He was to leave the Pottery in 1933 to start his own local workshop, becoming a furniture maker of some repute, and was the probable designer of the elegant three-legged potters' stools still in use at the Leach Studio to this day (see illustrations).

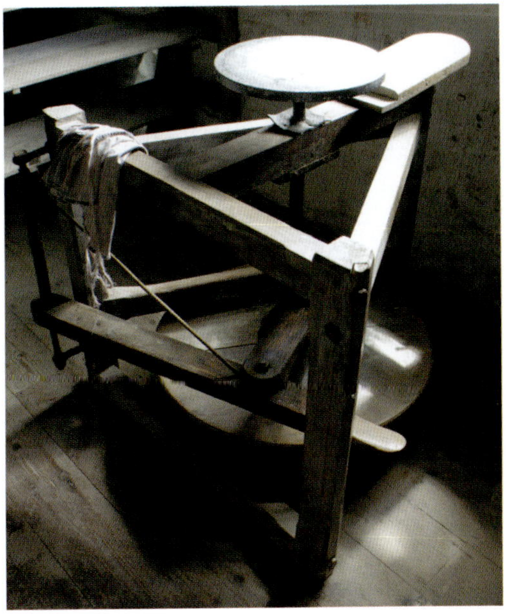

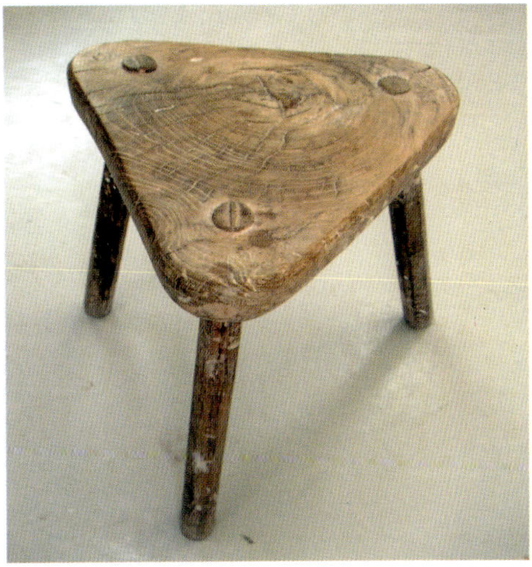

David Leach

David had become apprenticed to his father in 1930, and worked at Dartington in 1933-1934 before departing for a 3-year Pottery Managers Course at Staffordshire Polytechnic during 1934-1937, funded by the Elmhirsts. He taught at Dartington, probably had a hand in some early Dartington Pottery output otherwise bearing just the workshop 'D' seal, and may have assisted his father in some of the more unusual moulded dishes described above. A visual comparison should be made with the two late St Ives hump dishes of 1937 illustrated on page 111, which were claimed by Bernard during his lifetime but can now be ascribed with confidence to David.

Harry Davis

The Elmhirsts bankrolled the St Ives workshop, but it was Harry who made strenuous efforts to professionalise it during Leach's sojourn in Japan in 1934-1935, also funded by his Dartington benefactors. Interestingly, in *Hamada Potter*, Leach recalls: 'In 1934 I was invited to return to Japan, and Yanagi begged me to bring a batch of slipware, which I had not made for some years'. Leach was perhaps referring to the act of throwing, and that was the prime reason for the hire of Davis, who brought with him experience of all the main roles in running a pottery from his time at Broadstone Pottery, Bournemouth. Davis was to throw exhibition pots for Leach to finesse and finish, and he also taught David professional throwing techniques. Leach admired his throwing ability but felt his style was too mechanistic, and it is fair to say that there is an uncharacteristic sharpness and 'manufactured' quality to the St Ives output of the period 1934-1936, some of which is illustrated here. The overall design input of Leach can be clearly discerned in these, but the method of achievement somehow lacks the romance – some would say the unprofessionalism – of the Studio slipware pioneers.

St Ives standard slipwares (circa 1934-1937)

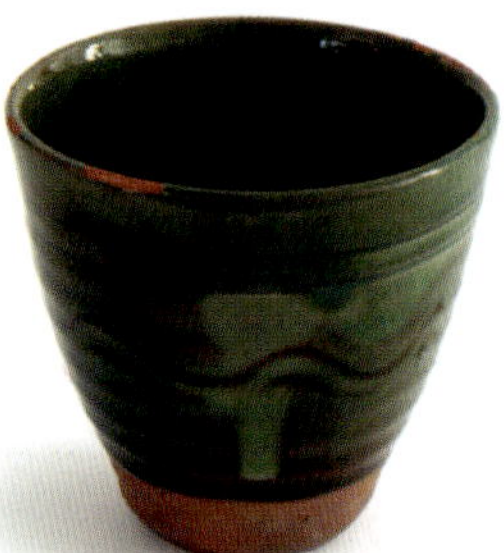

9 x 9cm.

Davis is acknowledged to have professionalised production at St Ives, both in modifying the clays and glazes to make wares more durable and also changing procedures for setting the round 1925 kiln to increase output and reduce firing losses. Indeed, under his management, the Leach Pottery showed a modest operating profit – an impressive turnaround from the dark days of the late 1920s and early 1930s. The dense quality of the underlying body fabric and sharp finish to the glazes on the following examples suggests that all were twice-fired. The raw glazing beloved of Cardew had the disadvantage of unpredictable results, and also demanded very careful and knowledgeable packing of the kiln, so it is understandable that with finances at a low ebb, unnecessary risks had to be avoided. Decorative techniques become standardised, with finger-wipe or combing predominant, although an occasional example of sgraffito is seen. Aside from this, Davis perfected the feathering and combing techniques admired by Leach and Hamada in the early days, but not previously brought to fruition on a large scale.

21 x 22cm.

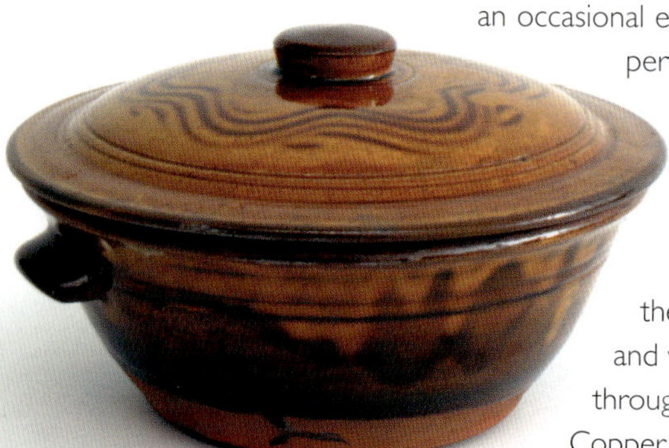

This lidded casserole is an epitome of output in these years, with its fine clay fabric, clear marking, and white background slip, with a meander decoration through to the body under an iron oxide tinted glaze. Copper was occasionally used to give a green finish, as this

13 x 13cm (excluding handle).

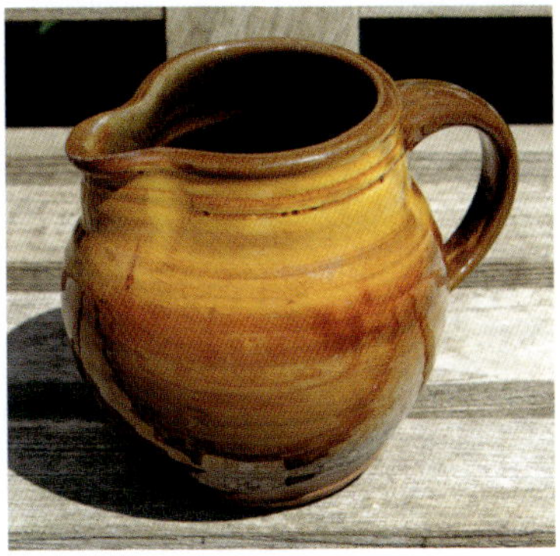

13 x 13cm (excluding handle).

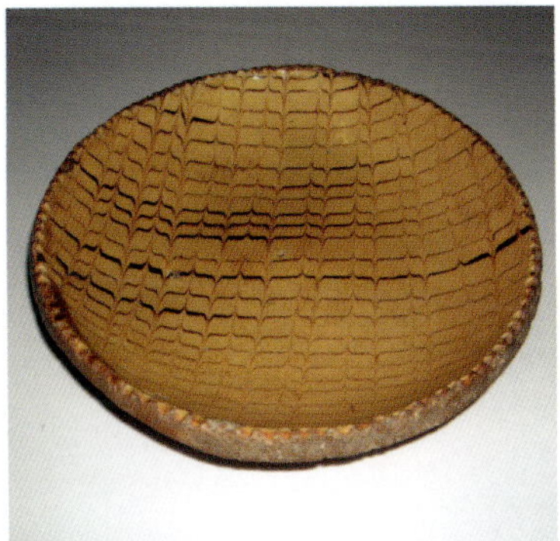

Diameter 19.5cm.

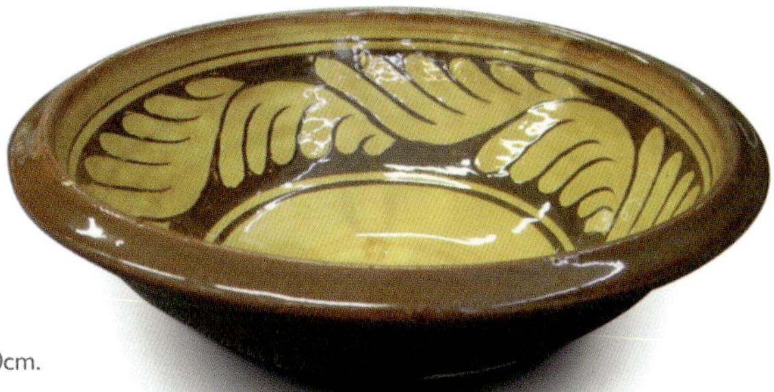

Diameter 20cm.

Diameter 19.5cm.

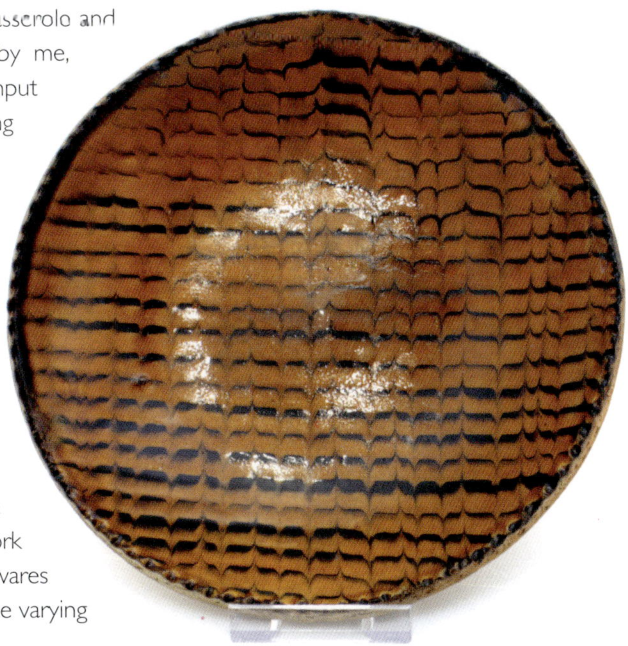

beaker demonstrates, and some forms were left undecorated, this jug being a good example. A similar casserole and an open handled dish have been seen by me, bearing a BL seal, confirming his design input before his departure for Japan. All standing forms of this period examined for this study have wire marks to their bases.

We also illustrate for the purposes of record two of the combed and feathered dishes produced in considerable volumes in these years. Lastly, we feature a footed fruit bowl with a running stylised foliate design in sgraffito within an enclosed band: visually it recalls some early work by Hamada, but it lacks the feeling and movement of the work that appears to have inspired it. All these wares bear either square or round SI seals, the size varying in line with the pot.

Winchcombe and *A potter's book*

Diameter 24cm.

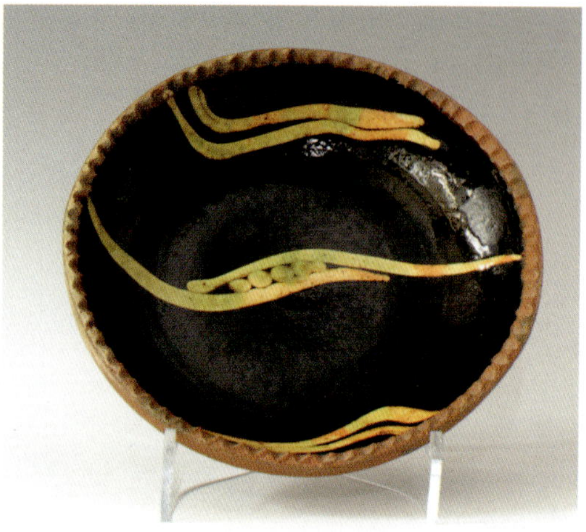

20 x 10cm.

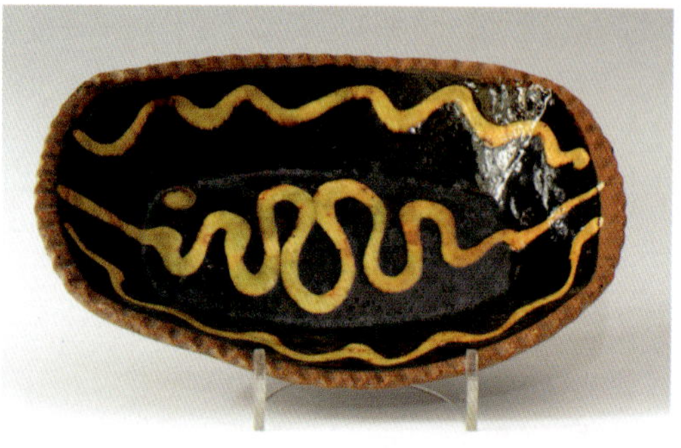

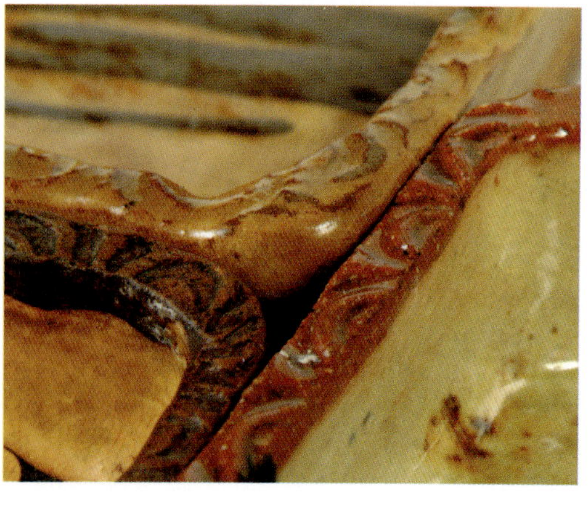

After his return from Japan and settling initially in Dartington in late 1935, Leach spent some time in summer 1936 revisiting old haunts such as the Ditchling Guild in Sussex, walking on the South Downs and sketching, before going on to stay with Cardew at Winchcombe for three months in the autumn of 1936, living in a caravan in the orchard behind the Pottery. The prime purpose of this visit to his erstwhile apprentice was to work on drafts of A potter's book, and the visit is recalled in the correspondence of Henry Bergen, as researched by Eileen Hampson in *Henry Bergen: Friend of Studio Potters* (op cit).

The relevance of this stay from the viewpoint of our present title is the influence that it had on specialised lines produced in the latter years of Cardew's time at Winchcombe, possibly prompting Leach to make similar wares after his eventual return to St Ives by 1937. Earlier in 1936, Cardew had been joined by Ray Finch as an apprentice, following some initial training in London. A fuller account of the circumstances and Finch's subsequent career at Winchcombe may be found in our title *Ray Finch Craftsman Potter of the Modern Age* (2006). In brief, with only two potters' wheels available and Sid Tustin the well-established lead production thrower, Ray was set to work making and decorating press moulded dishes, usually broadly oblong and with rudimentary notched edging.

Previous decorated pie and open baking dishes made at Winchcombe had relied on thrown and ovalled techniques revived by Cardew from the Fremington tradition, with the leading edges of pots left plain and as thrown. However, a new style of oblong shallow dish makes an appearance at this stage, with a rouletted top edge to the vertical sides but still using press-moulded techniques. A similar but square form is well known in the Japanese raku tradition, was favoured by Kenzan VI, Leach's original teacher, and was being actively made by Hamada in stoneware during Leach's 1934-1935 Japan visit.

Additionally, in the early days at St Ives, both Leach and Hamada favoured roulletting to reinforce the projecting edges of early hump dishes in Neriage, also chargers in the Toft tradition made in the period 1922-1926.

20 x 14 x 3.5cm.

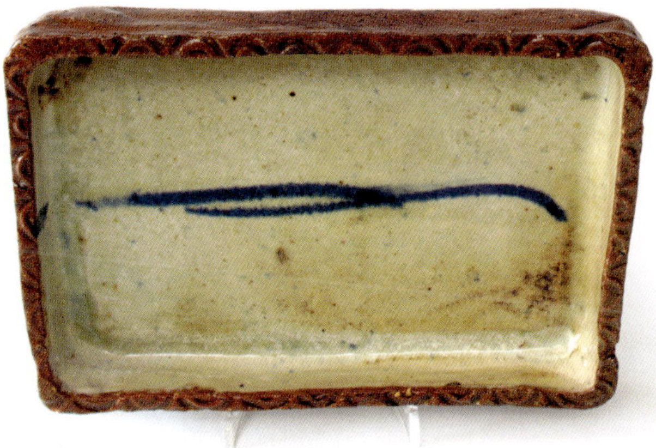

These oblong Winchcombe dishes proved popular in Scandinavia for food (pickled fish presumably) and the originals were used in a similar way for sushi and other traditional Japanese dishes. The two examples illustrated, probably dating from 1936, both have heavily grogged bodies: one has a glaze finish typical of that seen in 1920s St Ives raku and a Winchcombe brushwork-decorated plate from 1929 (see page 97), now believed to be a white lead-based raku glaze originally developed by Kenzan I (see Oliver Kent essay pages 128 -137). The feathering seen on the other is the only example I have come across in pre-war output at Winchcombe. While Leach had hitherto used such a technique very sparingly, we have learned above that Harris Davis specialised in this finish during his time in charge at St Ives, so this decorative technique may have been fresh in Leach's mind.

20 x 14 x 3.5cm.

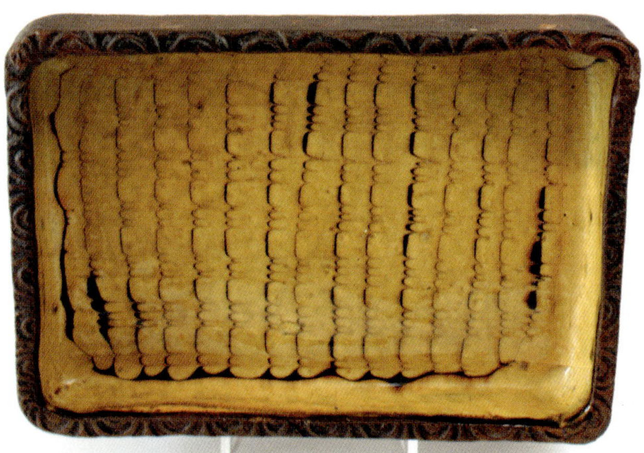

Late hump-moulded wares and other designs

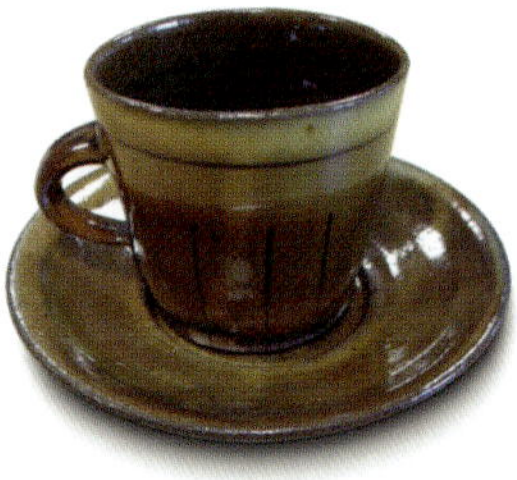

12 x 8cm.

Harry Davis, who had hoped for confirmation of a long-term post at the Leach Pottery, lost patience and went travelling, and David Leach, who had kept a watching brief on the workshop whilst following his course in Staffordshire, returned permanently by 1937. This rather tidy coffee cup and saucer with a turned base from the collection of the CSC may have been an outcome from his experience of 'the devil of Stoke' as his father referred to 'the Potteries', and it is a soulless and uninspiring thing.

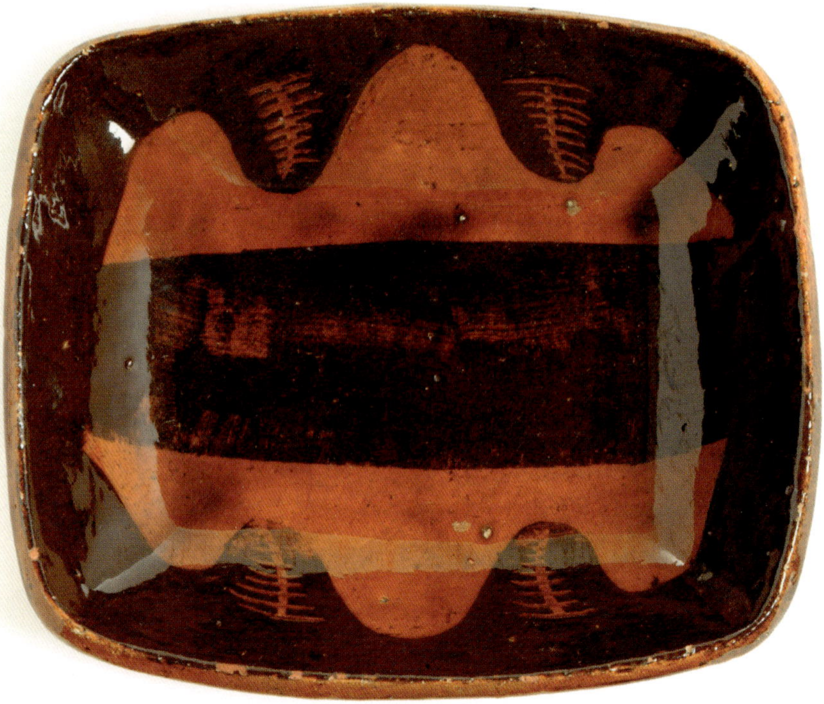

23 x 20 x 5cm.

On a more traditional note, the return of Leach father and son to the Pottery also saw a late crop of hump-moulded wares, with distinctive but different takes on the old tradition. This slightly crude but charming deep bowl bears a new version of Leach's personal seal, now redesigned as individual seriffed capitals, partnered with a distinctive square version of the SI seal also seen on hump dishes produced in 1934-1936 by Harry Davis. This Leach example employs landscape elements from his previous designs, achieved here through the use of a cut paper stencil applied symmetrically direct to the cream-coloured body before the application of a dark slip. The design is finished off with fir trees in sgraffito before the application of a purplish-brown (probably manganese-stained) lead glaze.

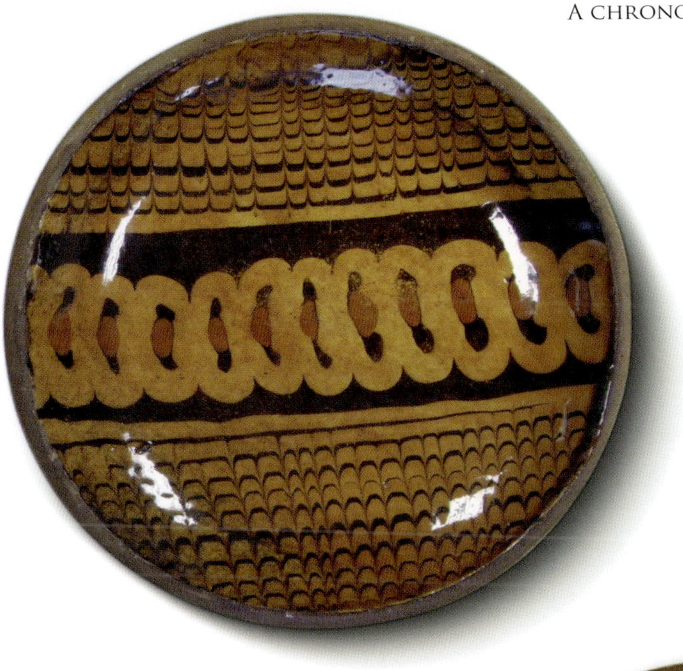

Both 20.5 x 3.5cm.

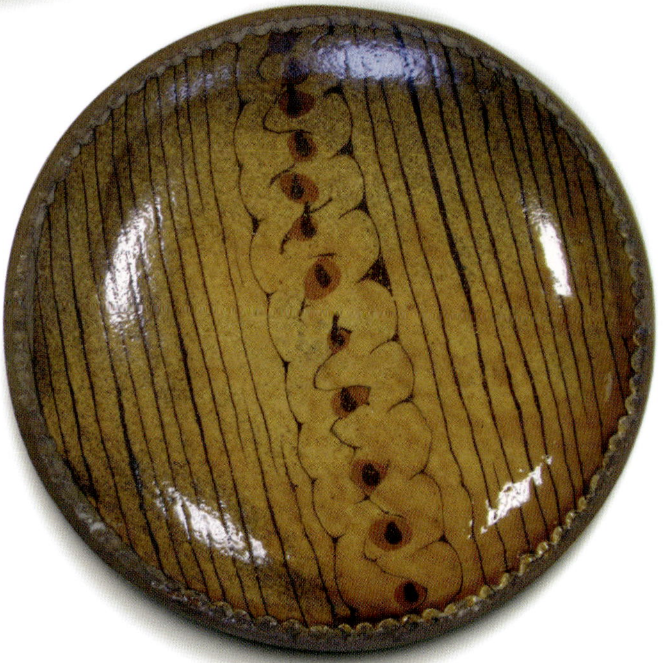

The same square seal is used on the back of these two well-known round hump dishes by David Leach in the CSC collection at Farnham. Both use a series of trailed and brush-painted colour overlays over a basic white background slip, with wax resist to provide a softer overall feel to the pattern. The laying of thin slip lines either side of a central motif also recalls the earlier unmarked Dartington dish illustrated on page 103.

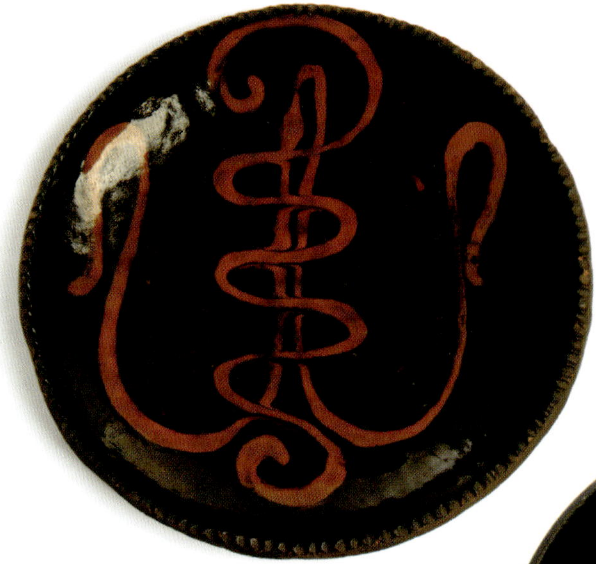

Leach dish. Diameter 28cm.

Traditional English dish
(18th century). 34 x 7cm.

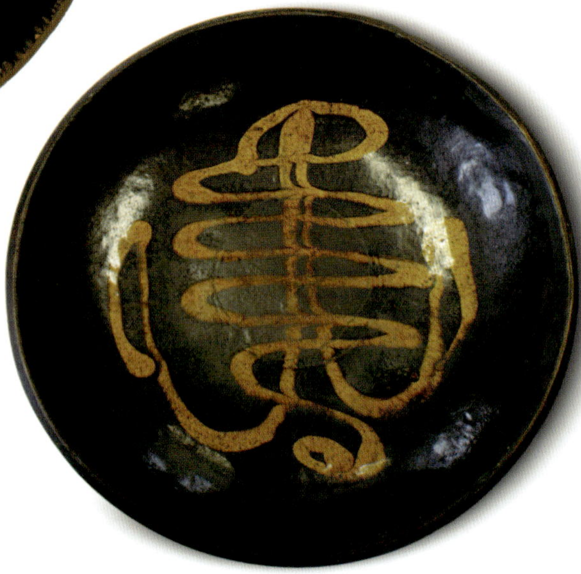

This final example, in effect a postscript to the main slipware years at St Ives, bears only the square SI seal but may be ascribed with confidence to Bernard. Dating it is difficult in the absence of his personal mark, and less successful versions appear to have been made at St Ives during his absence in Japan, leaving one to give a broad dateline of 1933-1937. Bernard owned a period version of this design, the 'boney pie' (see illustration from the CSC collection) and its strong sense of pattern and formality would have appealed to him. Other versions ascribed to Leach and identically marked have been seen. We hope in the near future to produce a related title on such hump-moulded period wares, both as a prequel to this book and to celebrate the superb slip-trailed traditions of the Midlands, Shropshire, Buckley and the North, so valued by Hamada, Kawai and Yanagi.

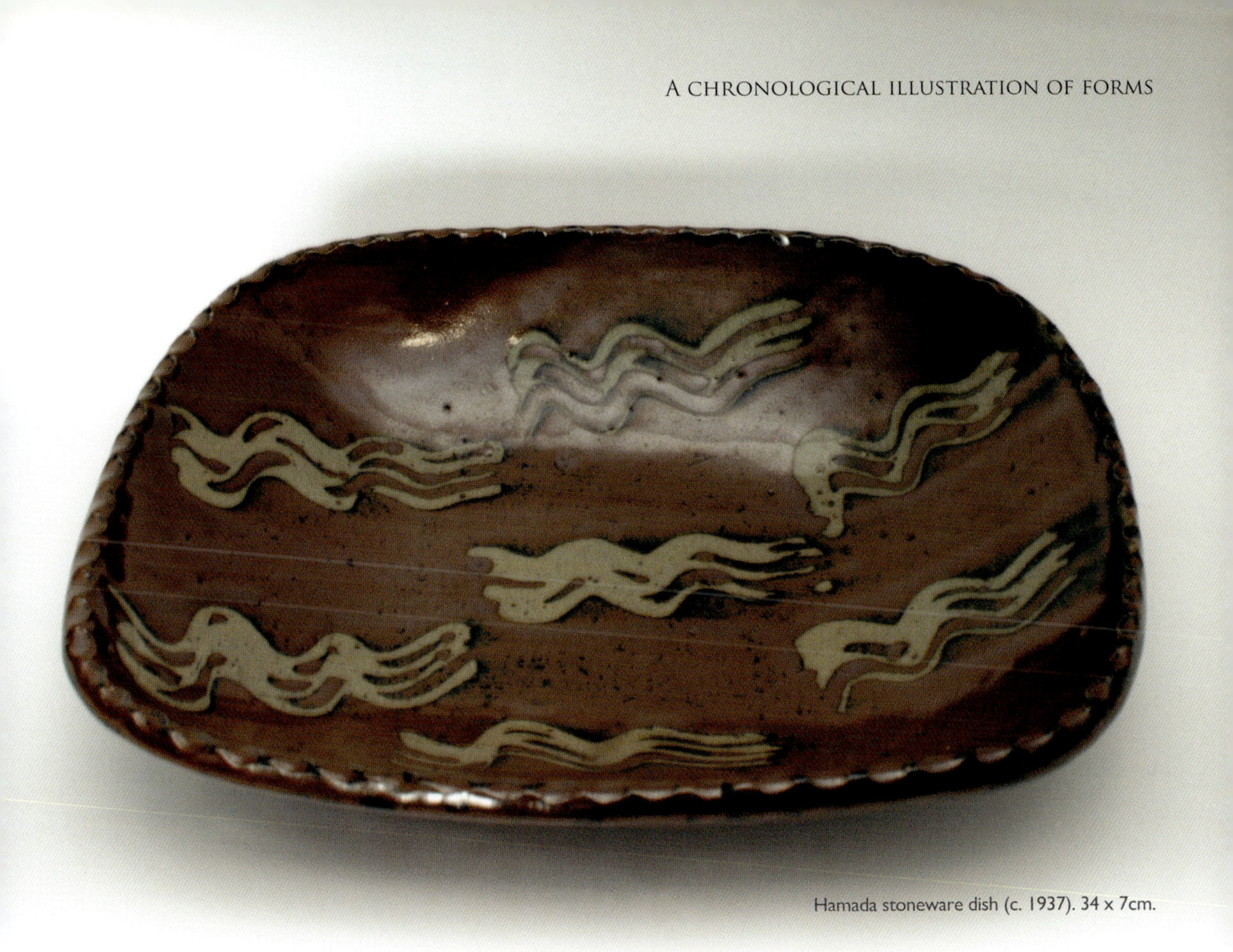

Hamada stoneware dish (c. 1937). 34 x 7cm.

Into stoneware

The interest of the Studio pioneers in slipware gradually declined after WW2, with Ray Finch, Cardew's successor at Winchcombe, finally moving over to stoneware after 1960. Nevertheless, the decorative techniques associated with both traditional wares and their pre-WW2 interpretation by Hamada and Cardew, strongly influenced stonewares made both in Mashiko and in Abuja, and latterly in England at Wenford Bridge and at Winchcombe. Cardew's apprentices were expert in the use of sgraffito techniques, but it was glaze trailing with spoon or ladle that was favoured by both Hamada and Finch throughout their potting careers, using both abstract and traditional designs and patterns to embellish form.

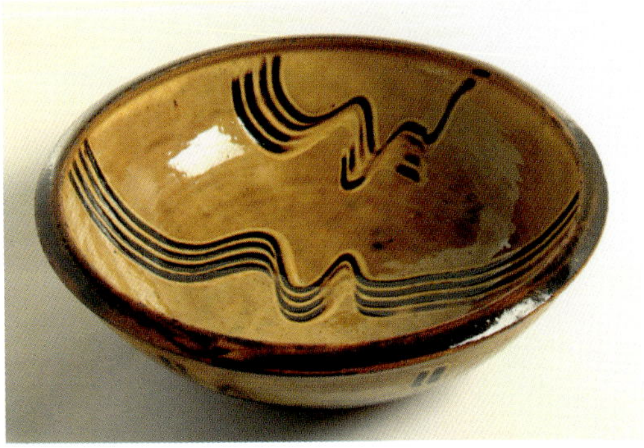

Ray Finch slipware bowl (c. 1938). 25 x 8cm.

Hamada stoneware tea-set (c. 1931). Teapot 18 x 18cm.

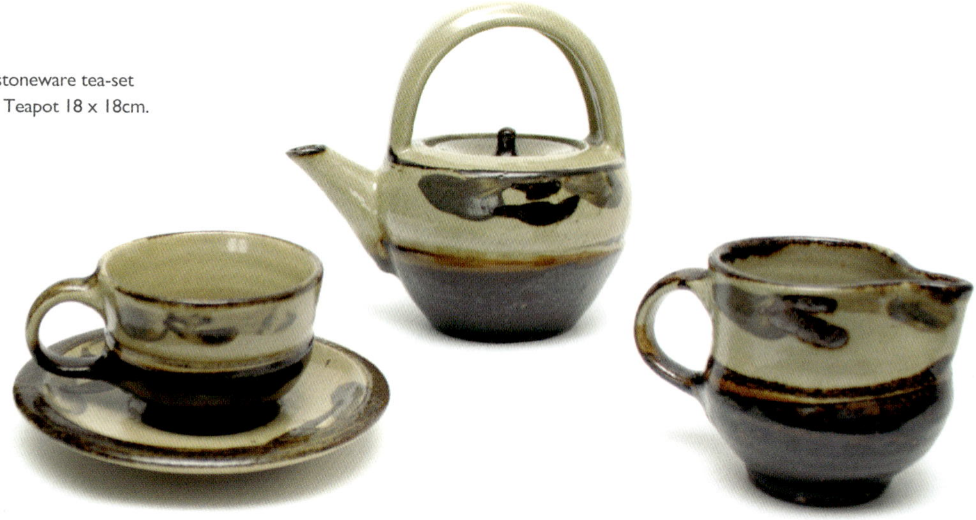

A 1950s slipware postscript

Ray Finch glaze-trailed dish (c. 1990). Diameter 30cm.

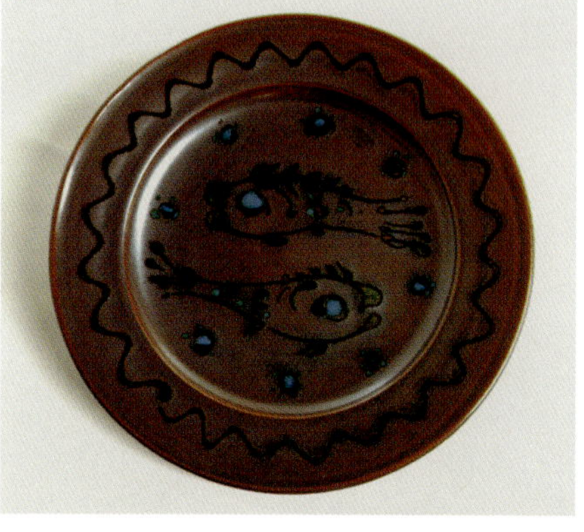

Although Leach decided, with the support of the Elmhirsts, to concentrate on stoneware production at St Ives from 1937, his supporters overseas both in the United States and Japan remained keen on St Ives slipwares. Both of his trips to Japan in 1934-1935 and later in 1952 therefore necessitated the design and making of slipwares bearing his monogram, which sold well at subsequent exhibitions in galleries and department stores. As has already been highlighted, Hamada had as early as 1923 become an avid collector of English and Welsh hump-moulded and slip-trailed dishes, and these were also much favoured by Yanagi who first saw a collection of such wares at the Guildhall Museum, London in 1929. For them, this was a medium that they saw as deeply rooted in English culture, and the words of Yanagi from the 1930s are relevant here: 'Leach's stoneware we admire, but we love his slipware, born not made'. It is understandable, coming as they did from a culture of stoneware ceramics, that it was slipware that primarily appealed rather than the western take on oriental ceramics that subsequently dominated at St Ives.

Ray Finch poured glaze dish (c. 2010).

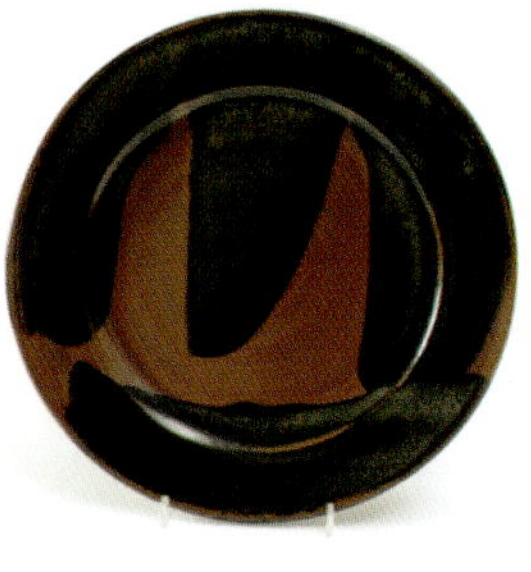

Leach also made and decorated ceramics during these overseas trips, which must have helped pay the bills. One such event was a ten-week lecture and demonstration tour of the United States in 1950, arranged by Robert Richman, director of the Institute of Contemporary Art in Washington, DC. As part of this stay, over three weeks were spent at Alfred University, New York State College, the leading institution for both industrial and studio techniques.

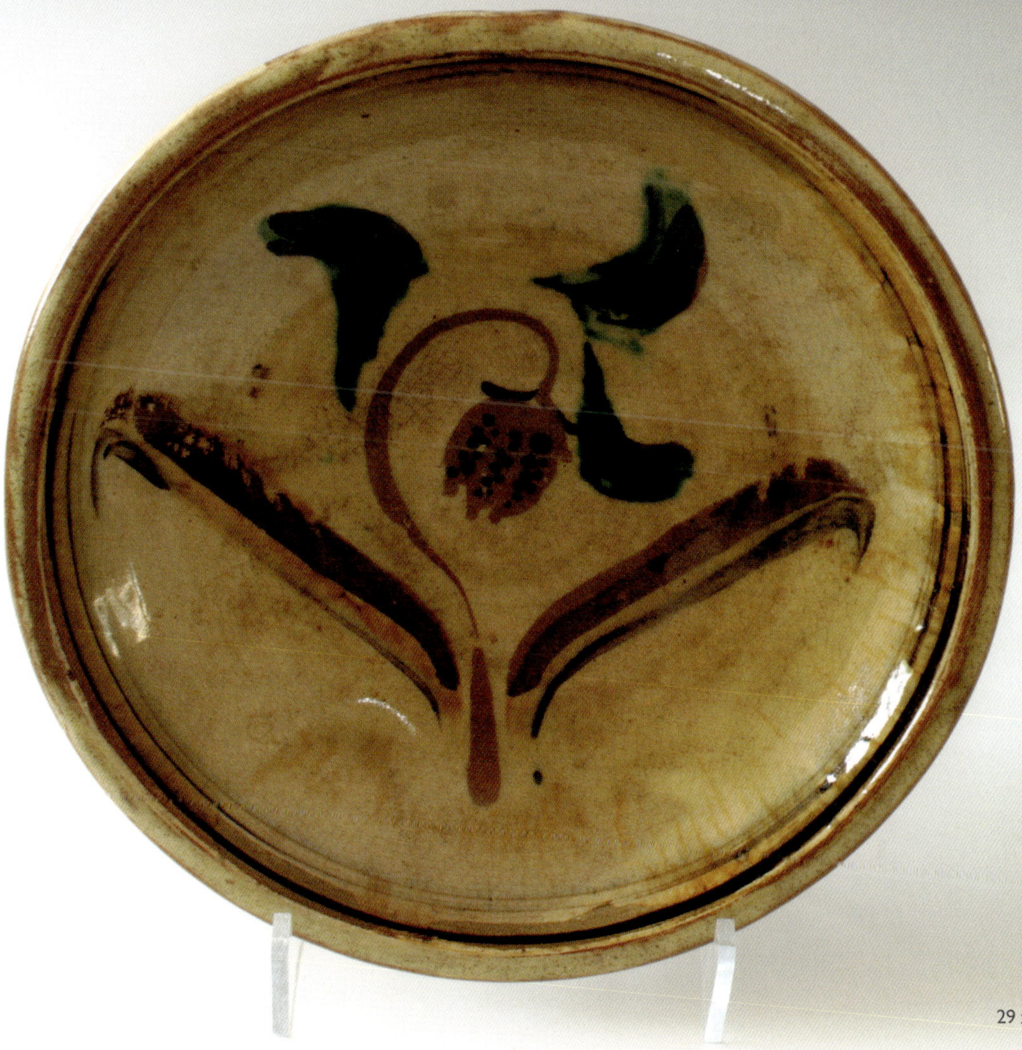

29 x 7cm.

The late slipware brushwork dish illustrated from a private collection, bearing only a BL brushwork monogram and the date 1950, was almost certainly made during this trip and was found recently in Washington State. The fritillary design is a favoured one for Leach and was first used as a motif on tiles in the mid-1920s. I have not come across any other US examples, either in our national collections or in published catalogues or books.

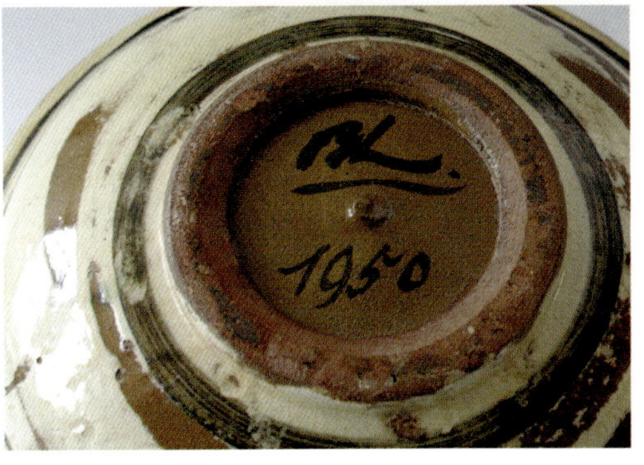

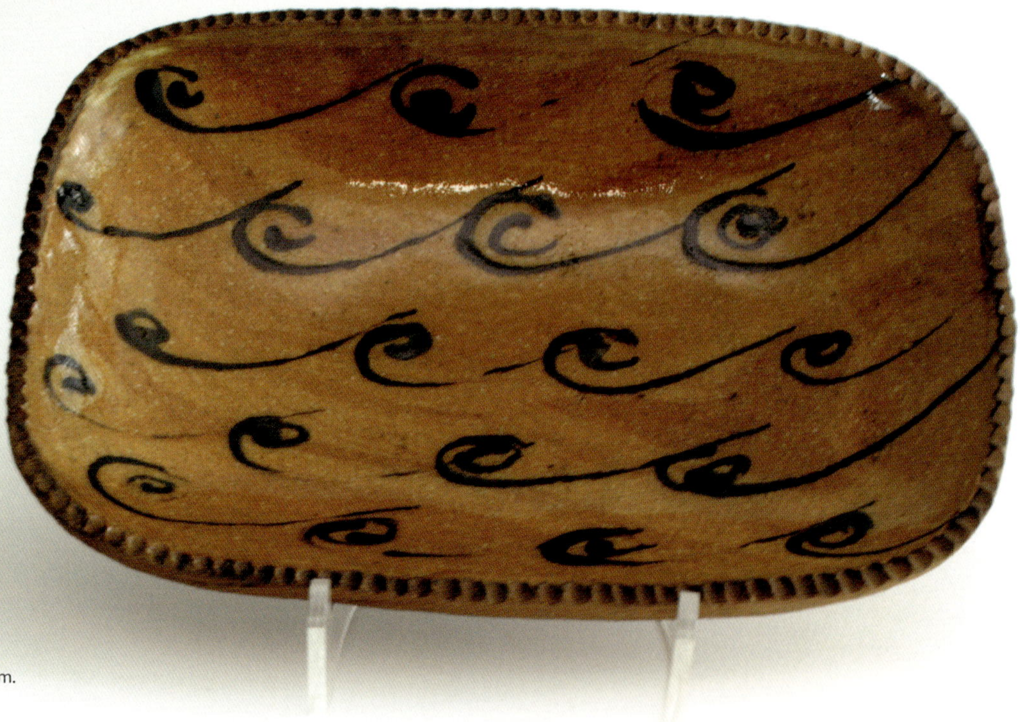

17 x 25cm.

Some beautifully decorated slipwares were made in anticipation of and during Leach's 1953 trip to Japan, which are now overseas and in private collections and were not available for photography. Readers are directed to Oliver Watson's excellent catalogue *Bernard Leach Potter and Artist* (1997), illustrations 131-135; the latter two were made at the Yumachi kiln, Matsue, owned by the Funaki family visited by Leach in 1934-1935. Hamada visited them in Matsue after his return to Japan in 1924 and had passed on many slipware techniques learnt during his time in England, and the Funaki family subsequently adopted the English slipware tradition as their own, creating forms in a similar spirit and style.

A continuing family slipware tradition

David Leach returned to slipware as a medium after founding his own Lowerdown workshop at Bovey Tracey, Devon in 1956 and this hump-moulded dish by him, which subtly relies in part on a mixed body clay for its aesthetic appeal, is fairly representative. David also decorated similar hump-moulded dishes prepared for him by Clive Bowen of Shebbear Pottery for a Millennium bottle kiln firing in Bideford, North Devon at the turn of this century.

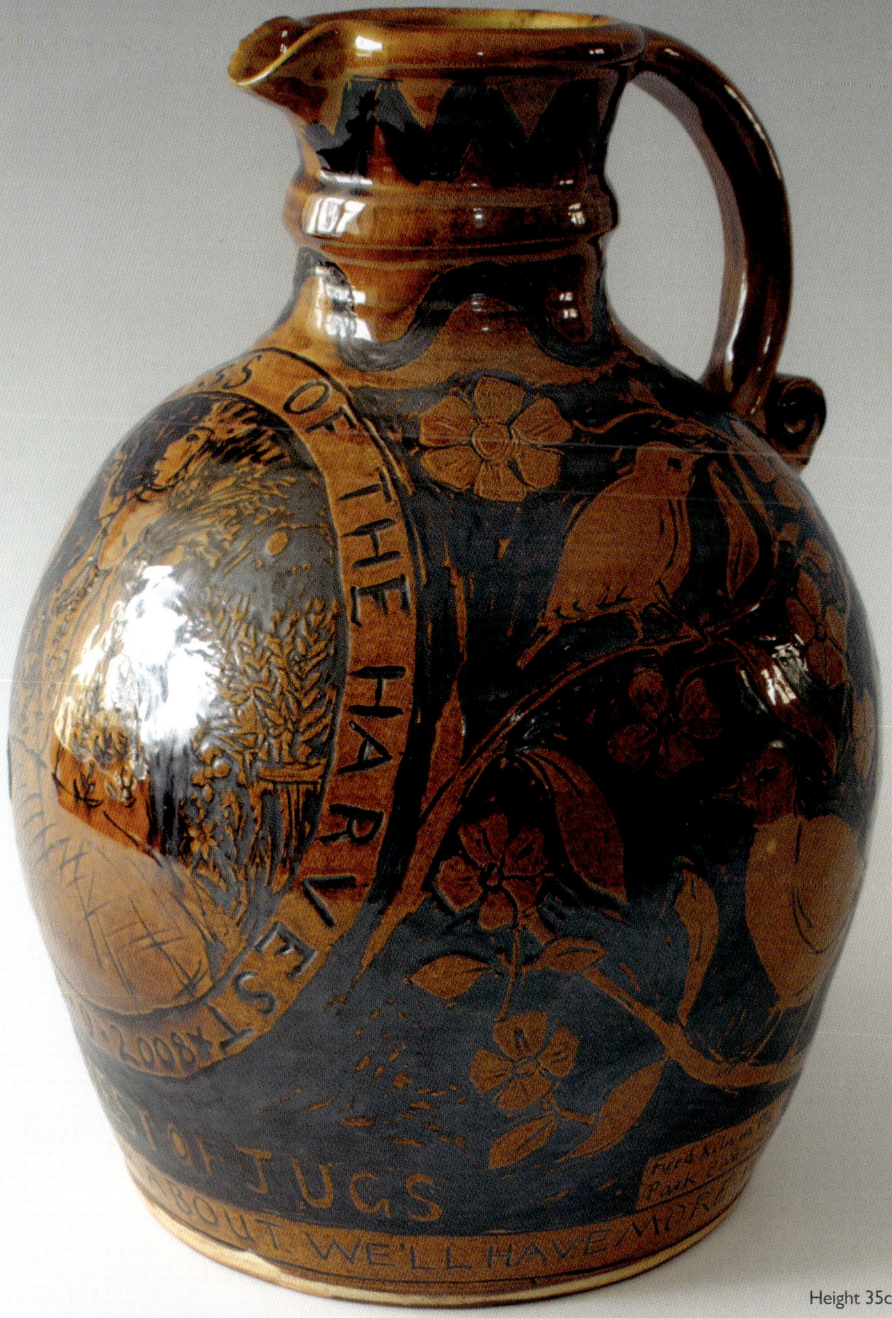

Height 35cm, width 24cm (maximum).

The family tradition of slipware is also continued to this day by Bernard's grandson, Philip and his wife Frannie at Springfield Pottery, Hartland, North Devon, and this harvest jug from the author's collection was made and fired by him, again at Bideford, in 2008.

SOME CLOSING THOUGHTS

It has been a challenging but rewarding task to pull together the material for this book and to research the diversity of the forms and the themes and sources of inspiration behind the early output of the Leach Pottery. Non-specialists understandably associate the St Ives workshop with its ubiquitous stoneware and alongside Winchcombe for its creation of synthesised everyday forms for the kitchen and dining table, and at the higher end with pots which can on occasions justify comparison with conventional art forms. But there is a germ of inspiration behind all creative and applied art, and I hope we have been able to reveal more fully an aesthetically and historically important slipware phase of the Pottery's development hitherto relatively unheralded in England, and in the process shed more light on early influences on the Studio movement, notably Richard Noall, thus far unacknowledged by commentators in general and Leach in particular.

Despite the quality and variety of low-temperature wares we have chronicled, I am, like Sid Tustin before me, a slipware man at heart, and am left with the clear impression that for Leach this distinctively English medium was primarily a source of early aesthetic inspiration and facilitated a learning phase in respect of form and style for the oriental stoneware that he primarily longed to create. The true revival of the slipware in the 20th century was to be achieved by Cardew at Winchcombe in 1926-1939, and in a different approach, its visceral aesthetics were captured and reinvented for a new age, culture and medium by Hamada at Mashiko. This is surely the true test of the best of contemporary artist craftsmen in taking on tradition as they both did and making it relevant for their present day, not in a codified Standard form but retaining something of the raw integrity of the original.

For me therefore, whilst I acknowledge Leach's undoubted ability as an arch synthesiser of form and decoration and his drive and ability to find the right people both technical, practical and financial at the right time, it is Hamada's technical tenacity in 1920-1923 in developing usable clay mediums that I most admire alongside the sterling work of Matsubayashi in 1923-1924 in reinventing for the western context an orientally inspired kiln that did its job well and stood the test of time. How they managed these feats out of their culture and environment and with such limited materials to hand fills me with admiration, but without them a truly Asian tradition of making and firing stonewares would not have been achieved at St Ives. And as to standing form, Cardew's time there produced some of the best of those slipware years, his sense of form widened and refined by Leach, and his desired vocation as a potter confirmed.

The exotic and unusual often interests and appeals, and so it was in Tokyo at the time of WWI, evidenced by the interest of the Shirakaba artists group in western aesthetics and culture. Similarly in England in the early 20th century, collectors of ceramics were strongly attracted by the hitherto unknown and only recently unearthed Chinese ceramics of the Sung dynasty – a taste for the exotic in both instances. In turn, the exotic and previously unheralded country craftsmanship was to be celebrated by the cosmopolitan Mingei movement, with Hamada and Kawai crossing cultures in their passion for and love of rural English slipwares. It is these products of our unknown craftsman rooted in our own traditions and culture that will continue to delight and inspire creative people of present and future generations.

John Edgeler
Queen Anne House, Winchcombe June 2010

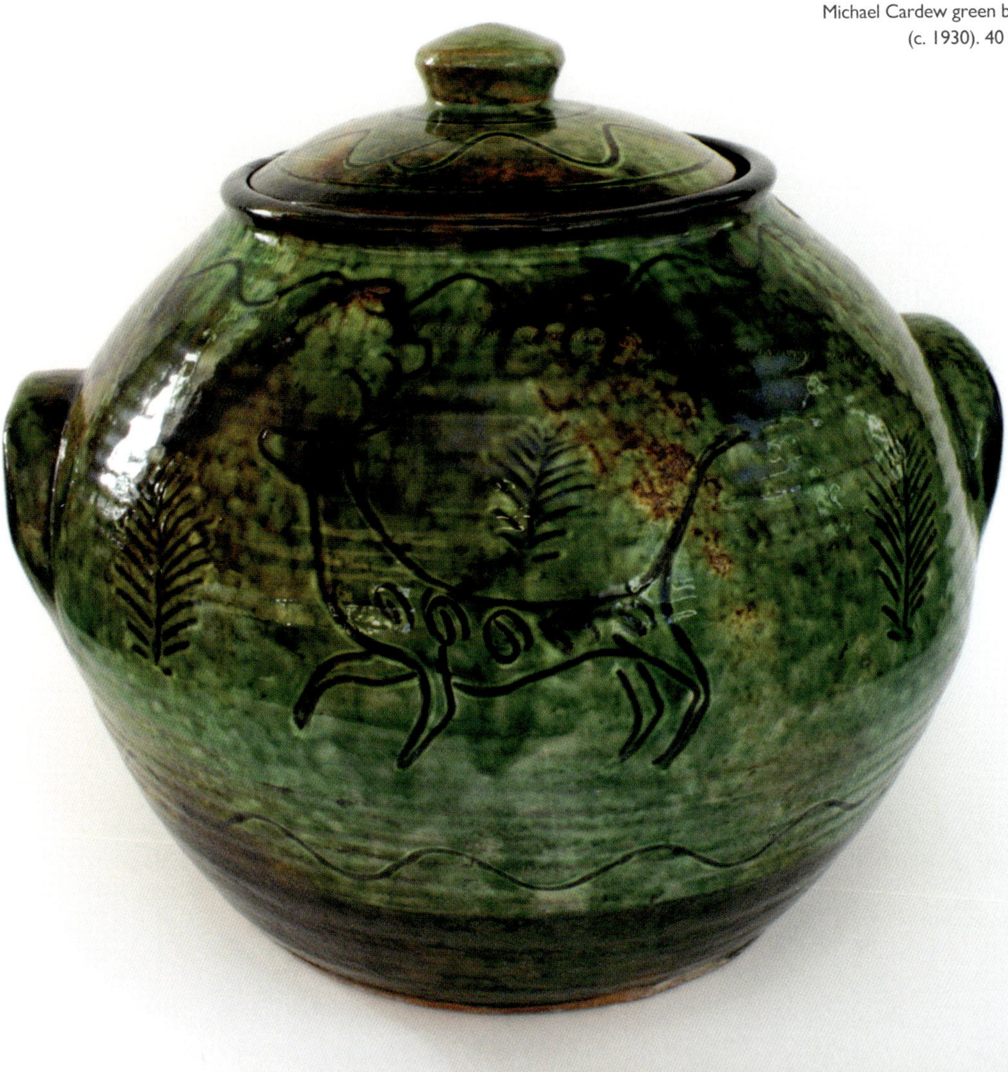

Michael Cardew green bread jar (c. 1930). 40 x 40cm.

4 INTERVIEWS

There follow three interviews with contemporary potters which give valuable insight on clays, making and tradition, chosen because of the relevance of their specialities and skills to help our understanding of early slipware production and the clays used at the Leach Pottery in 1920-1937, and the pots made by Leach and Hamada both in Cornwall and subsequently at Mashiko.

JOHN HUDSON – THE TOFT TRADITION

Whilst he originally trained as a teacher at St Paul's College, Cheltenham, John Hudson now pots full-time at his West Yorkshire workshop, and makes a range of low- and high-fired wares ranging from the practical to the highly decorated. He is possibly best known nationally for his reproductions of wares in the Thomas Toft tradition similar to those recreated by Bernard Leach at St Ives in the 1920s.

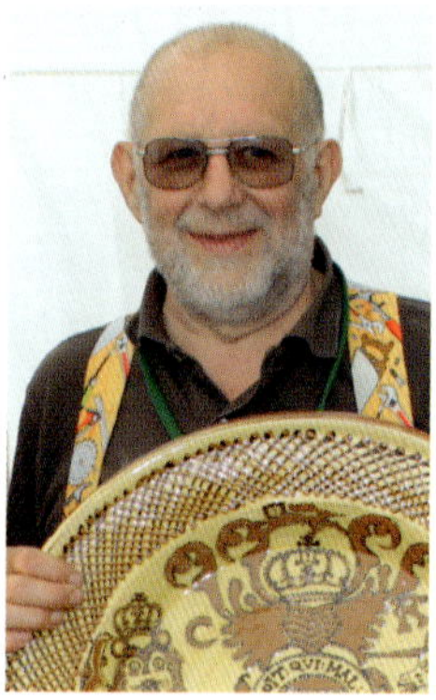

The time served tradition of using local materials is important to you, I understand, and you dig your own clay: with prepared materials readily available from Stoke – Etruria marl and the like – why do you prefer to win your own and what goes into the mix and glazes?

As you say, I use clay from a farm at Halifax , which is a West Yorkshire coal measures clay of a type used by Isaac Button, up at Soil Hill. These clays are over 350 million years old. I don't like using Etruria marl – if you read what Dr Plot says in his book, the Staffordshire potters only used it for their black slip. Mine starts off yellow (Fe2+ O3), turning red after firing when the water is driven off, and stands up well. I also use a yellow ochre from a stream at the bottom of our field. I pass the Halifax clay through a 30 gauge sieve, giving a fairly open sandy body which throws very well, and has a bit of a resistance to crazing, although it depends on how you fire it.

The clay I use is exactly the same as that used by Thomas Toft: if you go down to Hanley or Burslem, and see them digging holes in the road, you will see the yellow clay mentioned by Dr Plot. I also used to use a very nice buff firing clay, from the railway banking at the side of our house, but unfortunately some buggers have built houses on it, so it's not available, and as an alternative I use one part white firing Valentines clay to one part of my yellow clay. The black slip is my clay with about 10% iron oxide (or 5% iron and 5% manganese). I do need to be careful about the mix of the coloured slips as they will otherwise fall off, although that hasn't now happened to me for the last 15-20 years. As to glazes, I use Potclays P2002 with 10% of my own clay in it, together with 5% yellow ochre and 4% Bentonite, which helps

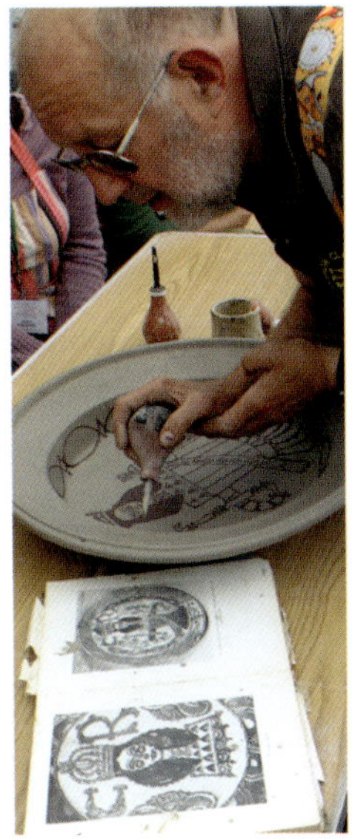

stop the glaze flaking off. I then fire to 1120°C , using an electric kiln I bought in 1977 with a Government loan: electric makes things very easy, as it buzzes quietly in the corner, and doesn't make many mistakes.

How did you come about acquiring the Toft style techniques you now use with such professionalism and fluency? Was this from books, trial and error, or looking at the original pots?

Well I looked at photographs and books, visited museums and the like, and eventually started to get things right. Probably the book I use most of all is Ronald Cooper's book on slipware dishes. I have two copies, one in my study, and the other, a rather beat up copy, in my workshop, a well thumbed and clay stained tome. Aside from looking in museums, the best thing I ever did was to join the Medieval Pottery Research group 21 years ago, and have become associated with a lot of people in the Museums and Archaeology world, which has opened doors for me. The Leeds Symposium on Food History is also a good organisation, and you have cross over figures and topics – Peter Brears springs to mind in particular. Most of the themes I use, I get from Museum collections, but people ask me to do all sorts of things, lots of pots using the style of Toft and other Staffordshire potters for wedding or birthday presents and christening gifts.

The number of pots I have thrown away and shards I have created is unbelievable. The first Coat of Arms charger I made was for Stuart Interiors of Somerset, and I made 22 before I got one right: most of them cracked or broke during drying, which in itself is very difficult to do and you have to follow a number of rules. I don't use any formers apart from the wheel head, which has a large disk which you can throw the big dishes on: at one time I used to lift them off but it's much easier using the disk which fits to a special wheel head, and which I suspect Tofty also used. With the Toft dishes, there is no turning of the bottoms, and they are just as they come off the wheel: then I knife trim them.

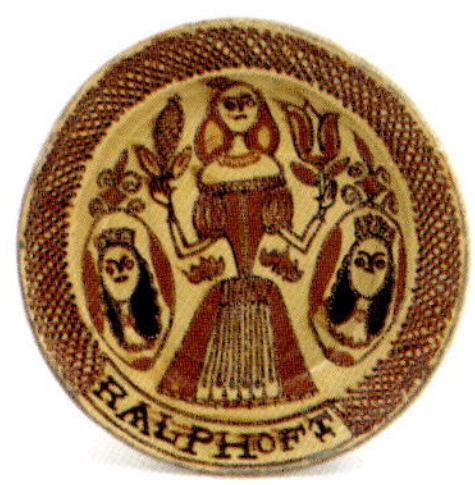

So I do free throw, but getting the rims down can be a real problem, and if you go too far, you can watch them sink slowly, but if you pull them down when they are too hard, the rims split: I was very gratified to find on a Thomas Toft dish that he had done exactly this, and there was a split that he repaired by putting a bob of clay either side of the plate and running his hand over it. It was quite clear how he did it, and I thought 'Well there really is a God' since if Tofty did it, then it's ok by me. The rims when you throw them are at an angle of 45° and as the pot stiffens up you gradually ease them down into an almost horizontal position, but not too far because when you fire them, they become dihedral, like a jet aircraft's wing, so you have almost got to leave then in an anti-hedral position, as it were, and then things will come out right.

I don't biscuit fire any of the large dishes: they are all once fired and I am sure Toft was the same, using galena glaze, which you can tell from the richness of the colours. Nor do I use props or stilts to support them in the firing. I do not fire them on their edges, otherwise they end up like Cornish pasties, as at the firing temperature of 1120°, the pots become super-pyro plastic and the y would bend right over almost like the Lion dish that Toft made, which is famous for the bend in it.

I do have two heroes in potting, one of course is Thomas Toft, and the other Isaac Button. Now you ask do I put anything in the clay: some years ago, Isaac who died in 1968 had been talking to someone from a museum or not involved in the industry, and he said *Thou knows I had a letter from that there Leach down in Devon (sic) and he wants to know what kind of sand I put in my clay to make big pots – but I spend most of my time taking the bloody stuff out!* Which is what I do.

ANDREW MCGARVA – HUMP-MOULDED DISHES

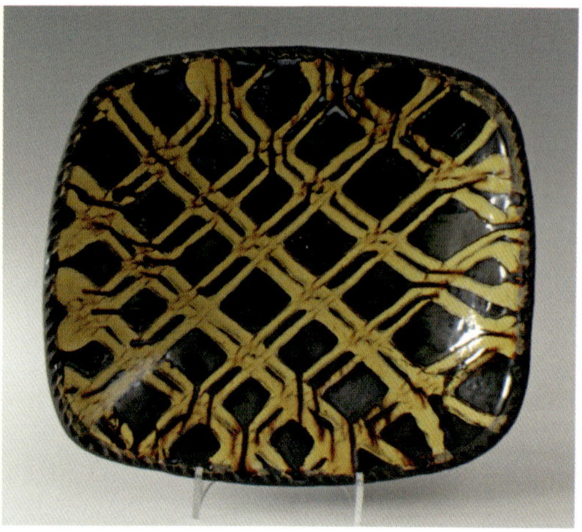

The potter Andrew McGarva has potted in the English, primarily earthenware tradition all his adult life, and after early researches into the tradition conducted with the help of David and Margaret Frith and other, he worked at Wobage with Mick and Sheila Casson, subsequently establishing his own workshop. The author of the book *Country Pottery* (A&C Black, 1990), he and his family current work and live at a country workshop in France.

I gather that you visited functional earthenware potteries such as Farnham whilst you were a student and love traditional making. What is it about these traditions that are so important to you?

Basically the design, because how tradition works is that all superfluous elements to the pots are honed down over the generations so that the pottery has a purity to it that there isn't anywhere else. When you are looking at 18th century wares, these are ones that they were making every day. I do a batch, and then I am off doing stoneware for a couple of months, every time trying to get back into it. To get it really spot on, you have got to have got to be doing it regularly, firing it regularly so that you are seeing what is coming through the process. The old pots give us the lesson – just don't get too complicated. Keep it simple – these are pots that are just complicated enough. It's also our heritage and I feel culturally that I come from England and that where I want to make my roots. We have the luxury of choice – some people want to make Korean pots, whilst I had rather make English ones.

How have you been able to pick up the necessary skills for your slip trailed hump moulded dishes?

Each one has to be made on a cloth, you have to have a whole lot of moulds which takes space. I have to fire them upside down so need a full set of proper pan rings, for either round or square dishes, so there is a whole lot of infrastructure, which is required. So it's the commitment to make them really all the way through in the way that I have to, to get the results. You can tell quite a lot by just looking at the old dishes, and saying 'why did they leave the edge unglazed, and which way is the glaze flowing, and why are they always curved. I tried some flat ones and they went concave: if you have an arch in a kiln, it stays up: that's why they are so clever – it comes from both the making and the visual side also. They work in the simplest way from that form, process, making and decorating, producing a good end result.

Colander (c. 1750-1850). Diameter 30cm.

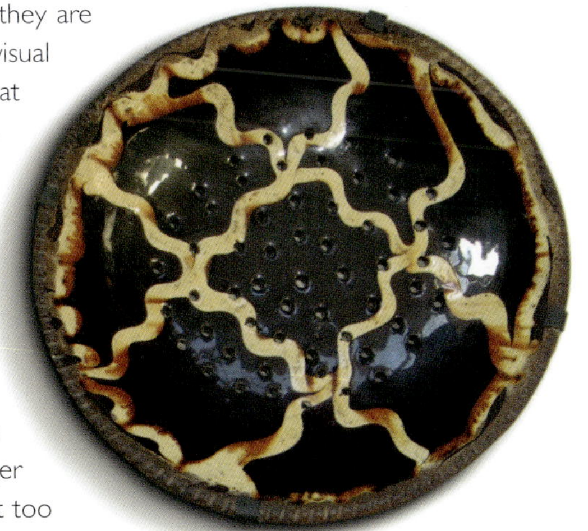

You sometimes refer to a particular dish as being 'juicy'; what are you referring to and is this down to a decorating or kiln process?

I like that extra drama when you have a bit of a flow to the glaze. The bleeding of the manganese gives you an extra dimension in the pot. The longer you fire, the more flow you get, but you don't want too much. Galena glazes are that much richer – you don't get the same result: the galena tends to soak it in so when its high fired the black slip tends to burn through, the white disappearing in places and just amalgamating with the glaze. I add a little iron to the glaze just to make it warmer.

I have noticed that you have a natural eye for decoration – why is decoration important to you and how much decoration is enough?

Well I started out making plainer things. I wanted to combine the qualities of slipware with the practicalities of French stonewares and make something new out of that, and the decorated ones sold better. Things develop and if you want to live by your craft, you have to sell it. Looking at the old pieces, dishes with cocks on and so on, they often used little space fillers just to accent the design, to fill in. The decoration doesn't have to be a literal depiction – they can be just abstract. But you have got to do it in one move, otherwise you will be lost. I tend to do a run of say three or four and try and get it better, second time around.

How do you know where to start drawing and trailing? I presume your dishes are humped and then decorated

No, everything is flat: you have to do it this way because otherwise it would all flow in as the slip is so liquid. Because they are mould made, you know that for a certain size of mould you need a certain size of slab, so you can actually make them quite accurately to fit within the edges: obviously you are going to cut the edge off when it's on the mould, but you have got parameters. Particularly with the feathered ones you want to see the change of direction. You have got to look at it and know that it's been done in one go: that's the whole game. When you look at old ones, there are always pairs of the trailed lines and you know it's been done in one continuous movement. When you put the whole thing on the mould, the whole thing skews: I try and get it right and then things happen. That part of the magic, sometimes things are just right...but it can be too perfect also...I quite like the humanity, where the things are quite perfect and have been allowed to follow the firing process, and have that freedom.

So do you set out to do a horse design say, with, I presume, seagulls

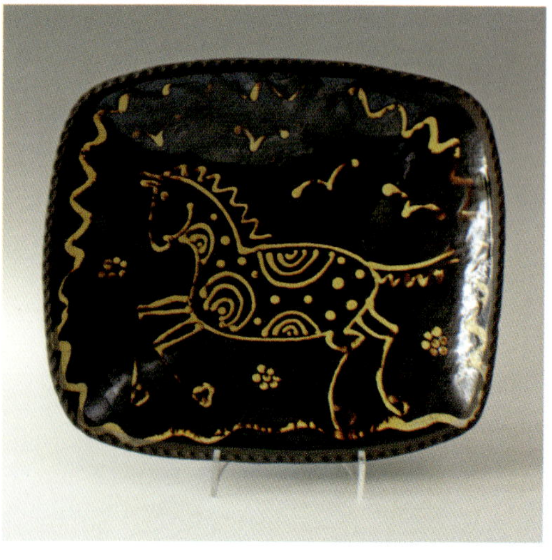

Yes, birds in the air and flowers below. Once you have done your main design, you have this big blank piece and I try and do a mix. With the painted pots over the years, I have tried to decorate less as it allows the shape of the piece to speak. But customers feel that they are getting their money worth with the surface filled. If you go to the trouble of making them in the right way, then they really ought to be decorated as they are not going to be valued if they are just plain. When I make them now, they are not everyday pie dishes, and they are deliberately made with feet so they are stable. The context in which they are made is changed, although they still have a function – when you put citrus fruit on them, they really stand out. The outside line holds and frames the whole thing, and they were also made for display on the dresser: if you own a dish like that, it means that you are a householder, and have power. On delft ware, the designs of the pots are making known your allegiances: people could understand your status from your display of things. And even on these you are saying 'Look I am making pies this big'. These are less formal than Toft and other wares made to order with a coat of arms or whatever – all the correct things.

POTS, CLAYS AND KILNS: A TECHNICAL AND AESTHETIC OVERVIEW BY PETER SMITH

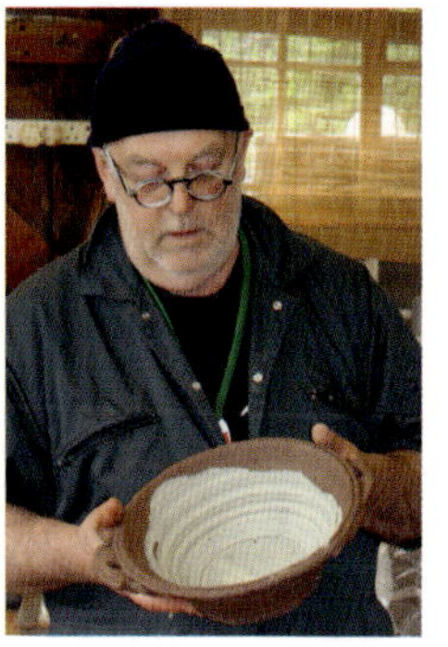

For those of you who have not come across Peter, he is probably one of the most original earthenware potters of his generation. He came to ceramics after attending an evening class and course with Robert and Sheila Fournier, and whilst a chemist and high temperature kiln specialist by training, he went on to produce original functional ceramics with a strong sculptural and textural flavour at his Pendeen, Cornwall workshop before concentrating on teaching, primarily at University College, Falmouth.

How did you unearth the information on Richard John Noall?

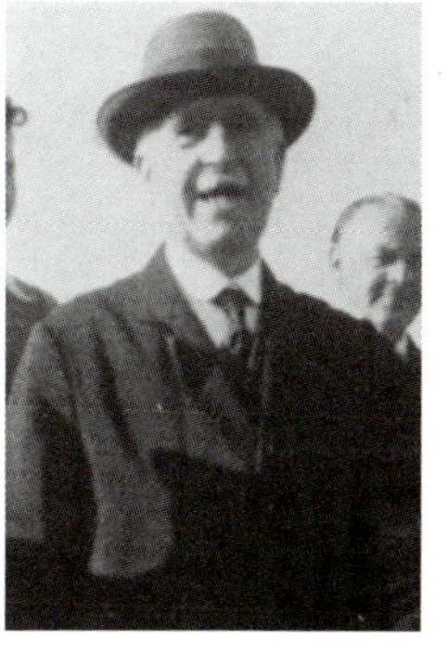

At a recent Leach Pottery show there was a fine hump-moulded dish by Hamada that caught the feel of English slipware perfectly. At the Penlee Museum a few weeks later, I saw a slipware dish on display that rang a bell – similar to the Hamada. The museum checked the provenance – it was given by RJ Noall in 1939. I researched Mr Noall and found that he lived just outside St Ives, virtually opposite the Leach Pottery until he died in 1944. Also he had a very good study collection of English pottery of the type Leach supported, the bulk of which he left to the RI in Truro. In fact part of the Noall collection was on show at the Pottery, including the Hamada dish. Noall was a well known antiquarian, and was an expert on early pottery, had trawled the fields for sherds and dug on sites. He is the man that Hamada mentions with the slipware in a cottage across the road. It is ironic or perhaps just desserts that part of his collection has finally re-appeared at the Leach Pottery, revealing a study collection on the 1920s doorstep and my Noall research continues!

You have given some valuable insights into the technical background of the early Leach Pottery

After we began to discuss technical aspects for your book, I researched the published side of Leach and Hamada looking for clues relating to the early period. Being in the area, I am familiar with the local materials that particularly interested Hamada, so the fired pot bodies for example look quite familiar to me and can be interpreted. It becomes obvious that Hamada came to St Ives with all the relevant technical skills and craft knowledge needed to start a far Eastern Pottery, and including local materials. Whilst it was Bernard who eventually codified the combined experience into A potter's book, it was Hamada who set the pottery direction in craft/aesthetic terms.

It is interesting to speculate what would have happened if Hamada had not come to St Ives. It is sure that the Pottery would have been very different (or not exist), possibly much more a Staite Murray kind of operation, but Bernard was used to having help. There would have be no informed driving force establishing production. Leach benefitted from three significant individuals in the early years, Hamada, Cardew and Matsubayashi, who in combination saw the Pottery through to a fully established production operation, with Hamada's aesthetic underlying it.

In 1923, the Hamada/Leach kiln needed to be fully rebuilt. From a study of available photographs, it was originally built in the casual Japanese manner which Hamada must have observed in Japan, since he mentioned forgetting to bring bamboo poles used to build the kiln roof. Leach mentions that Hamada formed blocks of unrefined china clay from Porthia with possibly some ball clay and fireclay in order to build the kiln. The blocks can clearly be seen in the photographs – also reclaimed bricks. So the 1920 kiln appears to be a mixture of fired and unfired material. Leach states that excessive use of wood caused the kiln to be corroded by ash glaze deposits – to the extent that holes appeared in the internal walls. He thought that they had used too much wood during the firings.

Rebuilding of firemouth of 1920 kiln using soft-fired cones (c. 1922).

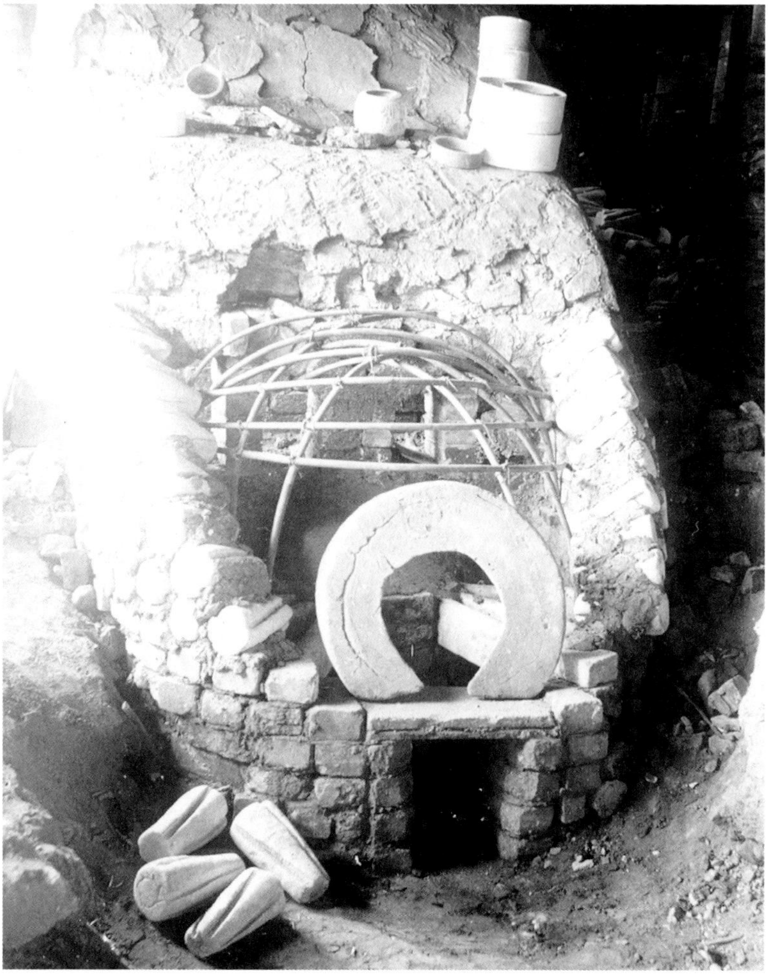

Coincidentally I use the non-clay sand and rock from china clay waste in my bodies – this material would have been in the unrefined china clay blocks formed by Hamada. In my bodies I use in excess of 30% of this material in various fractions from fine to coarse. Helping Peter Swanson to fire his anagama kiln, I made a stoneware piece with china clay material in the body, but unglazed. After firing, this piece ended up with a really thick overall glaze, including the base.

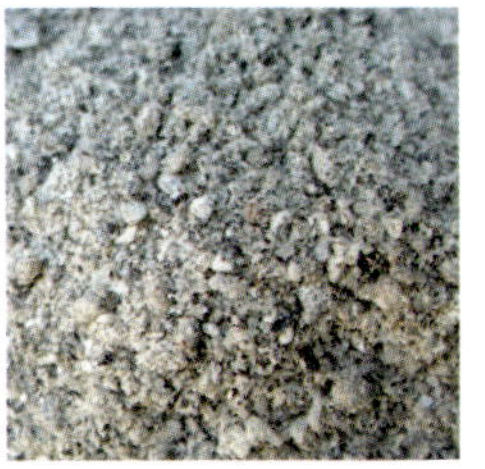

Raw china clay waste

This outcome made me think that a sodium/potassium vapour was generated in the high temperature wood firing, and that the vapour had in turn reacted with the china clay material, quartz, mica, feldspars and iron impurities to form a thick glaze. The china clay material is just waiting in the body for a flux (sodium/potassium) to appear in order to form a glaze. This china clay material is very effective for glaze production.

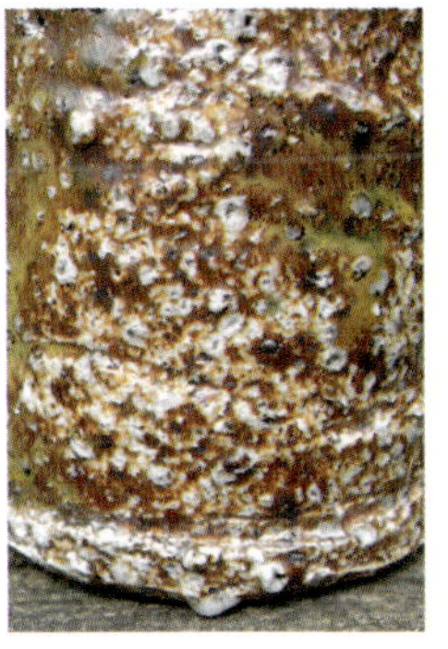

Anagama fired china clay body.

This effect explains why the first kiln in St Ives did not last since the same china clay material would react with vapour from the burning wood to form a thick glaze. This would be reinforced by subsequent firings. Hamada would not have known of this particular local material problem, nor would anybody else. If the kiln had been made of fireclay blocks then it would have survived much longer. So the kiln problem was an unfortunate and unforeseen consequence of the use of local materials. However, this failure brought Matsubayashi, who built a sophisticated kiln of mostly hard-fired brick. A professional job.

Subsequent tests in Peter Swanson's anagama kiln show the same outcomes, and I am hoping to assemble enough material to show the nature of vapour production in wood-burning kilns. It seems to me that the influence of Hamada is such that in the early days, the Leach workshop can be called Hamada's other Pottery, and his influence persisted until the Pottery closed. Hamada seems to be mentioned far more than Leach in conversations and publications today.

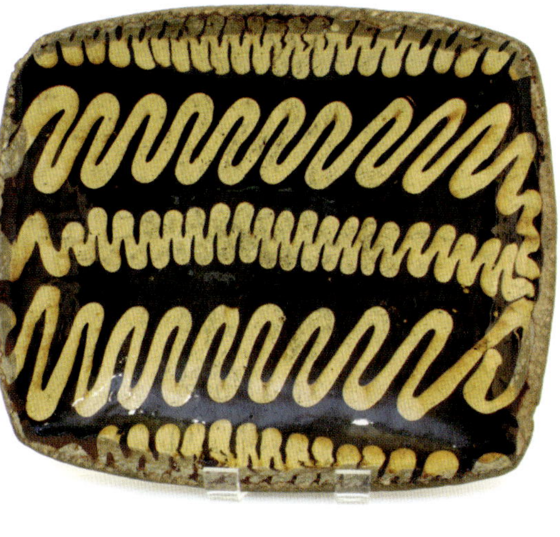

Hump-moulded and slip trailed dish (c. 1750-1850). Noall gift, Royal Cornwall Museum.

5 FIRING TECHNOLOGY AND THE SEARCH FOR THE 'ENGLISH TRADITION.':

AN ESSAY BY DR OLIVER KENT

A key element in the setting up of the pottery in St Ives was the conviction that an English ceramic tradition was ripe for revitalisation and Leach and Hamada brought with them an interest in English vernacular earthenwares, especially slipwares. Their starting points in Japan were inevitably the books available at the time. Leach mentions in particular Charles Lomax's *Quaint Old English Pottery*. Soetsu Yanagi had bought a copy in 1910 in Tokyo and was evidently excited by it. Pieces made in Japan by Leach include larger platters based on English slipwares that appear to be derived from its illustrations.

'My friend, the late Dr. Yanagi, with whom I was living, had a book... illustrating our pre-industrial earthenware – Lomax's *Quaint Old English Pottery* – which spoke to me with the warmth of blood relationship. So I set to work with a fresh impetus from home, in a technique which I knew, attempting to express something born rather than studied.' These pieces are fired in the Japanese manner and do not have the warm colour qualities of the English wares. The glazes are pale and slightly translucent, the slips reddish. To move on with them, one way or another, a more direct exploration of the source material was needed.

'When I returned to England in 1920 accompanied by Shoji Hamada, our first endeavour was to search for what remained of the English tradition. Books, museums and surviving country potteries, such as Truro, Verwood and Fremington were our chief sources of material.'

In *Towards a Standard* Leach draws attention to various types of Western ceramics that he feels fit his requirement for beauty emerging 'from a fusion of the individual character and culture of the potter with the nature of his materials – clay, pigment, glaze – and his management of the fire.' West Country representatives amongst his illustrations is a classic 'present day' pitcher from Lake's Cornish Pottery – 'sound form and good craftsmanship unchanged since the 18th century' – and a line drawing of a Fremington oval sgraffito-decorated dish. These are accompanied by two medieval slip-decorated jugs from London museum collections; one from Mill Green in Essex and the other from Cheam in Surrey.The juxtaposition of the Lake's and Cheam jugs on the same page is not accidental, drawing attention as it does to the similarity of form and the strength of the handles and the red slip decoration. It serves to suggest that the Cornish jug is in a long

English tradition of unselfconsciously made vessel form. The Mill Green jug is, relatively unusually for a medieval jug, decorated with combed sgraffito lines through a white slip, linking it in a similar way to the Fremington pie-dish. The key characteristics of these thrown forms are evident in many of those made at St Ives and especially in the Standard Wares – the Mill Green jug is the ancestor of the Leach Pottery tankard. The relevance of these pieces here is that they reaffirmed for Leach the long established nature of English pottery tradition and particularly the tradition of slip decoration.

This exploration was driven initially by an interest in the forms, glazes and decoration of the English wares; wares selected according to a particular view of what the English tradition might be. The visits to Lake's Cornish Pottery in Truro in particular seem to have had a strong influence, in part because of the welcoming attitude of the potters there. The nature of the resulting interaction is one of technology as much as design, especially so since these potters made little use of slips. The other major influence on the pots that they made came from the direct exploration of unfamiliar vernacular slipwares that they found in local houses, as sherds in the fields and ultimately in junkshops and salerooms.

An admiration for English pottery was not enough. The technology needed to be identified and explored in order to fully understand it as makers. When Leach and Hamada took up residence in St Ives their knowledge of making and firing technology was more or less entirely derived from Japan. A fine raku bottle by Hamada in the Potteries Museum and Art Gallery collection in red clay with a white slip under a clear glaze carries a paper label which reads 'Bernard Leach 1st Baking. B.320. Hamada Oct, 11, 1921.' (ref. 159/18169). The palette and physical quality of this piece is very close to the Leach slipware pieces made in Japan. The clear lead glaze is the same Kenzan glaze found on all the St Ives raku pieces; pale very slightly cloudy, crazing heavily and working well with slips or underglaze colour. Leach gives a recipe for a raku glaze derived from the *Sano Densho* in *A Potter's Book* that is presumably the one used on these pieces.

The raku produced by Leach at this time was carried out in the traditional Japanese way, glazed pots fired in a simple kiln and removed with tongs hot from the fire, to cool in air or water (the sawdust and smoke of the process popular amongst studio potters today originated in the USA in the 1960s). In Japanese tradition raku is essentially a term for earthenware. Instructions for building such a kiln are provided by Kenzan I in the *Sano Densho*. There are drawings of two including a portable one in his *Sano Kenzan Diaries* diary written in 1737 (Fig 1). These designs consist of a small round wood or charcoal-fired updraught kiln within which is a muffle, a ceramic container for the wares, which screened them from the flame and the kiln atmosphere.

(Re-drawn by Oliver Kent).

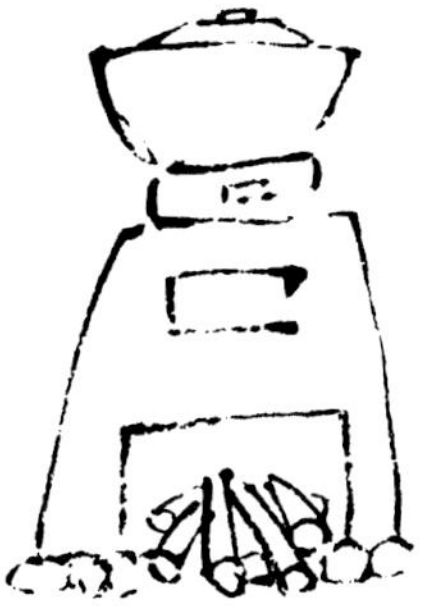

Kenzan talks about a space two fingers wide between the muffle and the kiln walls to allow the flame to pass. A door in the roof allows the potter to remove and replace pots during the firing.

Fig 2.

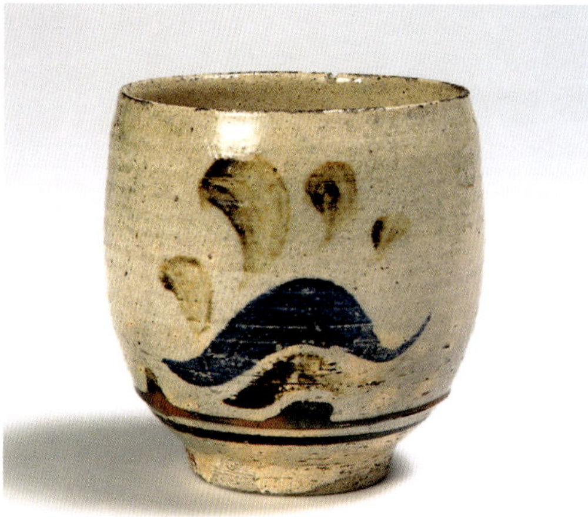

Leach and Hamada concluded that raku was unsuited to the English environment and it is clear that production was primarily for the purpose of attracting visitors to the pottery and entertaining them in the hope of selling ware (Fig 2). They began experiments with galena glazes on local clay, aided by knowledge of the methods used at Lake's. According to Hamada, some of the large lead-glazed dishes were made in the small biscuit kiln that they had built even before the original climbing kiln.

Although they had built the latter two-chamber kiln in 1920, problems with it lead them to turn to Japan for assistance and by May 1924 Tsuranosuke Matsubayashi had constructed a three-chamber kiln for them. The large kiln could in theory fire stoneware, earthenware and biscuit in different chambers, with careful firing. Cardew's description of the first firing in his biography records the failure of this process.The earlier raku kiln was also replaced with a new up-draught kiln for firing both earthenware and raku. This kiln is illustrated on a flyer for the Leach Pottery dating from around 1927, which shows a raku firing in progress (Fig 3). The woodblock print on the flyer shows the Matsubayashi three-chamber stoneware kiln in the background and places the raku/earthenware kiln in the corner of the kiln room where an up-draught kiln still stands to this day. It is clear from the photographs in the Leach Pottery collection that this kiln was also built by Matsubayashi, probably in 1925 (Fig 4).

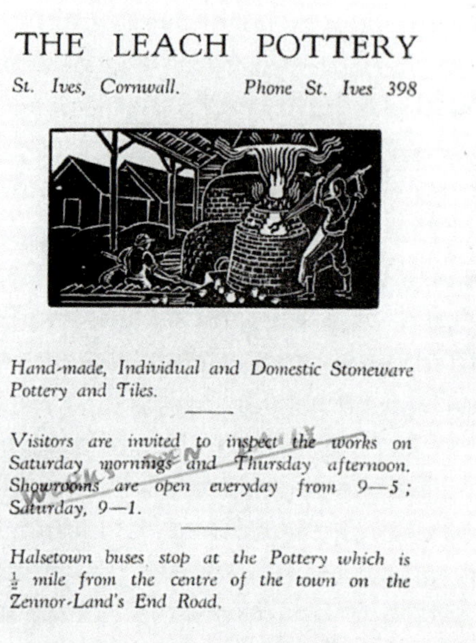

THE LEACH POTTERY

St. Ives, Cornwall. *Phone St. Ives 398*

Hand-made, Individual and Domestic Stoneware Pottery and Tiles.

Visitors are invited to inspect the works on Saturday mornings and Thursday afternoon. Showrooms are open everyday from 9—5; Saturday, 9—1.

Halsetown buses stop at the Pottery which is ½ mile from the centre of the town on the Zennor-Land's End Road.

Fig 3.

'we had a round kiln, about a yard in diameter inside and a yard in height… We also fired our glazed raku ware in this same round kiln, which was also used for the somewhat greater heat of English slipware, about 1000°C. This slipware was packed on perforated triangular shelves, tier upon tier, leaving something like a two-inch gap on the outside for the flames to rise to the top. The temperature at the top was a full one

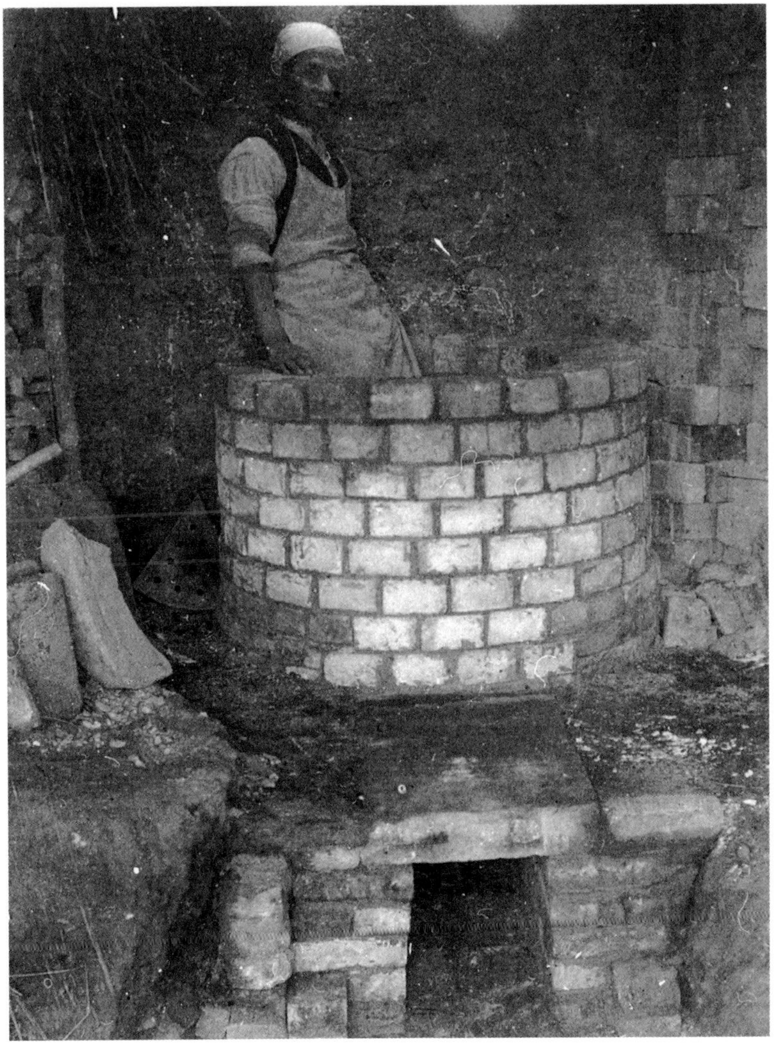

Fig 4. Matsu and the built shell of 1925 up-draught kiln.

hundred degrees lower than at the bottom, and it was on the top that the raku ware was fired.'

This kiln is interesting in combining ideas from both Japan and England. The St Ives kiln was larger than the Japanese up-draught raku kilns and not used in the conventional way. As illustrated in *A Potter's Book*, the kiln had elaborate perforated kiln shelves supported by props, a hood above to aid draught and a firebox with a grate and enclosing doors. This technical cross-over, however practically unsuccessful – temperature control was difficult and exploding raku pots were apt to shower shards onto the slipwares below them – provides a kind of metaphor for the 'meeting of East and West' that Leach in particular sought.

This kiln design is not one taken from the textbook or copied from some existing model. It is evidently the product of research and the exploration of the technology of the local potteries. Key seems to have been Lake's Pottery in Truro where Leach, Hamada, Cardew and Matsubayashi had all been made welcome. Michael Cardew's arrival at the pottery in 1923 had also brought his existing knowledge and contacts.

Cardew may not have listened attentively to Matsubayashi's lectures on chemistry but practical matters were much more to his taste. As he describes them in his autobiography, the visits he made to small potteries were always characterised by hands-on engagement with processes and activities. He tried out the wheels and made arrangements to be taught throwing; he arranged to stay to watch the packing and to take part in the firing of kilns. The influence of William Fishley Holland who provided throwing lessons for three weeks in 1921 is often cited. In practice it seems that it was Holland's successor at Braunton Fred Luscombe who allowed him to practice in the evenings when the working day was over and to keep his own wheel there. Whilst at St Ives, Cardew continued to explore. He visited the Burgess Hill Pottery in Sussex in 1925 and found the inactive Greet Pottery at Winchcombe. Once he had made the decision in 1926 to commit to starting up on his own, he set about exploring further and in more detail, persuading the Sims at the Cross Roads Pottery in Verwood and Mr Collins at Lake's to allow him to participate in firings. Verwood was quite different from the potteries he had so far seen, remote and operating with essentially pre-industrial technology. It is interesting that he turned to Mr Collins at Lake's for advice when he was in the process of deciding whether to buy the pottery at Winchcombe. It is clear that he interacted closely with Matsubayashi during the building of the kilns and his awareness of the design and operation of the Fremington and Braunton kilns must have been useful.

Hamada took careful note of local pottery that he saw in use and in the markets and shops and attracted by simple lead-glazed pitchers which he was told came from Truro, he early on visited Lake's pottery there where he was able to observe practical details of making, glazing and firing.

'There they used old hand-cranked, pulley-driven wheels and simple bottle (updraught) kilns, more than six feet in diameter and about fifteen feet in height. They used neither shelves nor saggers but piled up the pitchers in the kiln, using pieces of slate as shelves and supports. They used bundles of gorse as fuel.'

Lake's kiln was not in fact a true bottle-kiln but a hybrid converted in the 1870s from an open-topped kiln by adding a conical structure to its rim. In its original form it probably resembled the open-topped kilns in use at

Verwood in Hampshire and visited by Cardew. The purpose of the added structure at Lake's was to improve the draw and to lessen the difference in temperature between bottom and top. But whereas in a true bottle-kiln the cone sits above a shallow perforated dome that encloses the ware chamber below, Lake's kiln lacked the internal dome, the pots being covered with tiles and shards during firing just as they had been before. This is in effect a pre-industrial kiln amended by the addition of some more modern design elements, including the provision of grates and ash-pits in the fireboxes. Despite Hamada's description of the kiln as fired with furze, these fireboxes were designed for coal and the firebars were removed late in the firing to allow finishing with furze. Cardew describes this process at Lake's and records that a similar firing method was used at the Fremington Pottery. The kilns at Fremington, Braunton and Winchcombe were all standard bottle-kilns although the precise methods of firing varied (Fig 5).

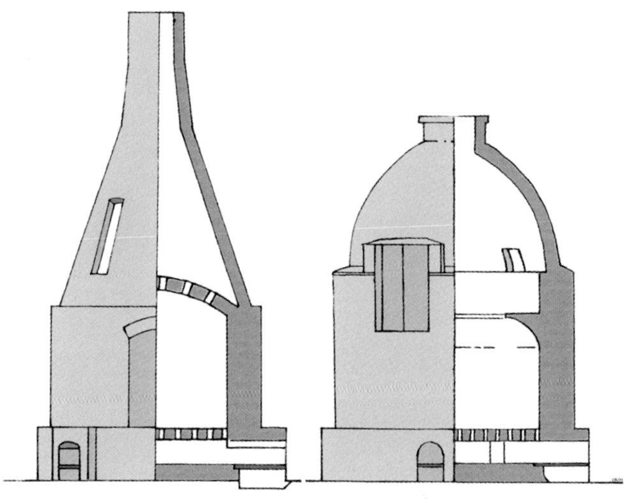

Fig 5. Winchcombe (left) and Truro kilns (drawn by Oliver Kent).

The 'top-loader' design of the Lake's kiln has a resonance with the Japanese raku kilns – a giant version with potters climbing in and out from above to load and unload the wares. The core elements of the Japanese kiln are there, a simple firebox, a perforated floor, a ware chamber with access from above. Although in *A Potter's Book*, Leach lumps the kilns at Winchcombe and Truro together as of the 'old English bottle-neck type,' it is the distinctive, pre-industrial, open-topped form of the Lake's kiln which the St Ives updraught kiln design most clearly references. As the illustration in *A Potter's Book* shows, the protective muffle used in the Japanese raku kiln to protect the pots from the direct action of the flame was abandoned. The pots are instead allowed to sit in the flame, but rather than stack them up one on another as at Lake's, perforated shelves are used to separate them. The firebox design is very similar to that used at Lake's as is the use of a perforated floor, a loose brick dome over the ware and a conical hood to assist the draw and take away fumes and smoke from the kiln shed. The coal firebox design is also shown in George Cox's *Pottery for Artists, Craftsmen and Teachers* published in 1914, one of the few handbooks recommended by Leach in *A Potter's Book* (Fig 6).

Fig 6.

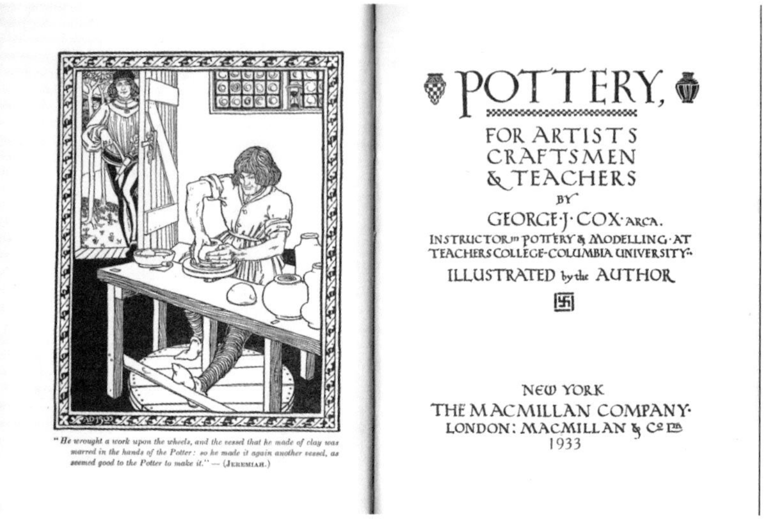

It is important not to see this design as an attempt to build an authentic 'folk' kiln. It is more an adaption of the Japanese earthenware kiln to new requirements, using aspects of what the St Ives potters had learnt in exploring the technology of the local potteries. Lake's and the Verwood kilns were unusual in being rooted in pre-industrial practices but it is unlikely that Bill Lake and his men could articulate that. The bottle kilns used by the majority of small potteries were industrial designs, usually built by professional kiln builders like the Pennys from Bristol. The modifications to Lake's kiln were probably done by one of these firms. Cox's book provides sound designs for small kilns that Leach and Hamada could have used but they chose not to. What the St Ives potters seem to be doing is exploring principles. This is learning by doing and the debate over the inconsistencies of firing atmosphere and fuel types is very much a part of that learning process.

At St Ives, despite difficulties obtaining fuel, the coal and furze model of the local potters was not taken up and the kilns were always fired with wood in the early days (conversion to oil firing came later). In retaining a preference for wood, Japanese experience was probably a factor, but the main reason was aesthetic. Lake's pots are notable for the flashing of the exposed body and irregular glaze colours that result from their direct contact with the coal and furze flame and ash. This was a consequence of inconsistent oxidising, reducing and re-oxidising conditions within the kiln and produced variations from oranges and yellows to greens and greys on glazed surfaces. It has been suggested that the characteristic yellow speckling found on some pieces, may result from contact with furze ash in the latter part of the firing. Closed saggers like those used at Braunton and in most industrial potteries at the time, would have maintained consistency but experience had show that the sulphur in the traditional country potters' galena glazes benefited from the free atmosphere of the kiln to burn off successfully.

Leach makes it clear that the irregularities that are so characteristic of the Lake's wares were too extreme to be appreciated on his slipwares. He wanted enough variation to give the glaze character but no more. This in effect is a dissonance between the search for a tradition and the experience of it. The reduced olive greens of the Lake's jugs are in harmony with medieval technology and colour rather than the post-medieval slipwares.

This calculatedly allowed the kiln atmosphere and the ash to affect the ware. The *Tree of Life* dish in the V&A collection, which is dated 1923, has Lakes-style flashes of reduced grey-green from irregular firing and may be an example of the early consequences of this decision (Fig 7). Later pieces are more controlled and the subtle variations in colour are not so intrusive. The open interior of the St Ives earthenware kiln reflects an oriental appreciation of the action of the flame whilst the use of wood, together with a growing experience of the firing process, avoids the perceived excesses of the Truro model. Clive Bowen, in firing lead-glazed earthenware today, talks about his love for the natural variation in the glaze and body colours from his wood-fired kiln at Shebbear. Ray Finch enjoys the golden speckles that sometimes appear on the Winchcombe tenmoku glazes when the wood ash settles on them.

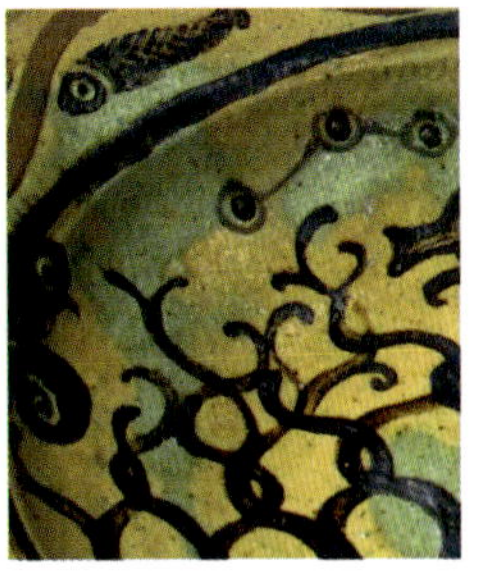

Fig 7.

The active exploration of the regional pottery-making practices of the South West of England provided the St Ives potters with a basis with which to construct a practical model of an English tradition. This was combined with an awareness of aspects of a wider British history of vernacular ceramics especially the slipwares of the Midlands and Wales built up through practical as well as visual research. The model they built does not entirely equate with ceramic history but was enough to provide them with a foothold with which to begin to work on the process of revitalisation as they saw it.

Earthenware and slipware production at the Leach Pottery had more of less ceased by 1938 and was not ever taken up again in any serious way. Exploration had been replaced by synthesis. The process of exploring the regional traditions of form and decoration had left their mark and the echoes can be seen the especially amongst the more utilitarian wares.

The Standard Ware jugs and tankards reference straight back to the Mill Green medieval jugs, fitted with pulled handles and the tankards with Fishley curled ends. Unglazed surfaces contrast with rich celadon and tenmoku glazes made from locally available materials. The power of the St Ives designs and the Potter's Book ethos is such that the same forms can be seen again and again amongst the canon of studio domestic-ware makers who often seem to regard them as traditional rather than a distillation of traditions – what jugs, tankards and mugs should look like.

Michael Cardew medieval style jug, St Ives (c. 1925). 22 x 19cm.

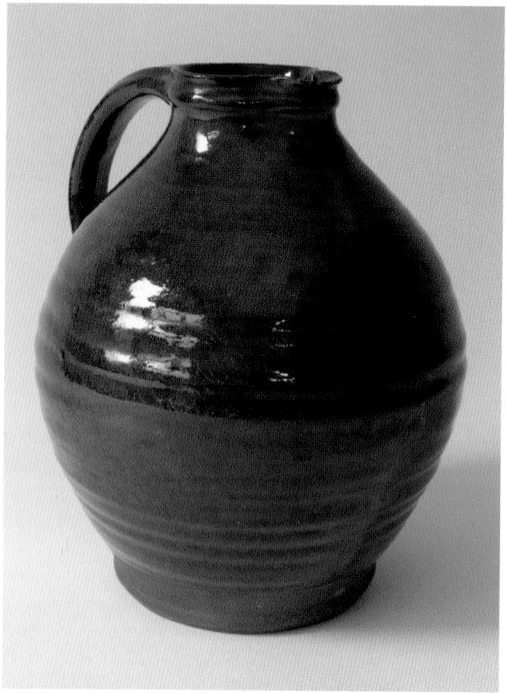

For Cardew the exploration of earthenware technology lead him to Winchcombe and resulted in a continuing thread which is currently most clearly visible in the work of Clive Bowen. The kiln that Clive uses is a direct descendent of that at Winchcombe albeit modified through Cardew's wider experience by providing a second chamber. For Hamada and other Japanese potters the slip itself is the lasting element. Hamada arguably took the lessons learned most fully into his mature work, building on the simple graphic possibilities of wet slip, blending East and West effortlessly. He seems to have looked closely at the Buckley-style trailed wares with their dark grounds rather than the yellow combed ones and taken in the freedom of drawing in the wet slip with a finger or a simple tool. Sometimes there is an obvious parallel but more often it is the spirit of the older pieces that is evident whether in earthenware or stoneware. The wet finger squiggle running across a dish or down the wall of a bottle provides a direct reference all the way back to the Fremington pie-dishes and the Mill Green jugs in the London Museum.

Bibliography:

Brears, Peter C. D., 1972, *'Techniques of the Truro Pottery,'* Folk Life, 10, 47-54.

Cardew, Michael, 1988, *Michael Cardew: A Pioneer Potter. An Autobiography*, London: Collins

Cox, George J., 1914, *Pottery, for Artists, Craftsmen and Teachers*, London: MacMillan.

Dawson, D. and Kent, O, 2008, *'The development of the bottle kiln in pottery manufacture in Britain,'* Post-Medieval Archaeology, 42, 1, 201-226.

De Waal, Edmund, 1998, *Bernard Leach. St Ives Artists*, London: Tate Gallery

Edgeler, John, 2008, *The Fishleys of Fremington: A Devon Slipware Tradition*, Winchcombe: Cotswold Living Publications

Kent, Oliver, 2006, *'The Account Book of Thomas and George Penny, Kiln Builders of Bristol 1882 – 1923,'* Bristol and Avon Archaeology, 21, (2006), 85-89.

Leach, Bernard, 1940, *A Potter's Book*, London: Faber & Faber.

Leach, Bernard, 1966, *Kenzan and his Tradition. The Lives and Times of Koetsu, Sotatsu, Korin and Kenzan*, London: Faber & Faber

Leach, Bernard, 1967, *Bernard Leach: A Potter's Work*, London: Adams & Dart

Leach, Bernard, 1976, *Hamada Potter*, London: Thames & Hudson

Lomax, Charles J., 1909, *Quaint Old English Pottery*, London: Sheratt and Hughes

McGarva, Andrew, 2000, *Country Pottery; Traditional Earthenware of Britain*, London: A & C Black

Olsen, Fred., 1983, (2nd ed), *The Kiln Book, materials, specifications and construction*, London: A & C Black.

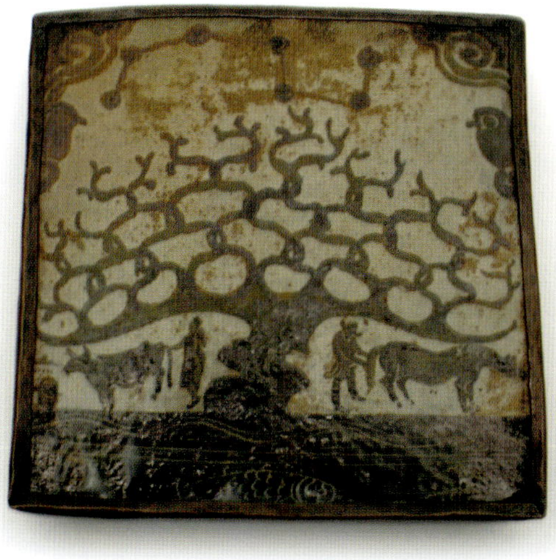

Teapot stand (c. 1927).
16 x 16 x 3cm.

6 APPENDICES

AN ANALYSIS OF POTS, CLAY BODIES AND MARKS

Making an educated guess from known information, throwing clays used for slipware were based around mixes of red St Erth, cream Porthia china clay sieved to various degrees of fineness and ball clay from Devon or Dorset, with the proportions changed to fit variable temperatures, the form in question and colour finish required. Some were also watered down as slips, both to change the apparent body colour and for under-glaze trailed and brushed decoration.

There follows a chronological illustrated analysis of pottery output at both St Ives and Dartington, with in each case a specimen image of a representative form accompanied by close-ups of the body and mark and supported by a brief commentary

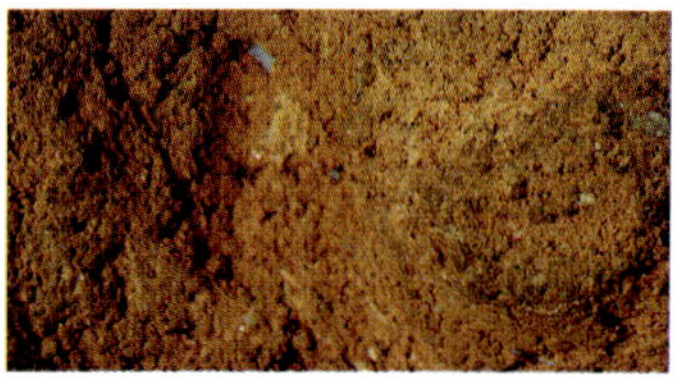

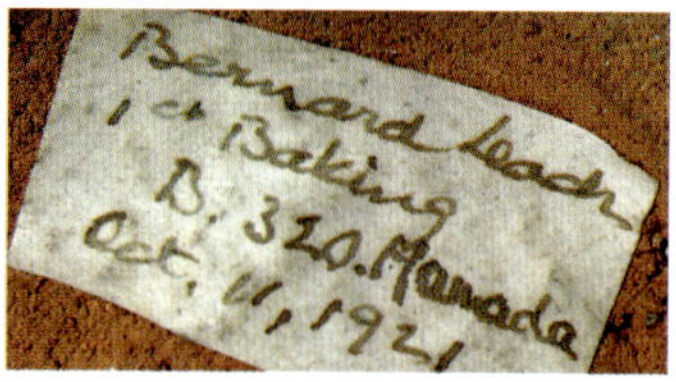

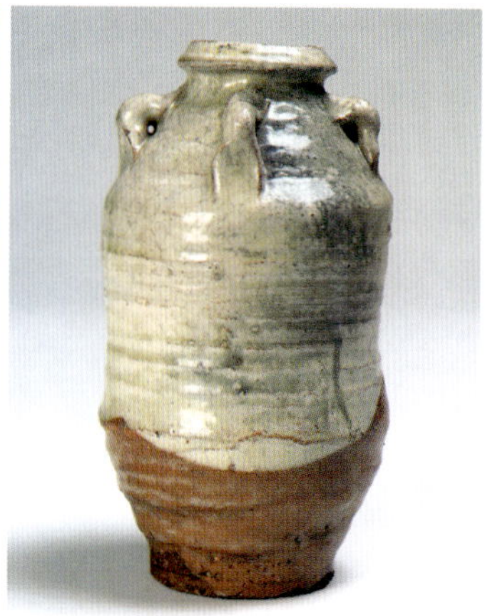

This coarse body was used in the earliest firings in the Autumn of 1921 and contained a high proportion of raw china clay. Pots of this type researched are not usually seal marked but bear a label. Some examples seen have their bases ground down presumably to avoid the scratching of polished surfaces in later use. The coarseness of the earliest clays is no doubt a reflection of Hamada's caution in developing bodies to cope with an unpredictable new kiln.

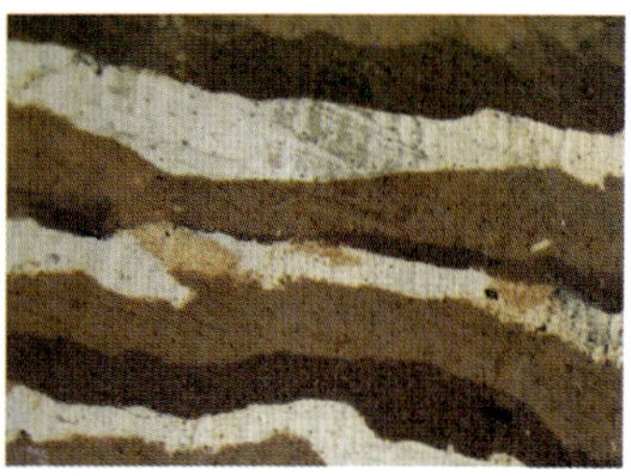

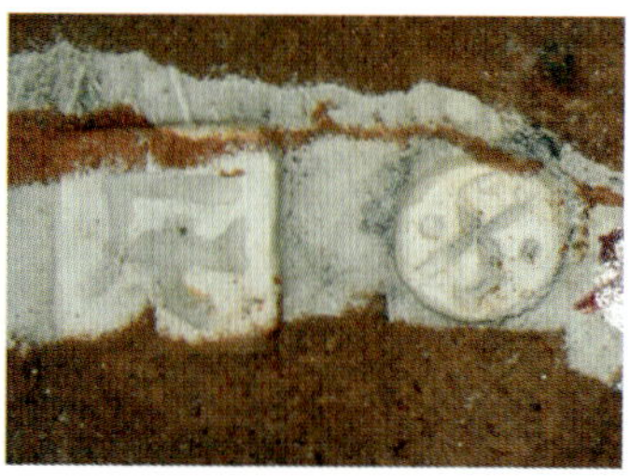

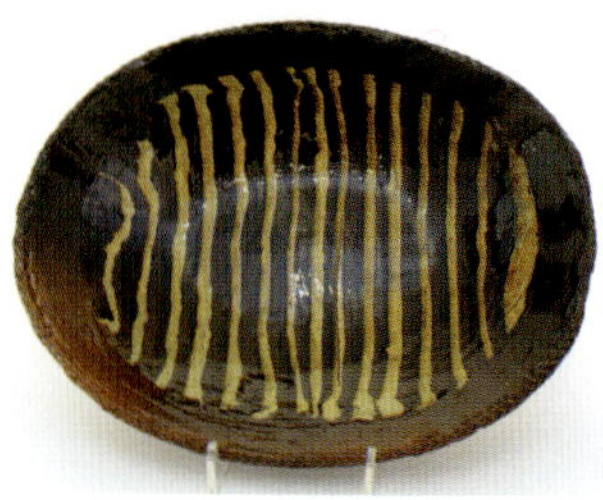

Hamada conducted trials of mixed clay moulded dishes in 1922, a technique called Neriage in Japan (syn. Agate ware) which are interesting as they show the grades of clay then available. The red layers no doubt contained some St Erth clay, and the white or cream either ball clay or sieved china clay. The latter medium was also used on its own in raku-style and higher-fired wares (see below).

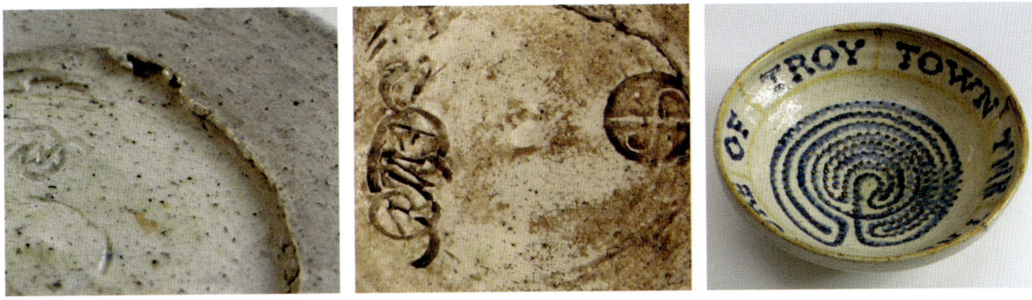

This raku-style body appears to have been created from a mixture of well sieved raw china clay with a proportion of white ball clay to aid throwing. The cracking seen is more likely to be due to turning on the wheel rather than occurring during drying. The medium was used by Hamada in Autumn 1922 for pieces decorated by RM Nance whose cursive initials they bear. The coarse nature of the local china clay used would have permitted a wide firing range of 900 – 1100 degrees, so ideal for an unpredictable kiln. A similar medium was employed for large and small turned and thrown platters and chargers.

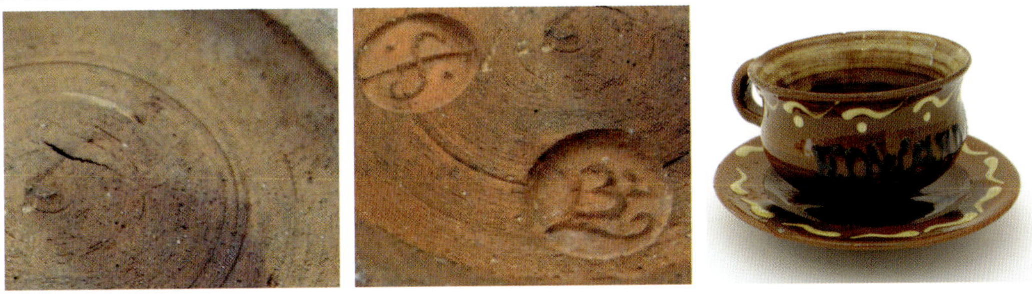

Relatively few pieces of handled standing form can be firmly attributed to Leach as maker in the early years. This cup and saucer made in around 1922 for Old Bassett, a friend of Leach and Hamada exhibits a relatively open textured red clay, possibly the 'brown bread' medium that Leach referred to in writings. A noticeably finer body than the example from 1921 above, with less raw china clay in the mix suggesting that Leach and Hamada were getting accustomed to the variability of the kiln.

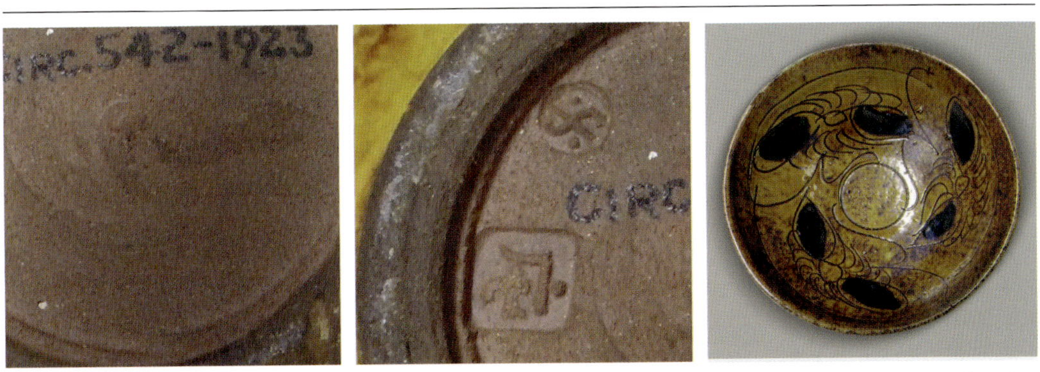

This footed bowl by Hamada, a form also seen in stoneware, shows a fine red earthenware throwing clay, as is evidenced by the clear impressed SI and personal seals.

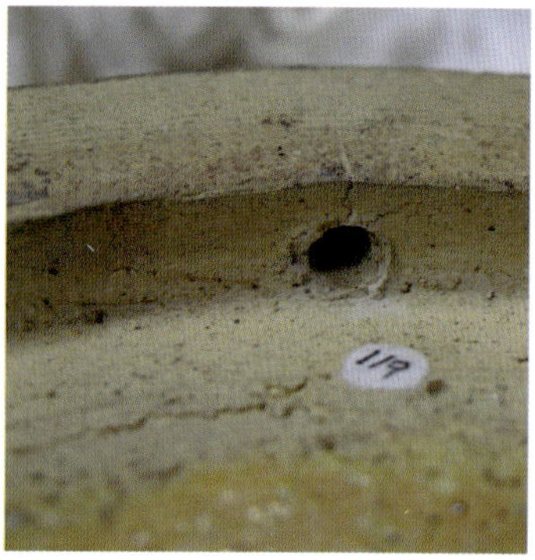
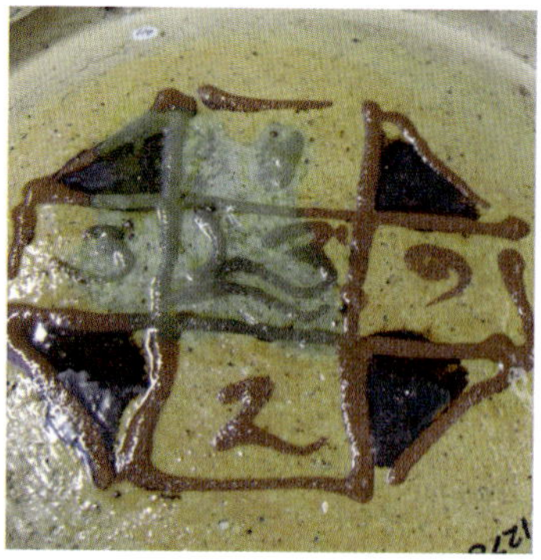
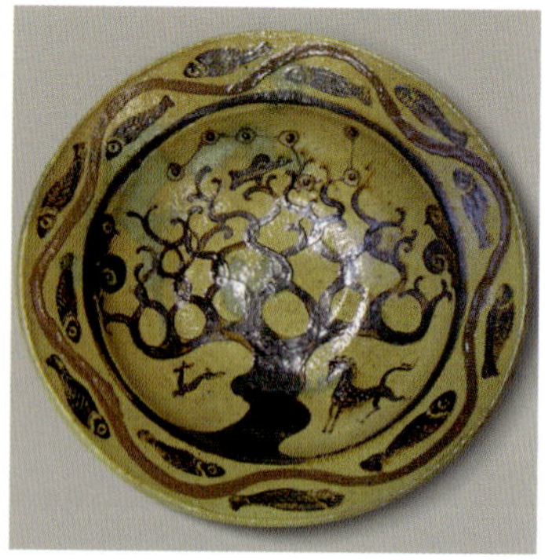

This large charger thrown over a former fixed to the wheel-head by Hamada prior to decoration by Leach is multiply interesting. It shows a further use of the raku-style medium of 1922 but here more highly fired. We believe it was biscuit-fired after decoration and then carefully glaze-fired in the upper chamber of the climbing kiln, seated on its foot rim rather than upside down as was usual. The greenish patches indicate temperature variation during firing, consistent with Leach's recollection of individually stoking one chamber and the importance and quality of this pot.

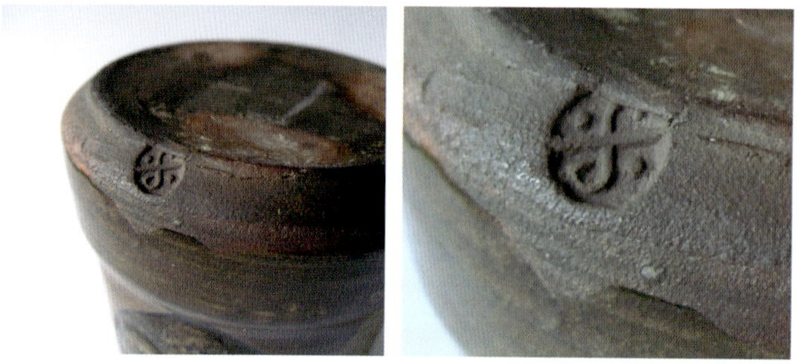
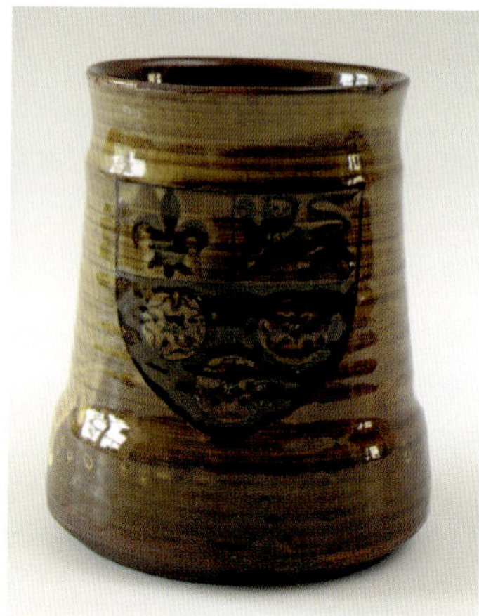

This early Cardew tankard of circa 1924 thrown to a Leach design shows a well thrown form in a finer sieved medium, probably St Erth with ball clay in the mix, sufficient to allow fine sgraffito work to the body. The base bears pad marks from its firing.

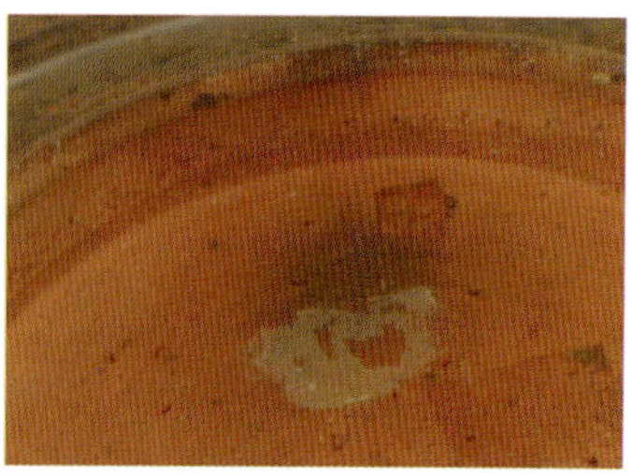
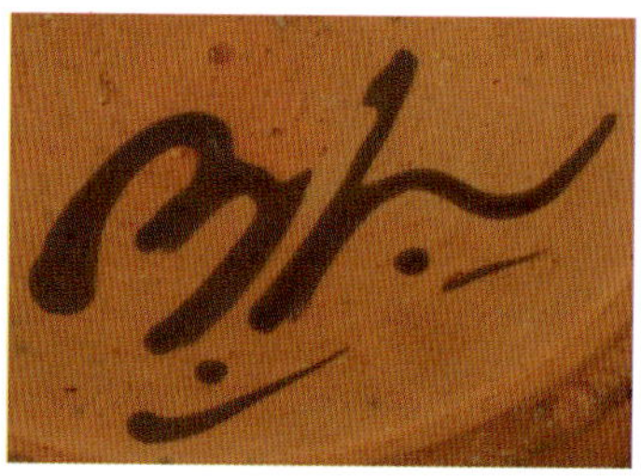
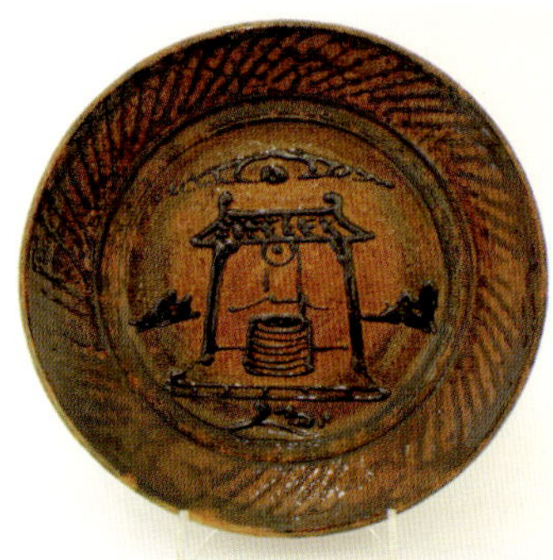

This charger from circa 1925 was probably wheel thrown by Cardew, using a slightly grittier medium. It bears a small square SI seal and the brushwork initials of Leach as decorator.

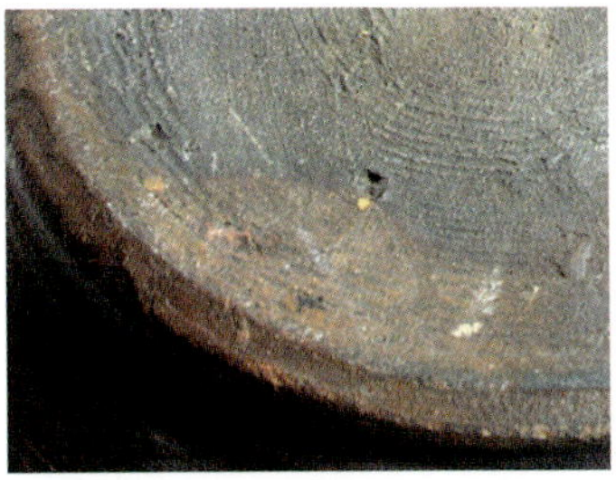
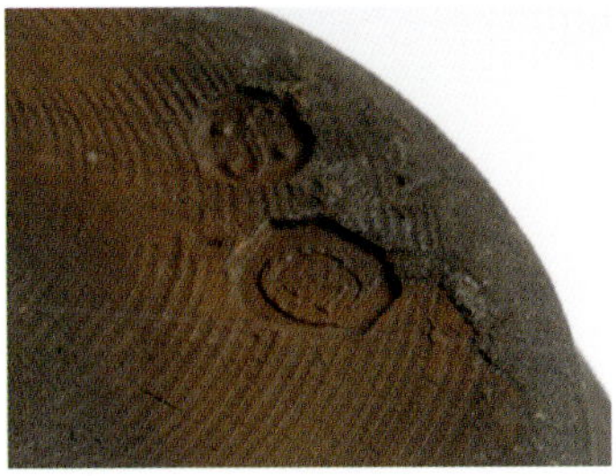
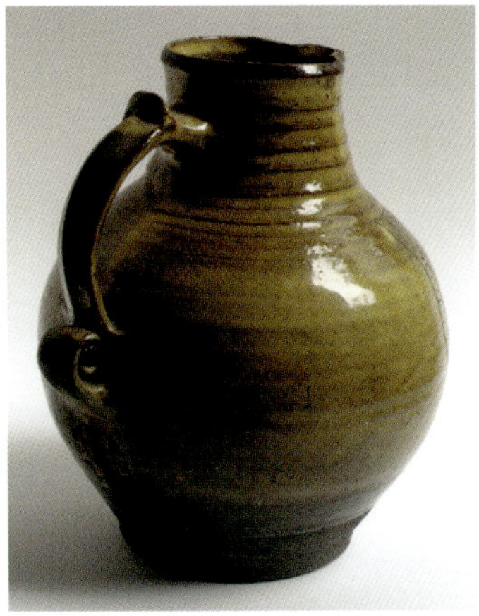

This well thrown jug bears Cardew's seal as thrower and the incised monogram of Leach as designer to the side of the body together with the date 1926. The clean appearance of this excellent example was probably fired in the new Matsu kiln, and indeed slipwares of 1925-1926 appear to have been more consistently fired.

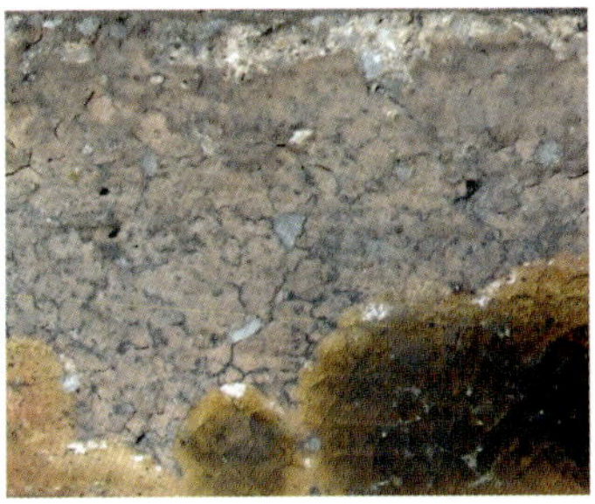
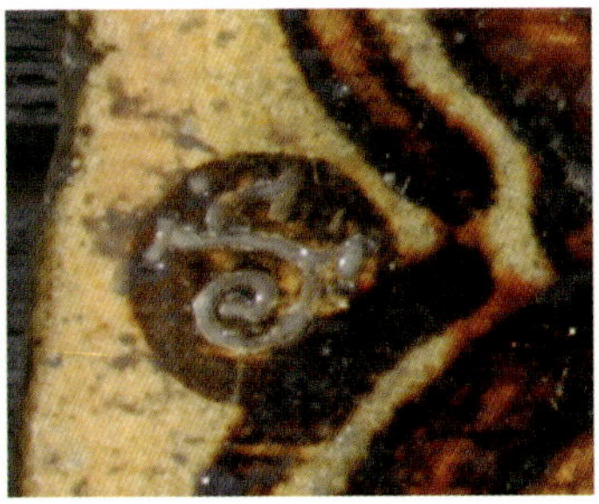
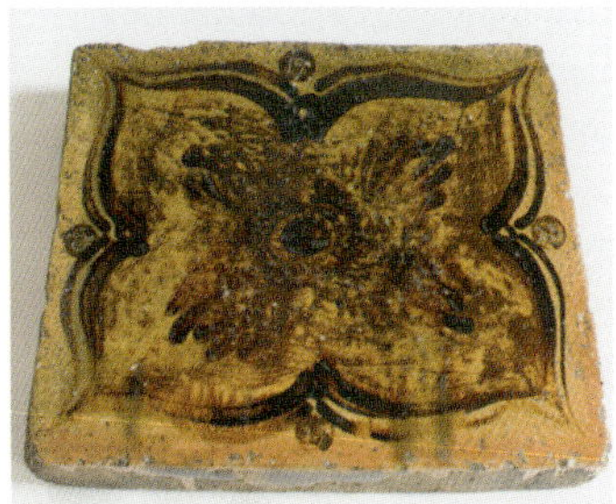

This one-off tile dated 1925 bears round black circles to its side consistent with it having been fired on a perforated kiln shelf. The clay medium is a form of fireclay which may have been brought in from further afield. We believe that Leach chose to decorate as a commemorative item of the 1st firing of the new Matsu kiln, one of several heavy kiln shelves fired for subsequent use in this kiln, as a test piece of his usual brushwork and glaze.

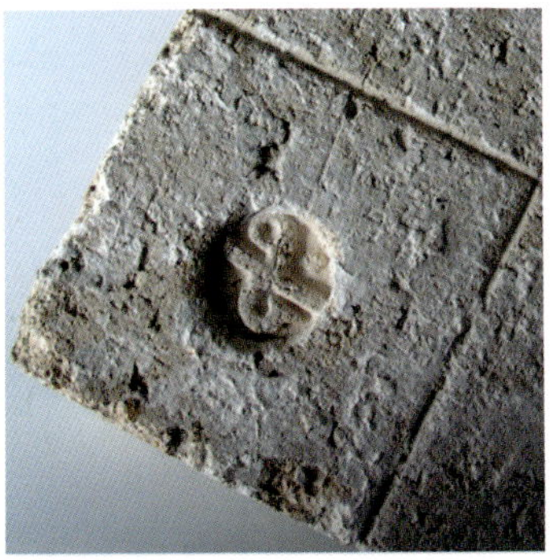
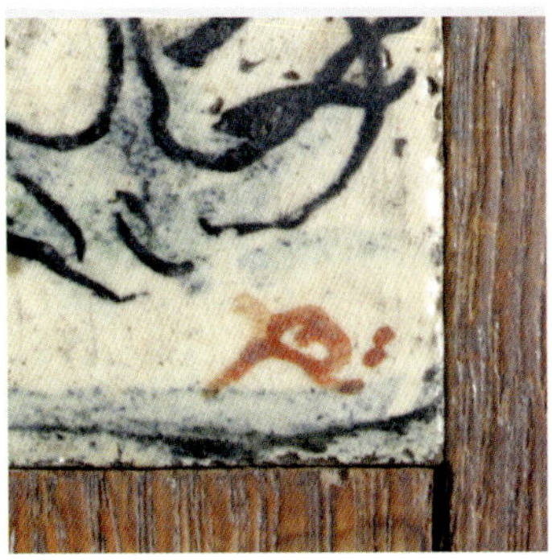
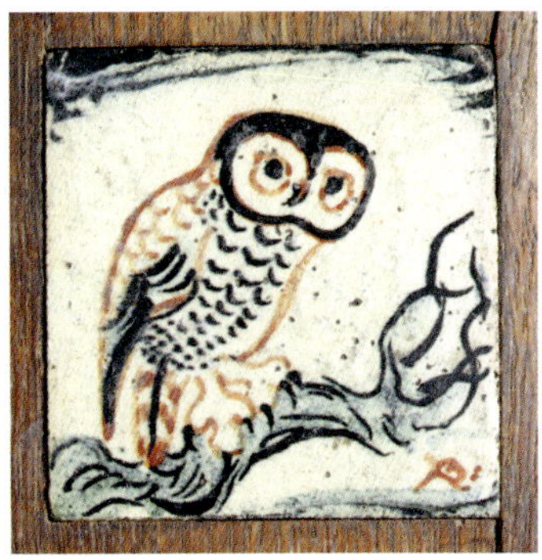

This unusual low-fired tile sits in an oak frame probably made by Dicon Nance, and is made of a chalky white medium. The back bears multiple SI seals similar to those of stoneware tiles of the period, although the fine crazing to the lead-rich glaze and freshness of the colours indicates an earthenware firing.

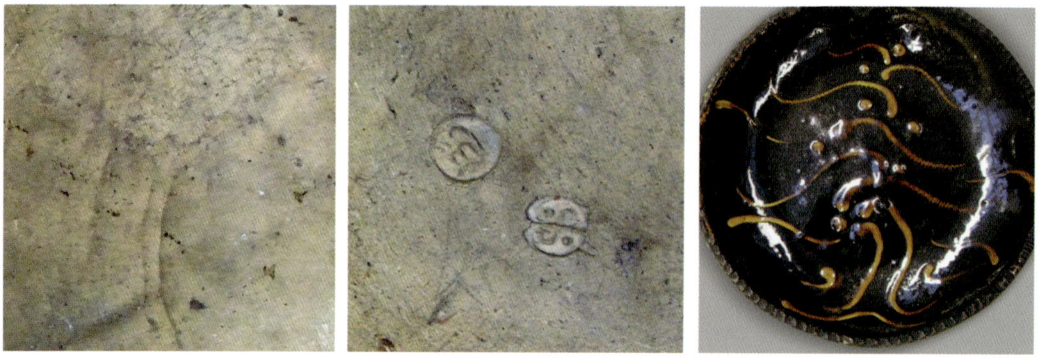

The first of a group of hump-moulded dishes made from circa 1930 using various fabrics, its dark finish disguises a pale cream body made of a fine and dense medium, probably well-sieved china clay with ball clay added to assist its plasticity.

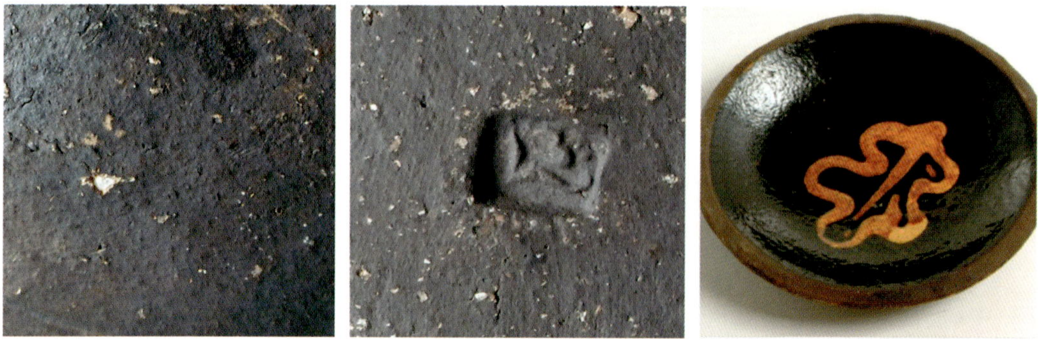

This Dartington example of 1932-1933, is believed to have been made from Fremington clay with grog added to open up the medium and assist drying and firing, the apparent colour being due to the application of a dark (probably manganese) slip.

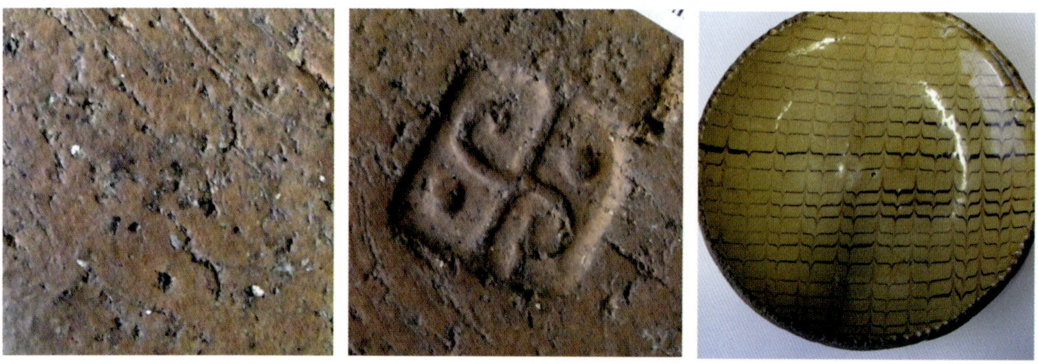

As a contrast, this St Ives example of 1934-1935 shows a much coarser medium, probably twice-fired. Whilst only bearing a workshop seal, it was probably the work of Harry Davis.

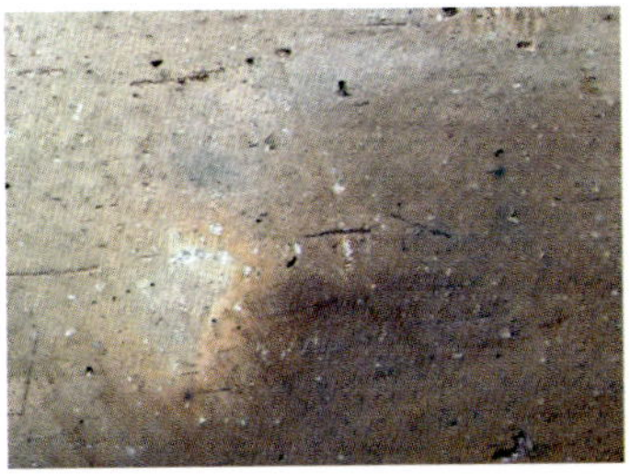
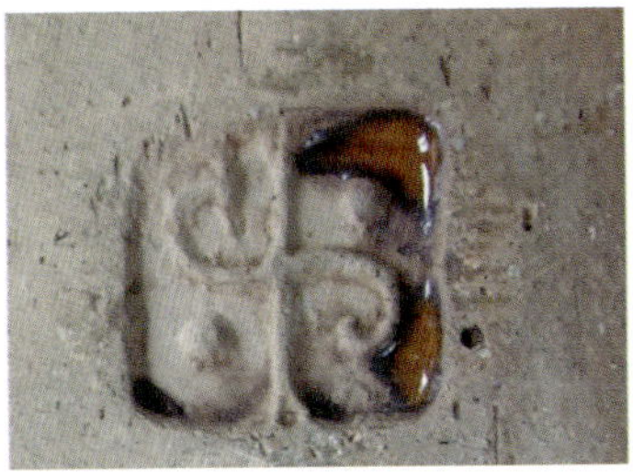
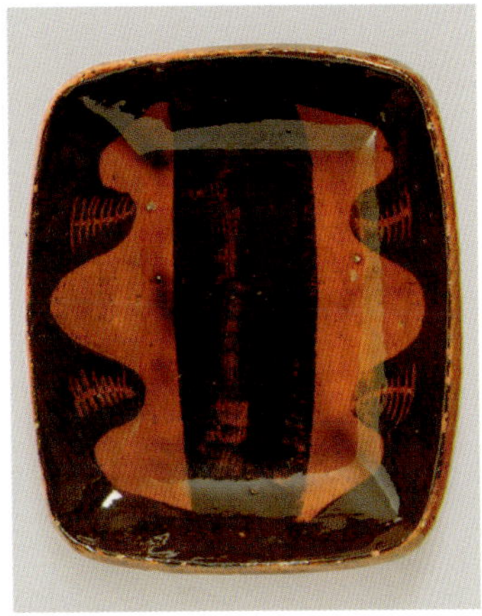

This late hump dish of around 1937 is of unusual form, possibly a one-off, and is made of a light coloured gritty medium showing little evidence of St Erth clay, and partly sieved china and ball clays seem the more likely sources. This is an early use of Leach's principal monogram seal of subsequent years.

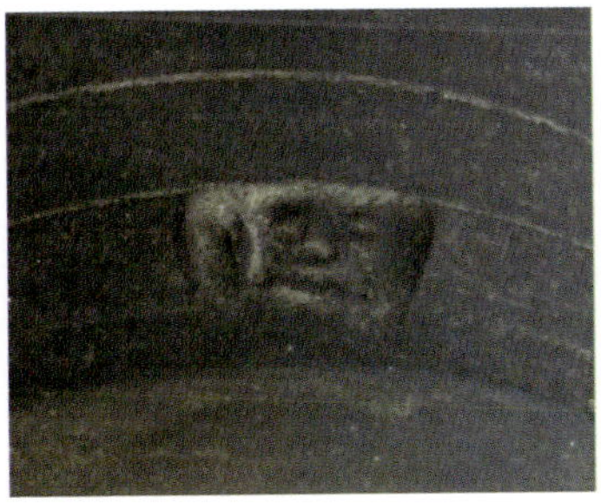
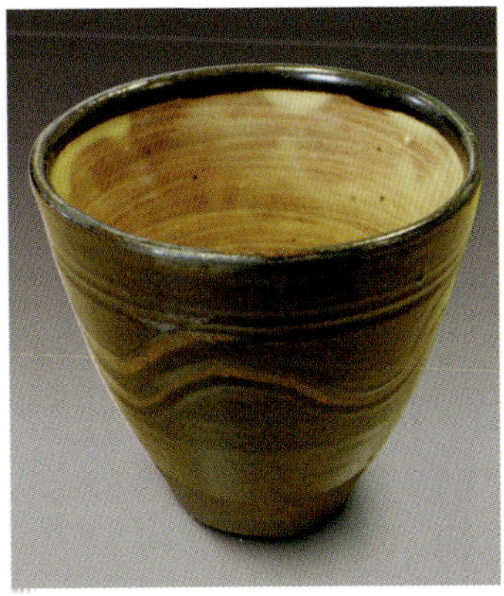

This beaker was part of a new range of standard forms developed at Dartington by Leach in 1932-1933, made using Fremington clay from North Devon, then covered in a dark (manganese) overall slip.

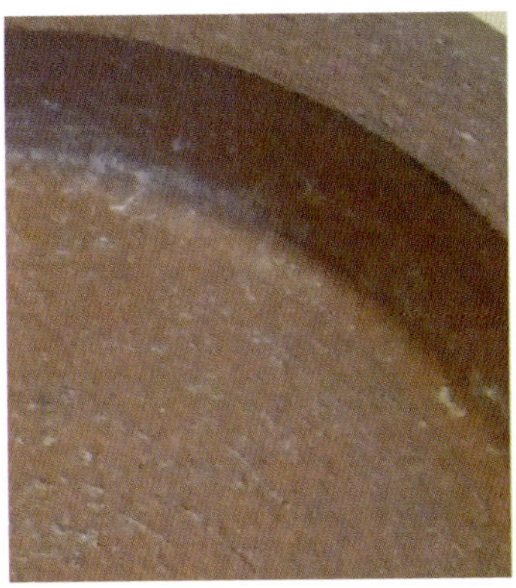

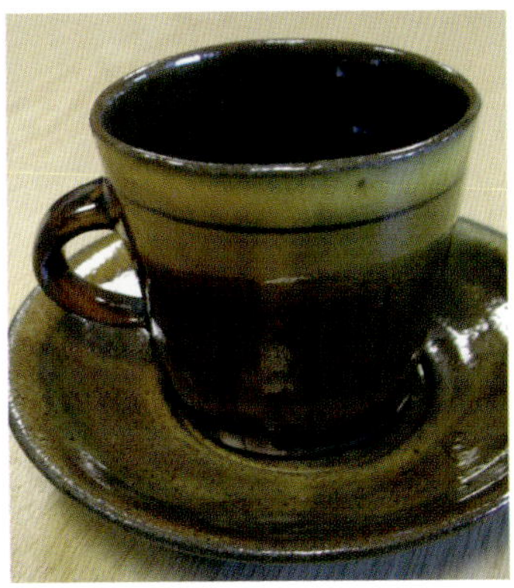

This postscript to slipware, a thrown and finely turned coffee cup and saucer, has something of the industrial and manufactured feel of Stoke, the possible source of the fine throwing medium employed. The likely maker, David Leach, had just returned permanently to St Ives from a 3 year course in Staffordshire. The painted SI seal would have been applied after turning when leather hard.

AN ILLUSTRATED REVIEW OF POTTERS MONOGRAMS

This area is fraught with uncertainty. The mere use of similar marks is no guarantee as to date, since these – particularly SI seals – would have lain around the Pottery over some years and been pressed into service if to hand. The actual authorship of wares is also vexatious, as Leach applied his personal mark on pots thrown to his order or design by a succession of lead throwers over the years. As a general rule he always marked his individual pieces. However, he also anonymously decorated standard forms in slipware (and later in stoneware) – mugs, bowls and small plates as well as hump moulded dishes – all of which bear just an SI seal. There also exist plain prototype forms from 1924-1925 with distinctive finishing, both to the body and base (see the 'Malpas' vases on page 68), which are experiments with themes and techniques used on other later wares bearing the Leach monogram.

In summary, it is usually (but not always) safe to assume that if the pot in question is decorated and bears a BL mark or seal then he was the one who added the design. In addition, his distinctive touch may also with care be attributed to wares just bearing a workshop seal. Lastly, on occasions, pots were marked by hand either with the brush or knib or by using a slip trailer where the bases were turned for stylistic and practical considerations. Since the hardened clay surface would not easily have taken an impressed mark, there was a need for alternatives.

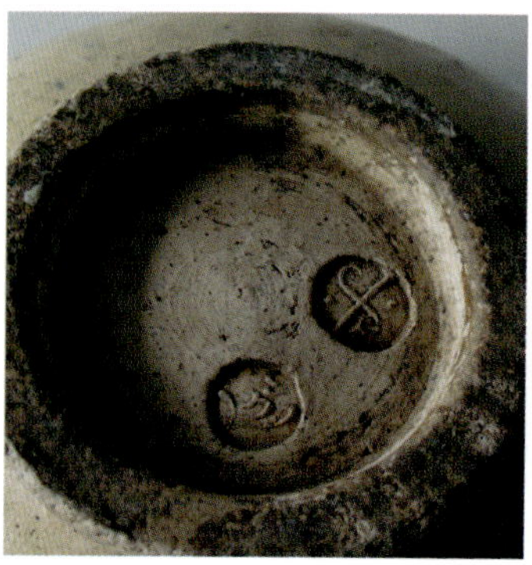

Leach 1922

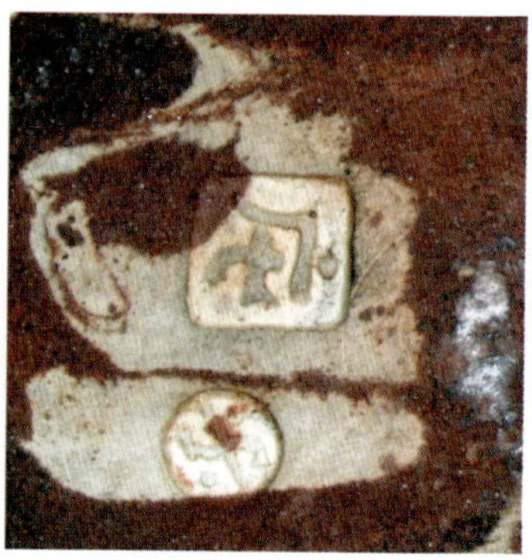

Hamada 1922

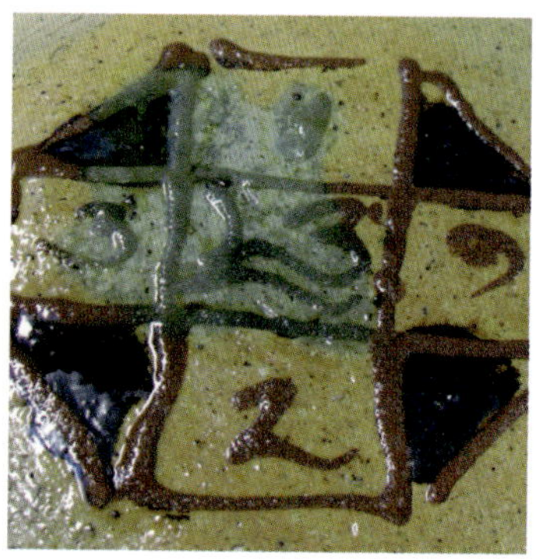

Leach 1923

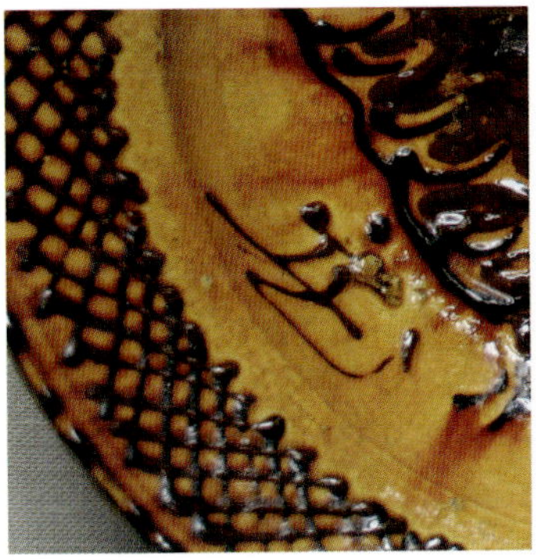

Hamada 1923

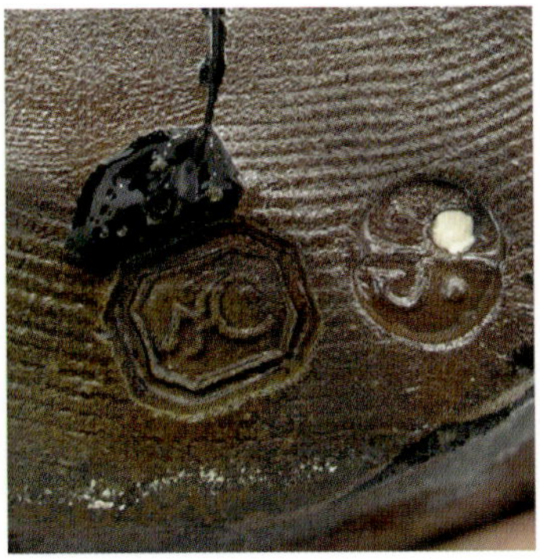

Cardew 1924

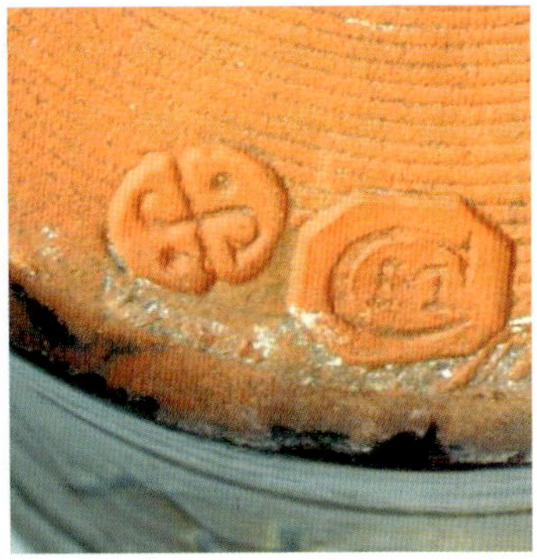

Cardew 1925

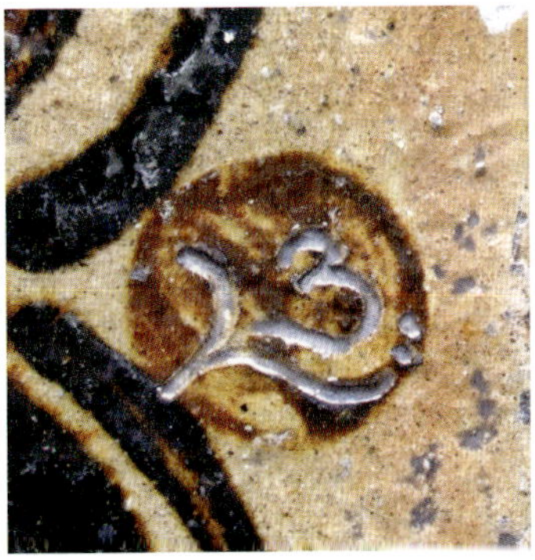

Leach 1925

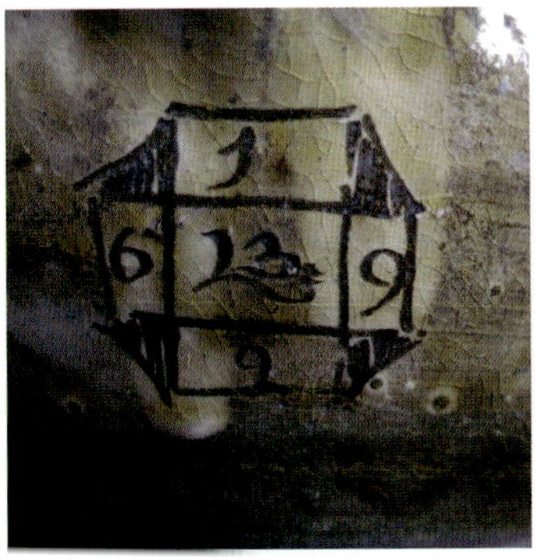

Leach 1926

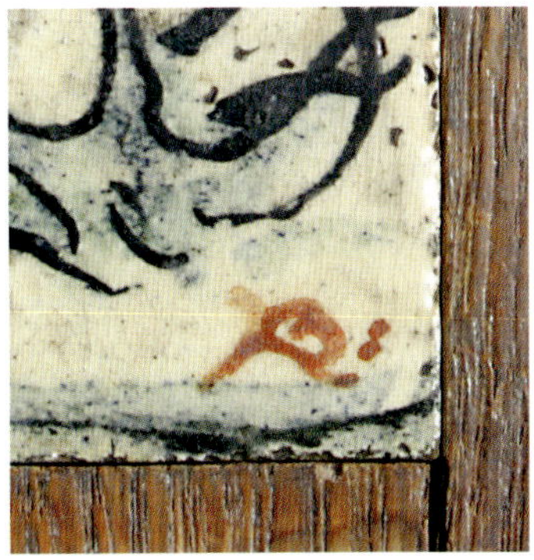

Leach 1927

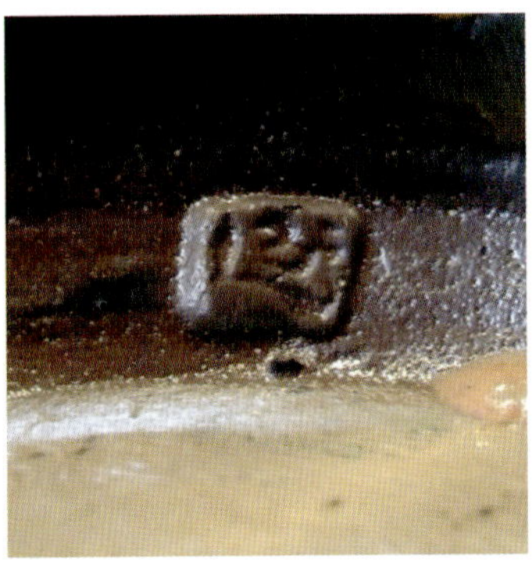

Leach 1930

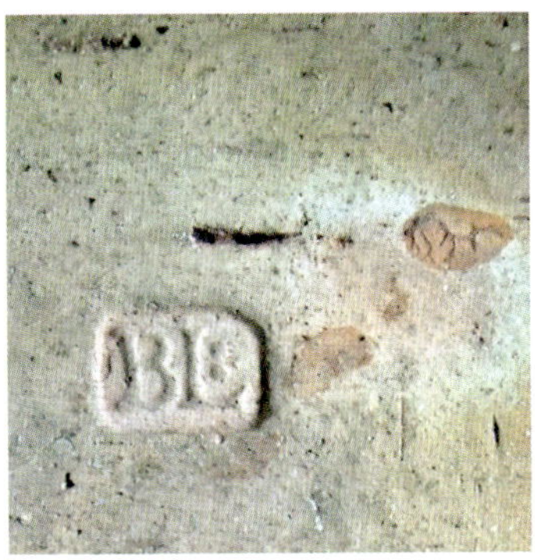

Leach 1937

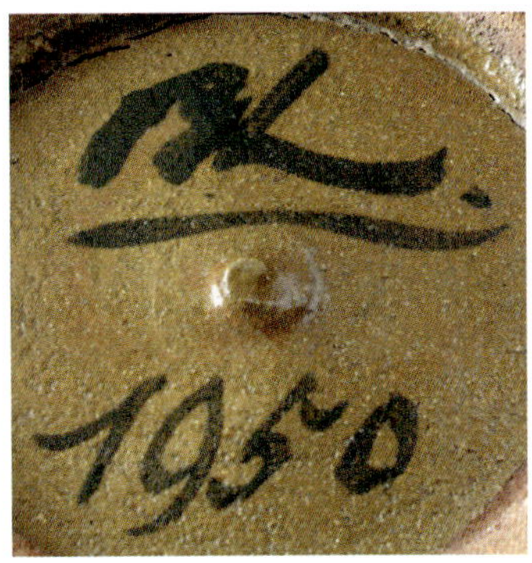

Leach 1950

AN ILLUSTRATED REVIEW OF FOOT RIMS

In the early years at St Ives, foot rims were employed primarily on bowl forms, unomis, larger plates and chargers, but were also used by Leach on his early jug, cup & saucer and vase forms. In contrast, standing forms thrown by Cardew in 1924-1926 had simple wire cut and flat bases, usually left untrimmed and with the wire scar still evident. Our illustrations are based just on a selection of pots illustrated elsewhere in this title and are not intended to be exhaustive. Some deeper foot rims may have been prepared separately on the wheel and then sprigged onto the base of pots.

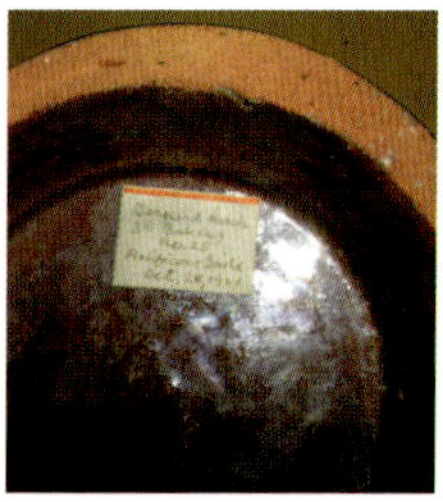

Leach 1921

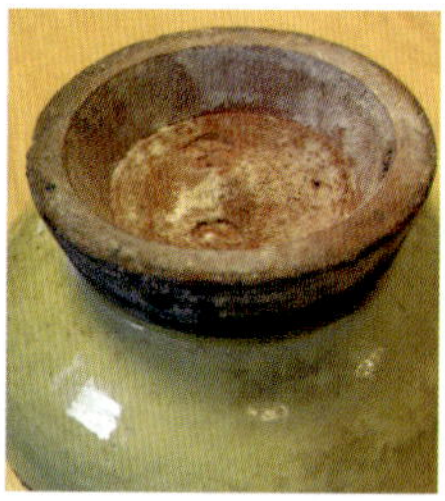

Leach 1922

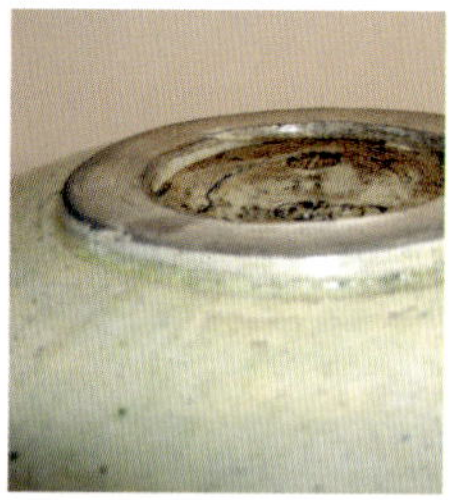

Hamada 1922

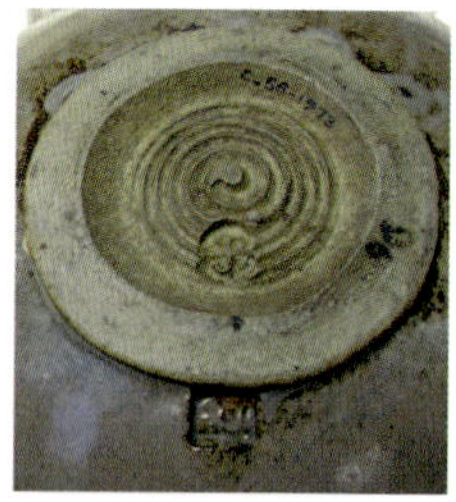

Hamada 1923

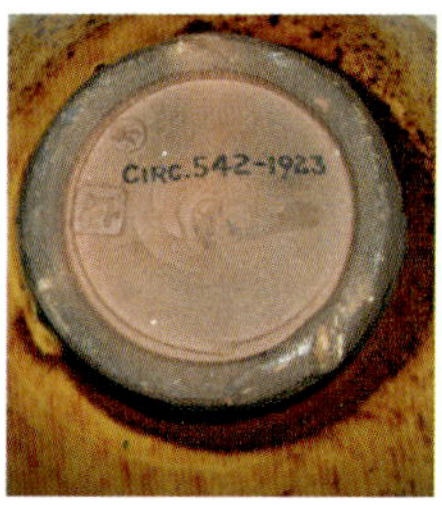

Hamada 1923

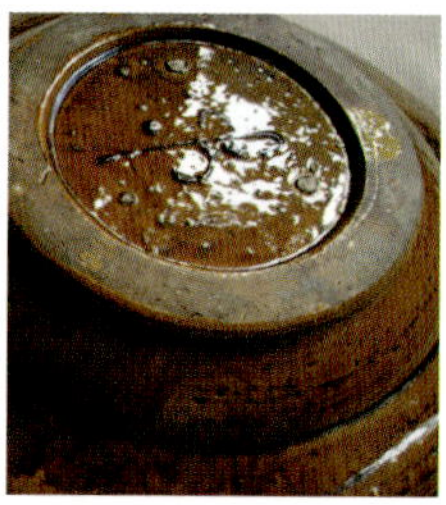

Hamada 1923

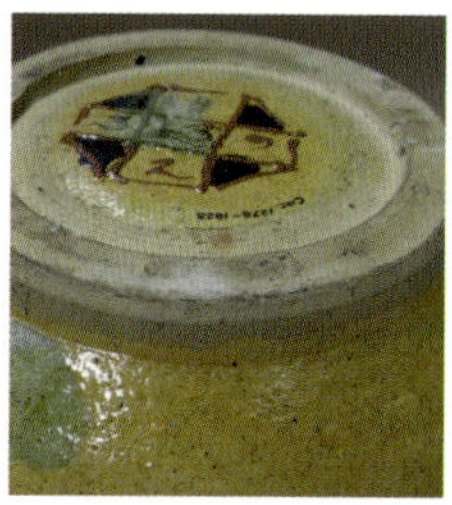

Leach 1923

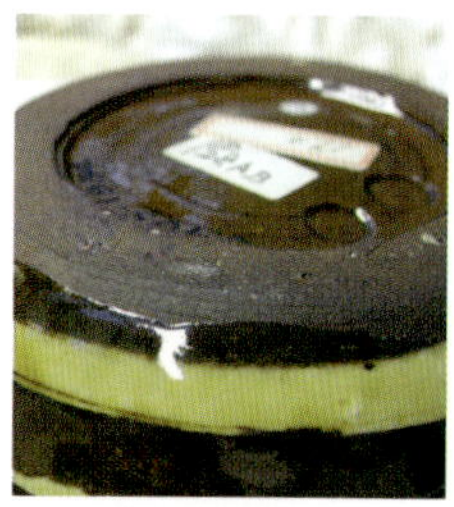

Leach 1924

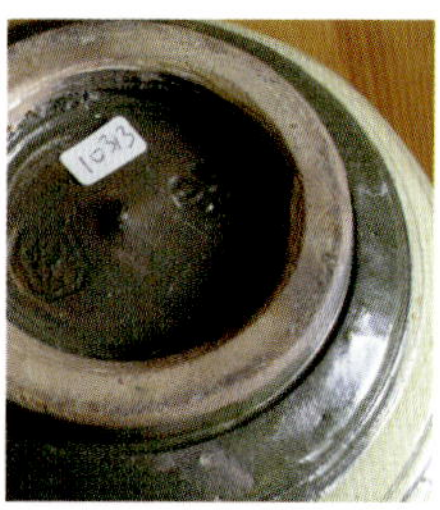

Cardew 1924

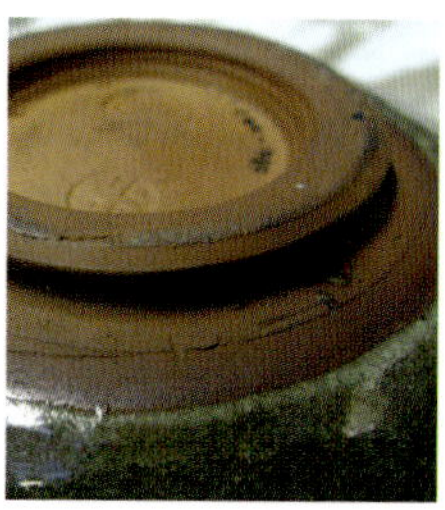

Cardew 1924

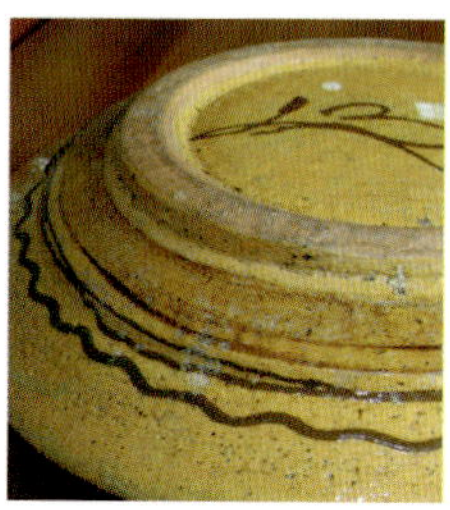

Leach 1929

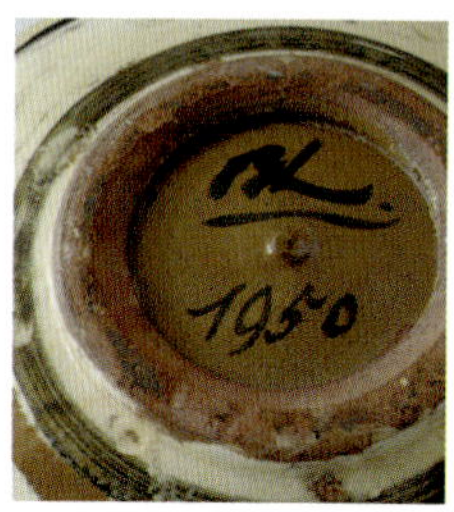

Leach 1950

AN ILLUSTRATED REVIEW OF HANDLES

Handled forms were relatively scarce in the period 1921-1923, but much more common after Cardew's arrival in late 1923, bringing with him some experience of throwing and Devon techniques of handle making. This level of output was not to resume until the 1930s and the arrival of Harry Davis. We illustrate here a number of handle types from marked St Ives pots. As with many country and studio potters, Cardew handles are almost akin to a signature in his later career at Winchcombe and elsewhere, but the range used on his standardised jugs and tankards of 1924-1926 are atypical, and reflect Leach's direction.

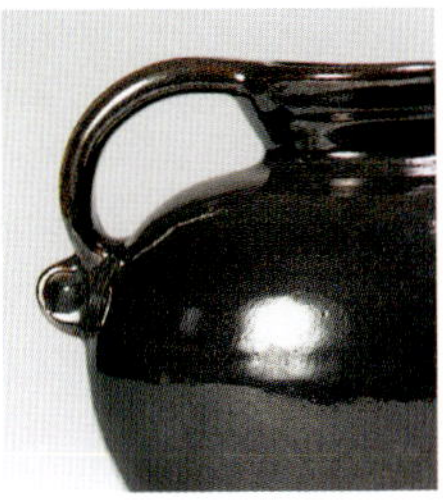

Hamada 1923

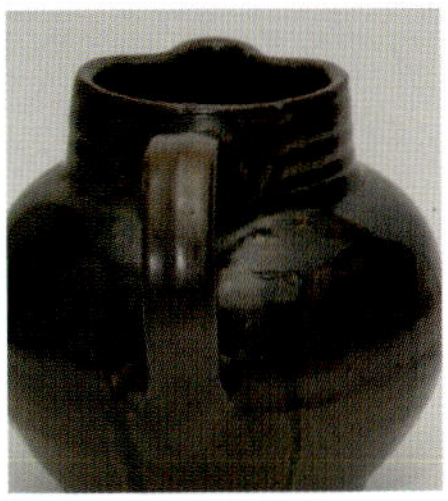

Hamada 1923

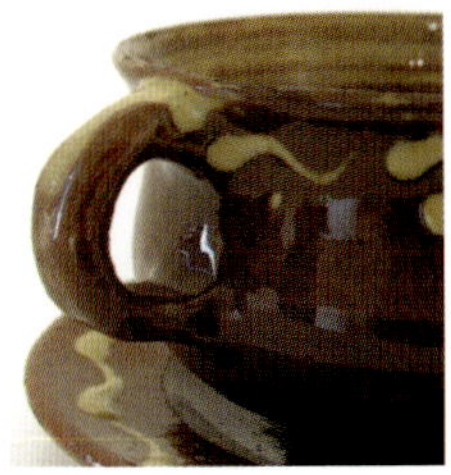

Leach 1922

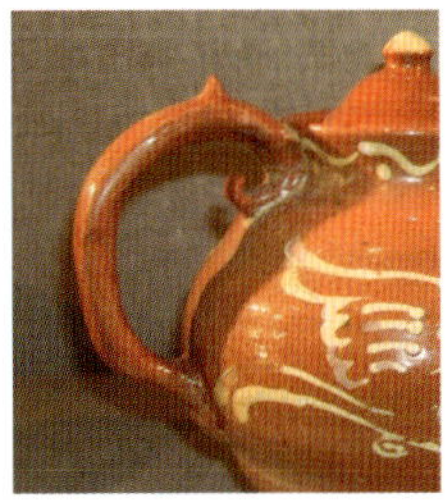

Leach 1923

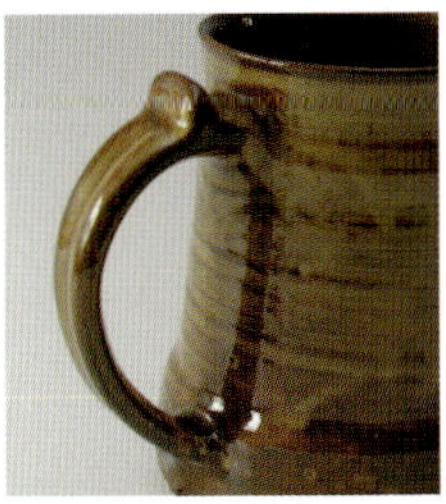

Cardew 1924

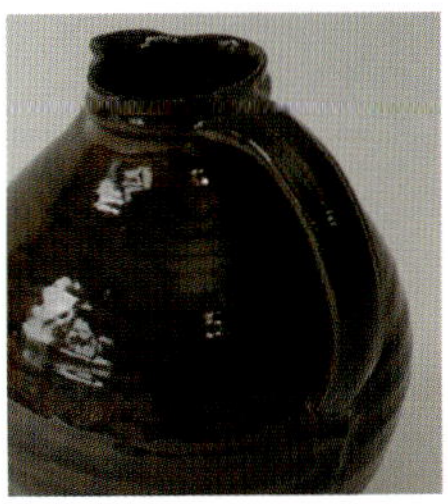

Cardew 1925

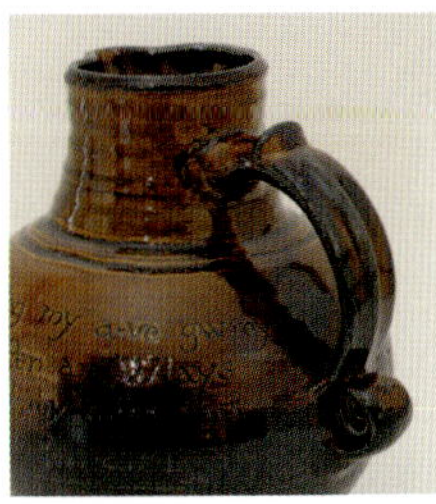

Cardew 1925

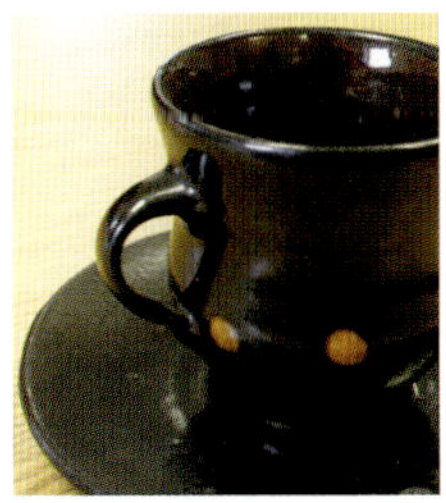

Leach 1932

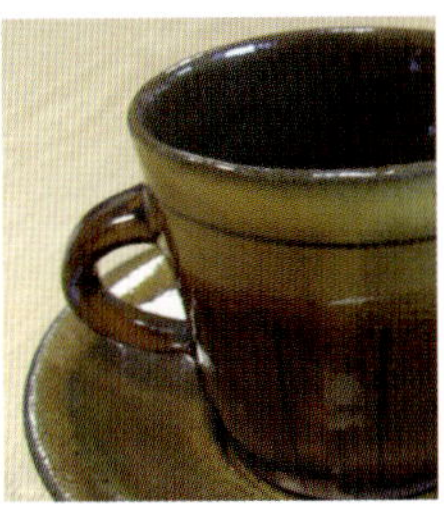

D Leach 1937

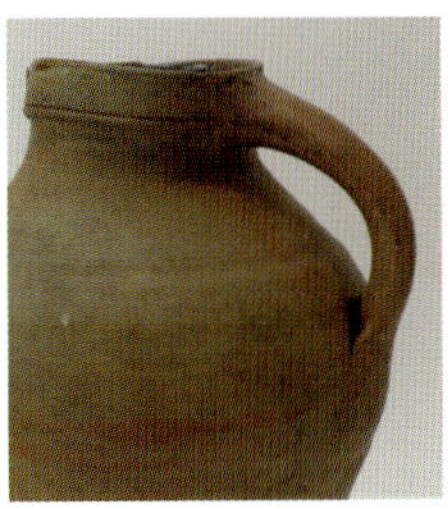

Lakes

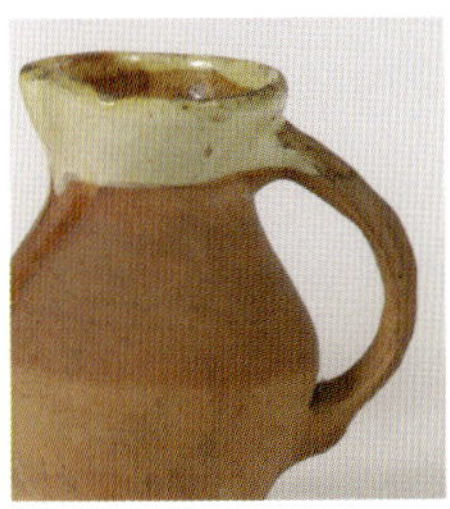

Fremington

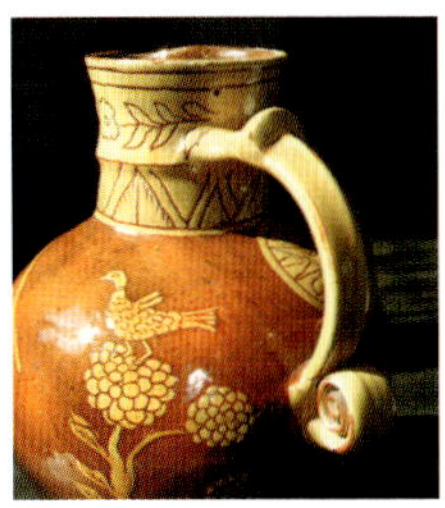

EB Fishley 1890

SOME TECHNICAL NOTES

Slipware glazes

The following glaze bases were used on St Ives slipwares in conjunction with a proportion of body clay and a colourant as required:

Galena (lead sulphide/PbS): This classic traditional glaze was slightly safer to use than white lead, but has the practical disadvantage of requiring oxidising firing conditions to allow it to mature at around 700°C, reacting with oxygen, losing its sulphur and converting to lead oxide ($2PbS + 3O_2 = 2PbO + 2SO_2$ gas). The presence of sulphur gives local reduction conditions around pots leading to unusual glaze finishes: these can sometimes be seen on the inside of deeper bowls and are valued by lovers of traditional slipwares. Hamada is known to have used a galena mix which he learnt from visiting Lakes in Truro, and it must have been used on a number of slipwares in the 1920s.

White lead (lead oxide/PbO_2): This was employed particularly, but not exclusively on raku style wares, and had a clear, glassy quality that facilitated very fresh, bright under-glaze colours. It was probably used to finish large wheel-head chargers fired in the climbing kiln, as it had the advantage of a wide temperature firing range of 900-1100°C.

Firing effects: Where iron brushwork has been used to decorate wares, high-lead glazes tend to dissolve some of the iron oxide leading to fugitive results. Movement under lead glazes is also seen, with a 'bleeding' or running of decoration.

The 1925 round slipware and raku kiln

The design of this new kiln built by Matsubayashi ('Matsu') in 1925 was bizarre as it employed perforated shelving designed in theory to allow gases and heat to penetrate to the upper part of the kiln. However, period photos of its construction show that these shelf holes were not big enough to allow the better gas flow required to achieve the more even temperatures required, and this is the evidence of the slipware pots produced from 1925 with some pots under-fired and others warped due to uneven firing.

Leach and members of his team are known to have visited traditional potteries at Truro (Lakes) and at Verwood in Dorset, both of which employed traditional bottle kilns open packed during setting with limited use of shelving. These were typically fired using coal, with furze (broom) employed towards the end of firings to finish off galena-based glazes. Such procedures were seen by members of the Leach team, and their subsequent choice of kiln design, setting procedure and firing materials is a curious one. Additionally, Leach did not seek advice when things went wrong, despite the good contacts that had been established at Lakes from as early as 1921, and were known to have continued after WW2 from contemporary correspondence seen, when he advised them on the availability of Rural Industries Bureau grants for kiln improvements. Oliver Kent's essay gives further consideration to these issues [pages 128-137].

Oxidised raku:

Most raku made nowadays is of the North American or European type, relying on reduction to create a variety of at times spectacular results. The true raku made for Thursday afternoon decorating demonstrations and lessons held at the Pottery during the summer was however fired in an oxidising environment, probably in the top of the 1925 Matsu round slipware up-draught kiln.

Such raku demonstrations must have provided convivial entertainment, and this style of work was recreated at Slipware workshops at Taena Pottery, Whitley Court, Upton St Leonards in the Cotswolds in the summers of 2009 and 2010 (see accompanying photographs). A variety of small forms were made in advance using a heavily grogged clay to open up the texture and help cope with the extra thermal shock entailed in the fast heating and cooling central to raku work. These were then brush-decorated by delegates following demonstrations by Potter-demonstrators.

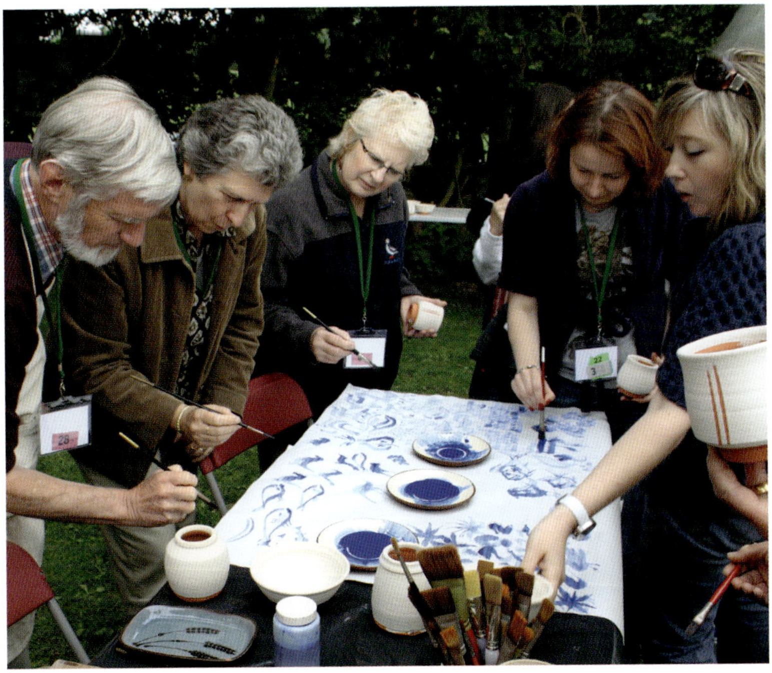

Laurence McGowan with delegates in 2009.

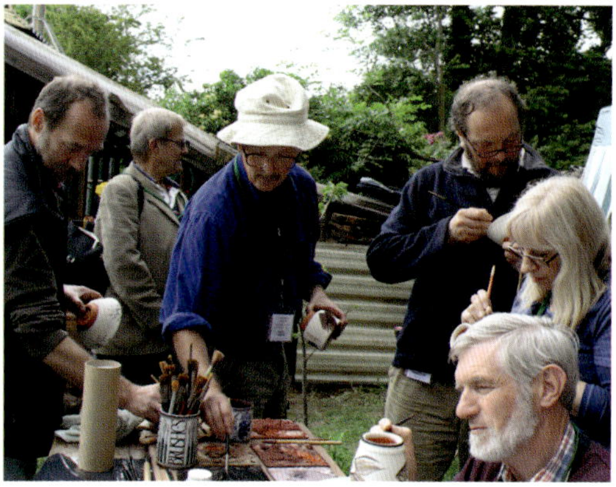

Paul Young, Philip Leach and Niek Hoogland decorating raku at Taena 2009.

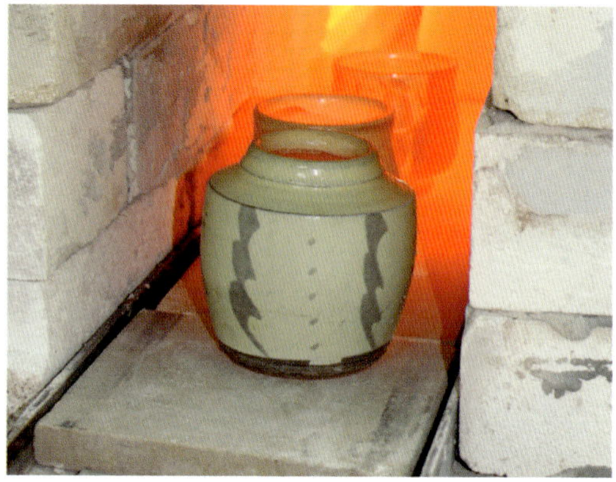

The pots were then gas-fired using a tunnel kiln adapted by Sean Casserley of Taena Pottery from an original design by Joe Finch. However, less formal brick-built structures can be just as effective, and were used by the Studio pioneers before WW2: the period photograph shows one built by Leach and Cardew at the Gordon Russell workshop in 1925 and the line engraving illustrates a design by Leach from *A potter's book*.

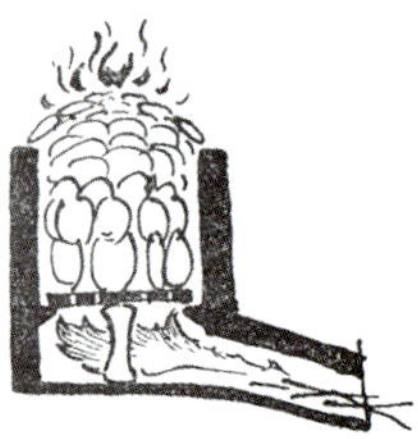

Simple round updraught kiln

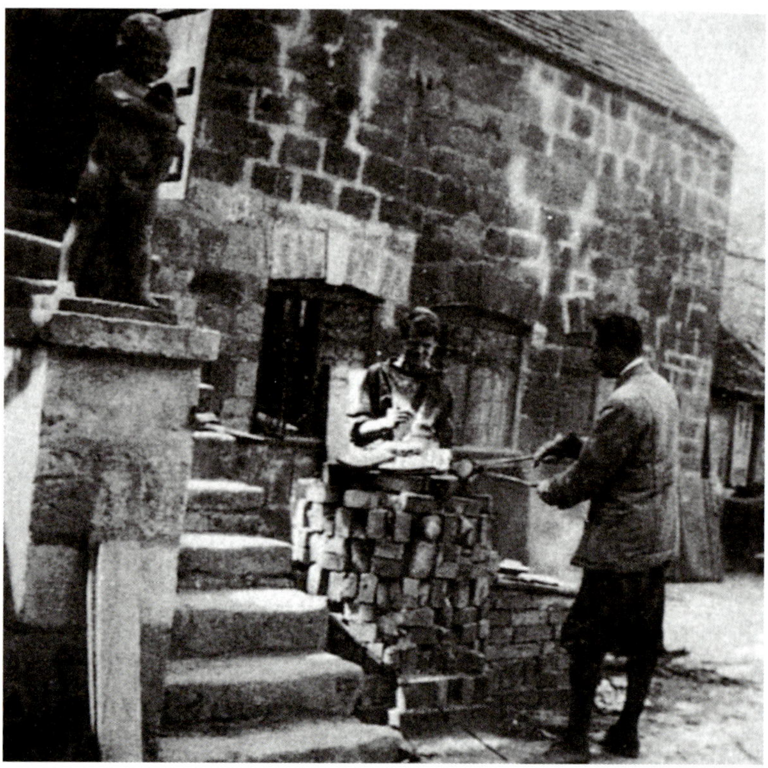

Leach and Cardew firing raku (c. 1925).

The materials used were provided by John Mathieson, to his own specifications:

Body: Sculpture terracotta from Valentine Clays Limited, The Sliphouse, 18-20 Chell Street, Hanley, Stoke-on-Trent, ST1 6BA. This throws well, and is smooth enough for domestic ware.

Slip: Hyplas 71 with 10-20% soft borax frit added for improved adhesion.

Glaze: Soft borax frit 85 / Grolleg China clay 15 / Bentonite 1. A suggested frit is Potclays 2264.

This glaze gives an open crackle when reduced in sawdust after a standard raku firing.

Pots are then fired to a nominal 900°C. Shining a torch into the kiln is surprisingly useful when checking glaze maturity. When the glaze is smooth the pots can be removed from the kiln and allowed to air cool. Caution – be very careful when first handling the pots. They may look cool but remain hot for a long time.

Unlike stoneware glazes, raku glazes tend to have a finite life. This can be prolonged by decanting the excess water and drying the glaze when it is not being used.

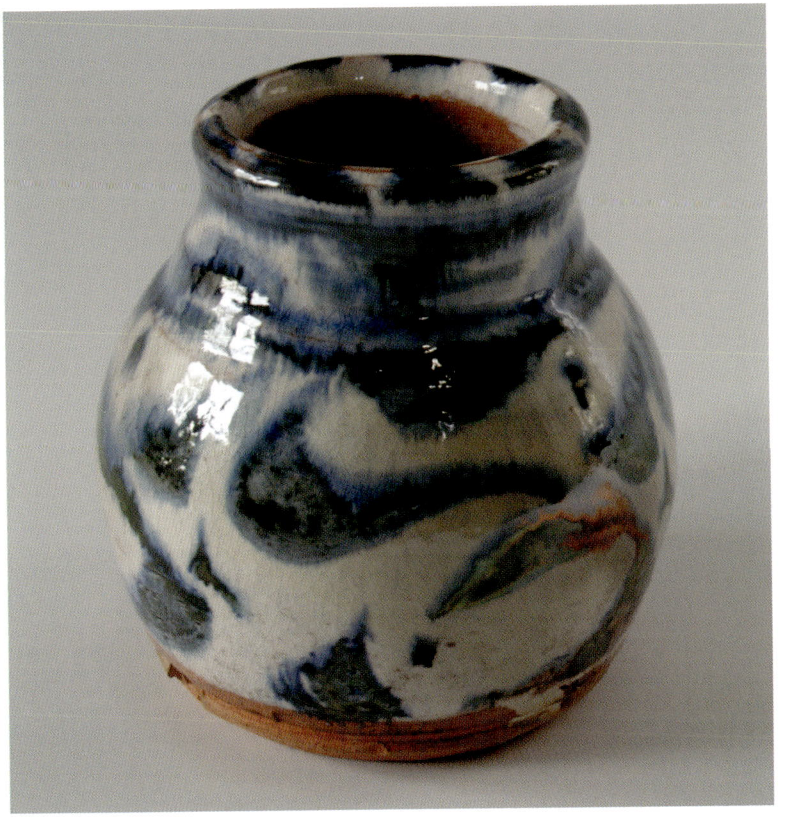

Taena raku from 2010 firing (brushwork by Andrew Hazelden using Aldermaston blue-green).

A SLIPWARE GLOSSARY

There are inevitably technical terms applicable to slipwares in general. The following covers those terms most often used in this volume, with some additions particular to the practice of Michael Cardew at Winchcombe in 1926-1939.

BALL CLAY: A plastic clay with a small particle size, so called because it was sold in measured balls. Mixed with water to thin it down, it is then used as a slip (q.v.).

BISCUIT FIRING: The firing of a pot at a lower temperature prior to the application of the glaze and its final firing. 'Biscuit' is the word used to describe the fired pot before it has been glazed.

BOTTLE KILN: A bottle-shaped round kiln, as used in traditional potteries, made out of tough firebricks, and tapering to the chimney at the top, often reinforced by wide iron bands.

BRUSHWORK: A decorative technique used at St Ives associated particularly but by no means exclusively with Chinese wares in the Tz'u-chou (now Cizhou) manner, using iron or other metallic oxides in suspension.

BUNG: A column or stack of saggars (q.v.), made stable by the use of 'snakes' or 'sausages' of clay between each succeeding saggar.

FURZE FIRING: The use of bunches of furze (syn. Gorse) in the later stages of kiln firing to raise the kiln temperature and 'flash', i.e. melt, the galena glaze.

GALENA: Lead sulphide, subject to reaction with acids and later made illegal as a glaze component. Gives a soft but shiny finish to the fired pot surface.

GLAZE: A mixture of clay, flint and galena applied to the surface to protect a pot and improve its impermeability.

GROG: Coarser material, often ground-up shards, added to fine clays to 'open' them thus making pots easier to throw and quicker to fire.

INCH: A measure used in the Imperial system in force during the whole period covered in this book.

1 inch = 2.54 cm

MEANDER: The wavy line decoration created by combing, extensively seen on North Devon wares of the 19th-century, notably at Fremington.

RAW GLAZING: The application of a glaze to a pot after it has dried sufficiently but before it has been fired.

REDUCTION: The effect of a lack of oxygen during firing. When iron ore is used in glazes, this is returned back eventually to the oxide, turning from a desired yellow or ochre to green, and through red eventually to black. Galena-based glazes can also bubble as a result, leaving round scars.

SAGGAR: A container, normally cylindrical, made of particularly robust fire clay, used both at St Ives and later at Winchcombe to protect wares from the flame during firing, with holes cut to allow oxygen to reach the pot surface and 'flash' (melt) the galena-based glaze. Saggars were not employed at the Fishley Pottery in Fremington, North Devon.

SCROLLWORK: A finishing detail to the base of handles used in the North Devon tradition: an extra piece of clay is left after the pulling of a handle and its application to the pot, which is then curled back on itself as a decoration.

SGRAFFITO: A decorative technique involving scratching a line through a layer of slip to the contrasting body colour of the pot.

SLIP: A suspension of clay in water applied after the throwing of a pot using white ball clay which is sometimes coloured in shades of pale brown through to black by the addition of iron oxide to the mix.

THUMBPIECE: A lateral piece of clay applied to the top of the handle of a jug or tankard to help balance the piece in the hand and ease its steady pouring.

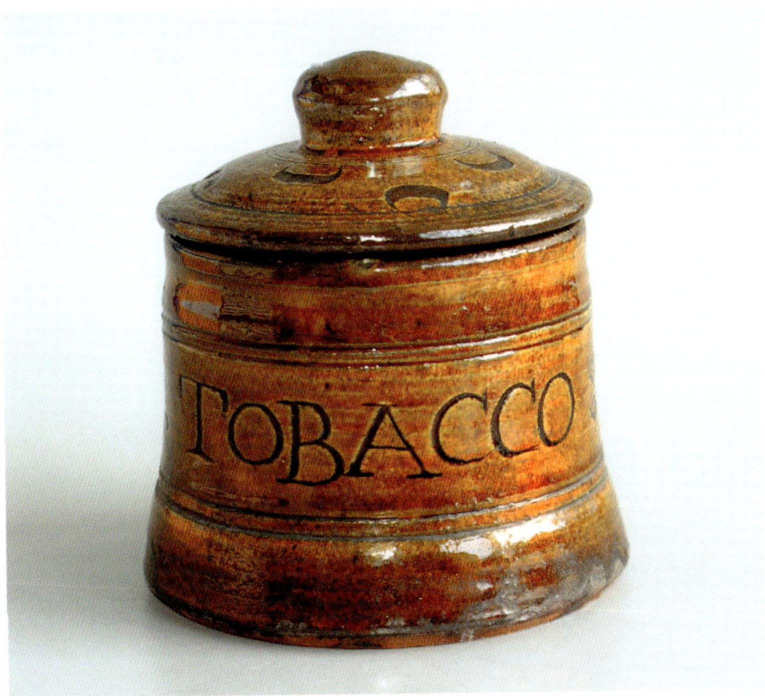

Michael Cardew baccy jar, St Ives (c. 1925).

SELECTED BIBLIOGRAPHY LISTED BY SUBJECT

Bernard Leach, Hamada Shoji and Studio Pottery generally

Birks, Tony and others, *Bernard Leach, Hamada & their circle*, Phaidon, Oxford, 1990.

Cooper, Emmanuel, *Bernard Leach: life and work*, Yale University Press, New Haven and London, 2003.

de Waal, Edmund, *Bernard Leach*, Tate Gallery Publishing 1999.

Hogben, Carol, *The art of Bernard Leach*, Faber & Faber, London, 1978.

Japan Association of Art Museums, *The, St Ives*, Setagaya, Japan, 1989.

Leach, Bernard, *A potter's book*, Faber & Faber, London, 1940.

Leach, Bernard, *A Potter's Portfolio*, Lund Humphries, London, 1951.

Leach, Bernard, *Hamada, Potter*, Kodansha International, Tokyo, 1975.

National Museum of Art, Tokyo, *The retrospective exhibition of Shoji Hamada*, Tokyo, 1977.

Petersen, Susan, *Shoji Hamada: a potter's way and work* (UK edition), A&C Black, London, 2004.

Riddick, Sarah, *Pioneer Studio Pottery*, The Milner-White Collection, Lund Humphries, London, 1990.

Rose, Muriel, *Artist Potters in England* (2nd edition), Faber & Faber, London, 1970.

Watson, Oliver, Bernard Leach: potter and artist, Crafts Council, London, 1997.

Watson, Oliver and others, *Shoji Hamada, Master Potter*, Lund Humphries, London, 1998

Whybrow, Marion, *Leach Pottery St Ives: the legacy of Bernard Leach*, Beach Books, St Ives, 2006.

Wingfield Digby, George, *The Work of the Modern Potter in England*, John Murray, London, 1952.

Yasuhiro, Yurugi and others, *The English Arts & Crafts Movement and Hamada Shoji*, Artis Inc, Tokyo, 1997.

English Earthenware

Ball Clay Heritage Society, *The Ball Clays of Devon and Dorset*, Newton Abbott, 2003

Barker, David and Crompton, Steve, *Slipware in the collection of The Potteries Museum* & Art Gallery, A&C Black, London, 2007.

Brears, Peter, *The English Country Pottery*, David & Charles, Newton Abbott, 1971.

Brears, Peter, *The Collectors Book of English Country Pottery*, David & Charles, Newton Abbott, 1974.

Buckley Clay Industries Committee, *Buckley Pottery*, Chester, 1975

Coleman-Smith, R and Pearson, T, *Excavations in the Donyatt Potteries*, Phillimore, Chichester, 1988.

Cooper, Ronald, *English Slipware Dishes*, Alec Tiranti, London, 1964.

Draper, Jo, *Dorset Country Pottery*, The Crowood Press, Marlborough, 2002.

Edgeler, John, *The Fishleys of Fremington: a Devon Slipware Tradition*, Cotswolds Living Publications, Winchcombe, 2008.

Fishley-Holland, William, *Fifty Years a Potter*, Pottery Quarterly, 1958.

Grant, Alison, *North Devon Pottery*, Edward Gaskell Publishers, Bideford, 2005.

Leary, Emmeline & Pearson, Jeremy, *By Potter's Art and Skill*, Royal Albert Memorial Museum, Exeter, 1984.

Lomax, Charles J, *Quaint English Pottery*, Sherratt & Hughes, London, Manchester, 1909.

McGarva, Andrew, *Country Pottery*, A&C Black, London, 2000.

Mingeikan, The Japanese Folk Craft Museum, *Slipware*, Exhibition Catalogue, Tokyo 2004.

Michael Cardew

Cardew, Michael, *Pioneer Pottery*, Longmans, London, 1969.

Cardew, Michael, *A Pioneer Potter: an autobiography*, Collins, London, 1988.

Clark, Garth, *Michael Cardew: a portrait*, Faber & Faber, London, 1978.

Dick, Peter & others, *Michael Cardew and Pupils*, York City Art Gallery, 1983.

Edgeler, John, *Michael Cardew and the West Country Slipware tradition*, Cotswolds Living Publications, Winchcombe, 2007.

Edgeler, John, *Michael Cardew and Stoneware: continuity and change*, Cotswolds Living Publications, Winchcombe, 2008.

Leach, Bernard et al., *Michael Cardew: a collection of essays*, Crafts Advisory Committee, London, 1976.

Winchcombe Pottery

Edgeler, John, *Ray Finch, Craftsman Potter of the modern age*, Cotswolds Living Publications, Winchcombe, 2006.

Wheeler, Ron, *Winchcombe Pottery: the Cardew-Finch tradition*, White Cockade Publishing, Oxford, 1998.

Wheeler, Ron and Edgeler, John, *Sid Tustin, Winchcombe potter: a celebration*, Cotswolds Living Publications, Winchcombe, 2005.

Other general reading

Binyon, Laurence, *The followers of William Blake*, Halton and Truscott Smith, London, 1925.

Harrod, Tanya, *The Crafts in Britain in the 20th Century*, Yale University Press, New Haven and London, 1999.

Hennell, Thomas, *The Countryman at Work*, Architectural Press, London, 1947.

MacCarthy, Fiona, *Eric Gill*, Faber & Faber, London, 1989.

Rackham, Bernard, *Medieval English Pottery*, Faber & Faber, London, 1947.

Williams, Margaret, *The Food of Love*, Halsgrove, Tiverton, 2007.

Height 27cm, width 20cm (maximum).

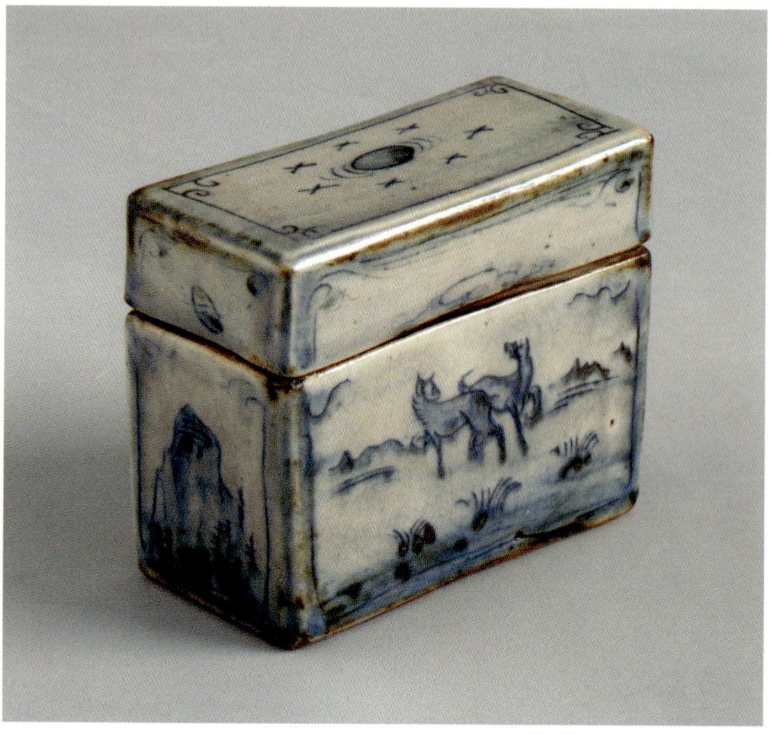

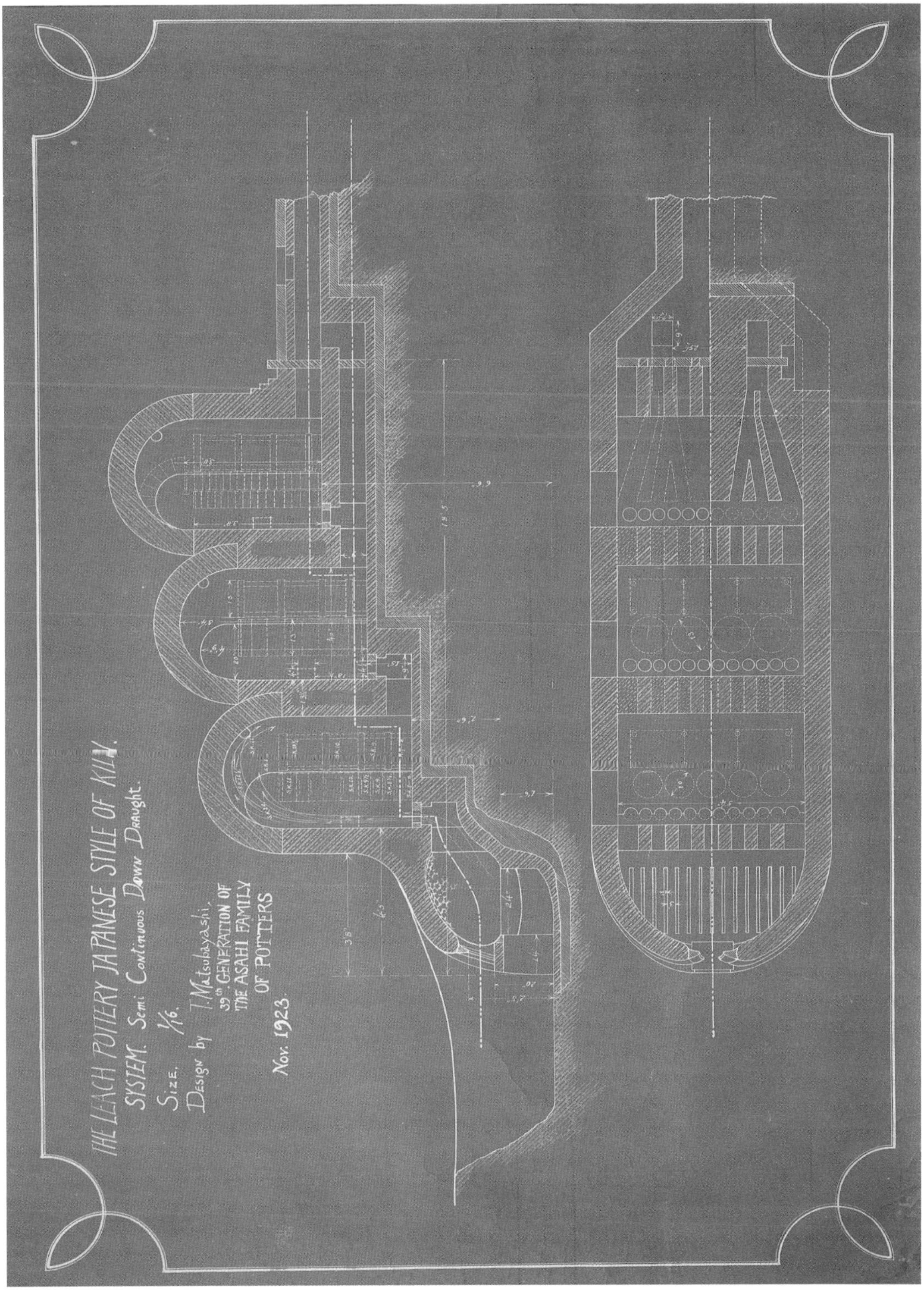
THE LEACH POTTERY JAPANESE STYLE OF KILN.
SYSTEM. Semi Continuous Down Draught.
Size. 1/16.
Design by T. Matsubayashi,
39th GENERATION OF
THE ASAHI FAMILY
OF POTTERS
Nov. 1923.

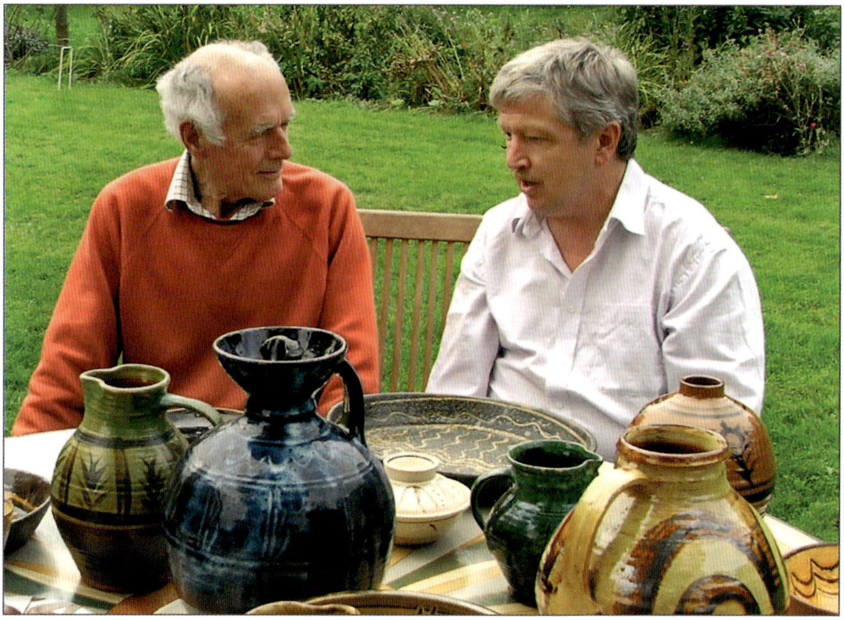

John Edgeler (right) in conversation with Alan Caiger-Smith in 2007.

THE AUTHOR:

A collector of ceramics from his early teens, John has lived in the town of Winchcombe in the heart of the Cotswolds since 1999, following a successful career in finance in the City of London. A dealer in and enthusiast for the work of the pioneering studio potter Michael Cardew for many years, in the period 2004 – 2008 he mounted a series of retrospectives at his Long Room Gallery with the help of local enthusiasts to honour the potters Sid Tustin, Ray Finch, and the work of Cardew in slipware and stoneware. Under his imprint, Cotswolds Living Publications, John has also written and published a series of related monographs based largely around pots exhibited in these retrospectives.

More recently, he has collaborated with outside organisations such as the Museum of Barnstaple and North Devon, co-curating a show there on the Fishleys of Fremington and the wider historic Harvest Jug tradition of North Devon. He has also worked with a number of leading slipware potters in co-organising and sponsoring pottery workshops and kiln wood-firings both in Devon and Gloucestershire. This new volume celebrating the pioneering slipware years of the St Ives Pottery in Cornwall and the early work there of Leach, Hamada and Cardew was launched at The Leach Pottery Studio and Museum in autumn 2010, as part of celebrations of the 90th anniversary of its foundation in 1920.